The Chief Justiceship of
MELVILLE W. FULLER

CHIEF JUSTICESHIPS OF THE UNITED STATES SUPREME COURT

Herbert A. Johnson, General Editor

The Chief Justiceship of Melville W. Fuller, 1888–1910
by James W. Ely, Jr.

The Supreme Court in the Early Republic:
The Chief Justiceships of John Jay and Oliver Ellsworth
by William R. Casto

The Chief Justiceship of
MELVILLE W. FULLER, 1888–1910

James W. Ely, Jr.

University of South Carolina Press

Published in Columbia, South Carolina, by the
University of South Carolina Press

Manufactured in the United States of America

Library of Congress Cataloging-in-Publication Data

Ely, James W., 1938–
    The chief justiceship of Melville W. Fuller, 1888–1910 / James W.
Ely, Jr.
      p. cm. — (Chief justiceships of the United States Supreme
    Court)
    Includes bibliographical references and index.
    ISBN 1–57003–018–9
    1. Fuller, Melville Weston, 1833–1910—Biography. 2. United
States. Supreme Court—History. 3. Judges—United States—
History. I. Title. II. Series.
KF8745.F8E44   1995
347.73'2634—dc20
B
347.3073534
B   94-18691

To my mother,
Edythe F. Ely,
and the memory of my father,
J. Wallace Ely

CONTENTS

EDITOR'S PREFACE

This series will provide readers with a convenient scholarly introduction to the work and achievements of the Supreme Court of the United States. Separate volumes will examine one or more chief justiceships, illuminating the Court's contribution to constitutional law, international law, and private law during that time period.

Assignment of volumes by chief justices' terms follows well-established historical traditions that may well be attributable to the now discredited view that Chief Justice John Marshall dominated his colleagues on the Supreme Court bench. However, this series organization is not intended to apotheosize the Chief Justices of the United States. Rather it seeks to place each chief justice into the context of his personal and professional relationships with other members of the Court. Thus its focus upon the chief justice is simply a means toward examination of all members of the Court. That viewpoint also facilitates examination of the way in which the Court conducted its business, since the chief justice is the primary manager of the flow of cases and opinions through the Court. Leadership in the collegial atmosphere of the Supreme Court is a function of interpersonal relationships, for the chief justice has no authority to command obedience. He must call upon the respect and deference that his associate justices are willing to accord him. Attention to the work of the chief justice inevitably requires close examination of all relationships among the justices.

Professor Ely's volume, as the first to be published in this series, provides high standards of scholarship and readability for those which follow it. His subject is the chief justiceship of Melville W. Fuller, a man of considerable ability elevated to the chief justice's position in part due to unusual political circumstances. Fuller was a successful Chicago lawyer well placed in the Democratic political organization. When nominated by

President Grover Cleveland he was ranked among the leadership of the Illinois bar, and was known for his conservative political philosophy. He brought to the Court a gift for efficient management and a talent for moderating discord. Fuller was the beneficiary of his wife's success as a hostess, and frequently entertained his Court colleagues at dinner. Rightly Ely refrains from pressing Fuller's claim to intellectual ascendancy among the justices. He gives due credit to the substantial and creative contributions of Justices Stephen J. Field, David Brewer, and Oliver Wendell Holmes.

The Fuller Court, and many of those following it, have been viewed in historical scholarship as proponents of *laissez faire* jurisprudence, based upon the supposed influence of social Darwinism in all areas of American life. It was this Court that decided *Lochner v. New York* (1905), providing reform-minded law professors and historians a new term of opprobrium, "The Lochner Era." Against this background Professor Ely's book is mildly revisionist. He demonstrates that while the Court favored economic growth and free competition as a general pattern, there are many decisions which delimit business and economic freedom when the public interest dictated that there be governmental restraint.

An intriguing aspect of this volume is Ely's description of a Supreme Court that seems to have had its feet firmly planted in nineteenth-century values of Jacksonian democracy. Yet it increasingly had to grapple with twentieth-century problems of economic regulation, complex federal-state relations, and international affairs. Beneath what appears to be a relatively calm period of the Court's history, the law's adaptation to societal change continued to gain momentum. Change was in the air during the Fuller years, and Professor Ely, without diverting attention from the Supreme Court, nevertheless makes the reader aware of the extra-judicial events of the day. They included the maturation of the labor union movement, the rise of agrarian discontent and revolt, and the growing political power of reform-minded individuals at the local, state, and national levels.

Written lucidly with a broad view of the place of the Supreme Court in American history and life, this volume provides readers with a comprehensive view of the Fuller years and helps to modify the pro-business stereotype that has so long discouraged scholars from taking a more balanced view of law in the Gilded Age.

Herbert A. Johnson

PREFACE

All commentators agree that the Supreme Court began to play an increasingly important role in the determination of public policy during the late nineteenth century. But historians have engaged in a fierce debate over the nature and extent of this judicial involvement. The aim of this volume is to provide a detailed analysis of the behavior of the Supreme Court during the pivotal tenure of Melville W. Fuller as chief justice.

This book is in the style of a judicial biography. Although one focus is on Fuller's leadership, careful attention is also given to the work of the Supreme Court as a whole and the course of decisions. How did Fuller guide the Court? How did the justices respond to the novel legal issues raised by the emerging industrial order? How did the Supreme Court under Fuller relate to the larger political and economic currents of American history? These are the questions that I have endeavored to answer. The conclusions may cause us to recast the conventional interpretation of the significance and impact of the Fuller Court.

Given the nature of this project, it was necessary to make difficult decisions regarding coverage of certain subjects. In many places this volume skims the surface of broad issues. Some individual topics treated briefly, such as railroad regulation, the liberty of contract, and the 1894 income tax, warrant a book in their own right.

Readers should also be aware of several features of this volume. The full citation for decisions discussed in the text can be found in the Table of Cases. In addition, an appendix indicating the tenure of all justices on the Supreme Court during Fuller's tenure has been placed at the end of the volume. Much of the information contained in this work was drawn from archival sources. I have used the following abbreviations in referring to these sources in the notes: LC: Library of Congress; and CHS: Chicago Historical Society.

The author of a book accumulates many obligations. I have benefited greatly from the generous help of many people in the course of writing this volume. Herbert A. Johnson, the general editor of the chief justices of the United States series, provided constant encouragement and sage advice. I am especially indebted to Herman Belz, Jon W. Bruce, Paul Kens, A. E. Keir Nash, Walter F. Pratt, Jr., and Nicholas S. Zeppos for reading some or all of the manuscript and offering thoughtful critiques. Donald J. Hall, Paul Janicke, Craig C. Joyce, and Robert K. Rasmussen made keen observations about particular sections of the text. R. Ben Brown and Linda Przybyszewski commented upon part of chapter 3 when I presented it as a paper at the American Society for Legal History in October 1993.

During the course of my research on this book, I have received valuable cooperation and assistance. I wish to thank especially Howard A. Hood and Peter J. Garland of the Massey Law Library of Vanderbilt University for their skill and patience in locating materials. J. Gordon Hylton kindly shared his study of voting patterns on the Fuller Court. I am also grateful for the help of the staffs of the Library of Congress, the Office of the Curator of the Supreme Court of the United States, the Chicago Historical Society, and the Heard Library of Vanderbilt Library, all of whom greatly facilitated my research. Dorris Baker typed the many revisions of the manuscript with efficiency and good humor. The editorial staff of the University of South Carolina Press was consistently supportive and helpful. Special thanks must go to my wife, Mickey, for her steady support and encouragement. Despite my reliance upon the assistance of others, I am of course solely responsible for any errors or omissions.

The Chief Justiceship of

MELVILLE W. FULLER

INTRODUCTION

The historical reputation of jurists is apt to ebb and flow as succeeding generations see the past with different eyes.[1] But Melville W. Fuller, despite being the subject of a sympathetic biography,[2] has never found a place in the pantheon of judicial giants. When President Grover Cleveland nominated Fuller for the center chair of the Supreme Court, one newspaper commented that "he will enjoy the distinction of being the most obscure man ever appointed chief justice of the United States."[3] Much of the historical literature has followed suit, picturing Fuller as a competent but undistinguished justice.[4] There is, moreover, no adequate treatment of the Supreme Court under Fuller's leadership. Historians have been all too prone to mimic the image, fixed by the Progressives, of a bench single-mindedly devoted to safeguarding corporate interests. But such explanations are simplistic and at best misleading.

Recent years have witnessed a revival of scholarly interest in the legal and economic order of the late nineteenth century. It is a propitious time, therefore, to take a fresh look at Fuller and the jurisprudence of the Fuller Court. The thesis presented here is that Fuller adroitly guided the Supreme Court during one of the most bold and creative periods of its history. Although Fuller never developed a grand theory of constitutional interpretation, there were certain recurring values—limited government, respect for private property, state autonomy—that infused his decision making. Fuller's judicial record marked him as a political and

---

1. See generally Richard A. Posner, *Cardozo: A Study in Reputation* (Chicago: University of Chicago Press, 1990).
2. Willard L. King, *Melville Weston Fuller: Chief Justice of the United States, 1888–1910* (New York: Macmillan, 1950, reprint Chicago: University of Chicago Press, 1967).
3. *Philadelphia Press*, May 1, 1888.
4. David P. Currie, *The Constitution in the Supreme Court: The Second Century, 1888–1986* (Chicago: University of Chicago Press, 1990), 79–83.

1

economic conservative, but he was willing to innovate in many fields of law. In his philosophy and practice, for instance, the substance of property rights was not frozen in the past but evolved to meet changing conditions over time. Nor was Fuller hesitant to review decisions of the political branches or to overturn earlier precedent. In so doing, he led the Court to articulate novel constitutional doctrines to reflect emerging economic conditions and the needs of interstate business enterprise.

Fuller and his colleagues effected a synthesis between property rights and individual liberty. Assigning a high value to economic freedom and the rights of property owners, they viewed attempts to redistribute resources or to benefit special groups as exceeding the limits of appropriate legislative authority. In many cases the justices probed the boundary between legitimate governmental power and the enjoyment of private economic rights. Their judicial commitment to entrepreneurial liberty fitted neatly with utilitarian considerations. The Fuller Court pursued instrumental goals to protect investment capital and guard the national market. Embracing the commercial outlook of modern society, the justices ratified and defended the changes that were transforming American society at the end of the nineteenth century.

Even as the Fuller Court became increasingly involved in supervising the economy, however, its overall record was more complex than standard accounts allow. The Court during Fuller's tenure did cramp legislative power, but not in all respects and not always with the same emphasis. Despite a professed faith in free-market forces, the justices did not consistently follow any economic theory in resolving cases. They were far from doctrinaire adherents of laissez-faire principles. Indeed, contrary to the exaggerated charges of Populist and Progressive critics, the justices upheld most of the business regulations enacted by legislators. Fuller and his colleagues were suspicious of regulatory agencies, yet their decisions on the whole accommodated the rise of the administrative state.

Although the justices invalidated state laws that infringed upon property rights or interfered with the free flow of interstate commerce, the members of the Fuller Court took federalism seriously. To their minds the federal nature of government gave states wide leeway for social experimentation. The justices were reluctant to disturb the traditional balance of state-federal relations in such areas as criminal justice, race relations, and public morals. This dedication to federalism led the Fuller Court to resist an expansive application of the Bill of Rights to the states.

The Fuller years also marked a watershed in the evolution of federal judicial power. The Supreme Court assumed a more prominent role in governance and actively shaped policy. Fuller and his associates did much to establish the federal courts as the primary protectors of constitutionally guaranteed rights. They provided the basis for subsequent growth of federal judicial authority.

For all its trailblazing decisions, the Supreme Court under Fuller was a product of its time and place. The justices generally acted in accordance with the main currents of public opinion. Their work corroborates Lawrence M. Friedman's insight that law is "a mirror of society" and that legal developments are "molded by economy and society."[5]

---

5. Lawrence M. Friedman, *A History of American Law,* 2nd ed. (New York: Simon and Schuster, 1985), 12.

1

A Gentleman and a Scholar

Augusta, the capital of Maine, was a small frontier community in the 1830s. Into this rustic environment Melville Weston Fuller, the second son of Frederick Augustus Fuller and his wife, Catherine Martin Weston, was born on February 11, 1833. Family tradition pointed Fuller on the path to a legal career. His father was an attorney in Augusta, and an uncle was a lawyer in Bangor. Fuller's maternal grandfather, Nathan Weston, sat on the Supreme Court of Maine for many years and served as chief justice from 1834 to 1841. His paternal grandfather, Henry Weld Fuller, was a probate judge in Kennebec County.[1]

The experiences of his childhood would leave a deep mark on Fuller's intellectual development. Three months after Fuller's birth, his mother filed suit for divorce from his father on grounds of adultery. This was an unusual development since divorce was uncommon in antebellum America. As a result of the uncontested divorce decree, Fuller's father had no role in his son's upbringing. Catherine moved with her two children into the home of her father, Judge Weston. The future chief justice spent his formative years under the influence of his grandfather. An ardent Democrat, Judge Weston preached the virtues of Jacksonian politics and frugality in financial matters. He also maintained a fine library and transmitted his love of literature to the young Fuller. Under Judge Weston's tutelage Fuller early acquired lifelong commitments to the Democratic Party and literary pursuits. He was raised as an Episcopalian and remained in that faith until his death. For several years after her di-

---

1. For the career of Nathan Weston see James W. North, *The History of Augusta* (Augusta, Maine: Clapp and North, 1870), 502–505; William Willis, *A History of the Law, the Courts, and the Lawyers of Maine* (Portland: Bailey and Noyes, 1863), 510–517. For the career of Henry Weld Fuller see North, *History of Augusta*, 516–517; Willis, *History of the Law*, 700–702.

vorce Fuller's mother earned a living by giving piano lessons. She remarried in 1844 despite the jealous protests of her second son, then eleven. The remarriage proved difficult for Fuller to accept, and he continued to live most of the time with his grandparents.[2]

At the age of sixteen, in September 1849, Fuller entered Bowdoin College. His mother and grandmother shared the cost of his college education. At Bowdoin Fuller was active in the Athenaean Society, a literary and debating organization, and was elected president of it during his junior year. He became an avid debater and pursued his passion for writing poetry. Democratic Party politics also claimed his attention. In 1852 Fuller helped form a Granite Club at Bowdoin to support Franklin Pierce's campaign for the presidency. Elected to Phi Beta Kappa, Fuller graduated from Bowdoin in September 1853.[3]

Fuller commenced his legal studies promptly after his graduation. As was then the common practice, he received most of his legal training by apprenticeship. Fuller studied law in the Bangor office of his uncle, George Melville Weston. In fall 1854 Fuller entered Harvard Law School, where he attended lectures for six months. Admitted to the Maine bar in 1855, Fuller moved back to Augusta and began to practice law with another uncle. His principal occupation, however, was as associate editor of the *Augusta Age,* the leading Democratic Party newspaper in Maine. A political career also beckoned. In March 1856 Fuller was elected to the Augusta common council. He was promptly appointed both president of the council and Augusta city solicitor.[4]

Despite his early political success and his advantageous family contacts, at the age of twenty-three Fuller abruptly decided to move to Chicago. Several factors influenced his relocation. For an ambitious young attorney Chicago offered much wider professional opportunities than static Augusta. Political considerations also played a role. Fueled by outrage over the Kansas-Nebraska Act of 1854, the Republican Party gained ascendancy in Maine. This in turn induced Fuller, a loyal Democrat, to pursue his political fortunes in a more hospitable state. Last, he was escaping from the pain of a broken marriage engagement.[5]

2. Willard L. King, *Melville Weston Fuller: Chief Justice of the United States, 1888–1910* (New York: Macmillan, 1950, reprint Chicago: University of Chicago Press, 1967), 10–17.

3. King, *Fuller,* 18–26; Louis C. Hatch, *The History of Bowdoin College* (Portland: Loring, Short & Harmon, 1927), 115–116.

4. King, *Fuller,* 26–31; "Chief Justice Fuller," 1 *Green Bag* 2 (1889); Louis Clinton Hatch, *Maine: A History: Biographical* (New York: American Historical Society, 1919), 3–4.

5. King, *Fuller,* 31–34.

There was nothing exceptional about Fuller's western move. Lured by rich soil and burgeoning commerce, many New Englanders migrated to the Midwest in the 1850s. Chicago, with its expanding railroads and rapid industrial growth, was a magnet for aspiring attorneys. The city's population, about eighty-five thousand when Fuller arrived in May 1856, increased steadily as Chicago became the commercial center of the West.

Fuller lacked a ready entrée to Chicago's corporate and professional elite. Shortly after his arrival, Fuller accepted a salaried post (at fifty dollars a month) with Samuel K. Dow, another native of Maine and a successful attorney. Several months later he formed a partnership with Dow. This arrangement, which was the first of several short-lived partnerships, was dissolved in 1860. Fuller appeared regularly in court and earned recognition as a skillful appellate advocate. In 1861, for instance, he argued eight cases before the Supreme Court of Illinois. Despite his hard work, Fuller found it difficult to establish a financially successful law practice. His professional income was meager, and he had to borrow money from his grandfather and uncles.[6]

Immediately after his move to Chicago, Fuller became deeply involved in Illinois politics. Since this aspect of Fuller's career left a bitter legacy, it is essential to consider his political activities in some detail. Sectional differences over the extension of slavery sharply divided Americans on the eve of the Civil War. Like most New Englanders, Fuller strongly disapproved of slavery. While a student at Bowdoin College, he had written a paper criticizing its "tyrannical cruelties." But Fuller regarded slavery as a domestic institution under state control and thus immune from federal interference. Fuller defended the controversial Kansas-Nebraska Act on grounds that it would limit the spread of slavery. Sharply critical of both secessionists and abolitionists, Fuller espoused compromise to resolve the looming sectional crisis.[7] He became an outspoken supporter of Stephen A. Douglas in the famous 1858 senatorial campaign between Douglas and Abraham Lincoln. Two years later Fuller vigorously worked for Douglas in the presidential election.

The election of Lincoln to the presidency and the outbreak of the Civil War in April 1861 left Fuller in an awkward political position. Loyal to the Union, he favored military action to crush secession. Nonetheless, he continued to oppose abolitionism and grew unhappy about the Lincoln administration's conduct of the war. Fuller did not serve in the army. In-

---

6. *Ibid.*, 35–40, 61–63; John M. Palmer, ed., *The Bench and Bar of Illinois* (Chicago: Lewis, 1899), vol. 1, 561–562. For a sketch of Samuel K. Dow see *Bench and Bar of Chicago* (Chicago: American Biographical, 1883), 274–279.

7. King, *Fuller*, 41–46.

stead he spent the war years pursuing partisan goals and denouncing many of Lincoln's policies as unconstitutional.

In November 1861 Fuller was elected a delegate from Chicago to the Illinois constitutional convention. Overshadowed by the war, the 1862 convention did not meet under propitious circumstances. The convention was controlled by the Democrats, and strong partisan feelings dominated its proceedings. Democratic leaders sought to embarrass the state administration of Republican governor Richard Yates and adopted a legislative apportionment highly favorable to their party. Fuller played a prominent role in convention deliberations. Reflecting the racial attitudes of many Northerners, Fuller joined with his Democratic colleagues to adopt constitutional provisions that prevented the immigration of blacks into the state and denied blacks the right to vote. He was also instrumental in framing a blatantly partisan congressional apportionment scheme.[8] Not all of Fuller's positions were so controversial. He worked for a more efficient judicial system and successfully urged the convention to prohibit the issuance of paper money by banks. Although he was a Democratic loyalist, Fuller handled himself well at the convention. A Republican delegate recalled that Fuller "was most eminently fair and considerate in everything."[9] It was indicative of his kindly nature that he obtained permission to use the convention hall "to deliver a poem for the benefit of a blind girl."[10]

All of Fuller's efforts at the convention, however, were in vain. In order to improve the prospects for popular acceptance of the constitution, the Democrats decided to submit the provisions on congressional apportionment and restrictions on blacks as separate measures. Aroused by the gerrymandered apportionment schemes, the Republicans bitterly assailed the proposed constitution as a secessionist document. To Fuller's disappointment, the voters rejected the work of the convention in June 1862. It was revealing that only the sections prohibiting black settlement and suffrage carried.[11]

---

8. Oliver M. Dickerson, *The Illinois Constitutional Convention of 1862* (Urbana, Ill.: University Press, 1905); Arthur Charles Cole, *The Centennial History of Illinois, Volume Three, The Era of the Civil War, 1848–1870* (Springfield: Illinois Centennial Commission, 1919), 267–270; D. W. Lusk, *Eighty Years of Illinois: Politics and Politicians, 1809–1889*, 3rd ed., (Springfield, Ill.: H. W. Rokker, 1889), 142–144. See generally *Journal of the Constitutional Convention of the State of Illinois* (Springfield, 1862).

9. Elliot Anthony, *The Constitutional History of Illinois* (Chicago: Chicago Legal News Print, 1891), 114.

10. *Journal of the Constitutional Convention*, 450.

11. Dickerson, *Illinois Constitutional Convention*, 20–26; Cole, *Centennial History of Illinois, Volume Three*, 270–272.

Fuller privately vowed to take no further part in active political life until his law practice was more firmly established. Yet in less than a year he was elected to the Illinois House of Representatives from a usually Republican Chicago district. Fueled by resentment of the Emancipation Proclamation, the Democrats captured control of both houses of the legislature in November 1862. Fuller's margin of victory was narrow, and the election results were disputed. He petitioned the Supreme Court of Illinois for a writ of mandamus and was declared duly elected.[12] It might have been better if Fuller had lost this contest. The 1863 legislative session, known as the "peace" legislature, was perhaps the most contentious in Illinois history. Once again Fuller found himself in the center of controversy.

Democrats unsparingly denounced Lincoln's policies and engaged in running battles with Governor Yates. Emerging as a leader of the Democrats in the House, Fuller was linked to a host of controversial measures. He urged ratification of the Corwin Amendment to the federal constitution, a provision that prohibited interference with slavery by the federal government. Moreover, to many Democrats the Emancipation Proclamation was a particularly sensitive issue. They believed Lincoln had broken his repeated pledges that the war was to restore the Union, not free the slaves. Fuller supported a resolution that denounced the Proclamation as "unconstitutional, contrary to the rules and usages of civilized warfare," and "calculated to bring shame, disgrace and eternal infamy" upon the United States. He delivered a major speech harshly attacking Lincoln's steps to end slavery in the rebellious states. "The Emancipation Proclamation," Fuller maintained, "is predicated upon the idea that the President may so annul the constitution and laws of sovereign states, overthrow their domestic relations, deprive loyal men of their property, and disloyal as well without trial or condemnation."[13] Fuller was also quick to decry violations of civil liberties by the Lincoln administration. He denounced Lincoln's suspension of habeas corpus and presented a resolution deploring suppression of the *Chicago Times* by the military as "subversive of constitutional and natural right." Similarly Fuller assailed the arbitrary arrests of administration critics. Fuller supported a resolution denouncing the arrest and banishment of former Democratic congressman Clement L. Vallandigham, a vitriolic opponent of Lincoln, as a step toward "reducing the country to an absolute despotism."[14]

---

12. *People ex rel Fuller v. Hilyard*, 29 Ill. 413 (1862).

13. *Journal of the House of Representatives of the Twenty-Third General Assembly of the State of Illinois* (Springfield, 1865), 83; King, *Fuller*, 55–56. See generally Lusk, *Eighty Years of Illinois*, 148–162.

14. *Journal of the House of Representatives*, 661, 674, 715.

Utterly exasperated, on June 10 Governor Yates prorogued the legislature for the first time in Illinois history. He acted on the basis of a provision in the state constitution empowering the governor to act in case of a disagreement between the houses with respect to adjournment. The Democrats were outraged. A majority of the lawmakers signed a protest, drafted by Fuller, that branded the governor's action a "monstrous and revolutionary usurpation of power."[15] The matter did not end there. Fuller served as counsel in a court challenge to the legality of the prorogation. The Supreme Court of Illinois, however, sustained the governor's position on grounds that the lawmakers themselves had acted as if the session were terminated.[16]

Soured by his legislative experience, Fuller never again held elective office.[17] Despite the constant wrangling, he was one of the few leading Democrats to win the respect of the Republicans. Fuller remained active in Democratic Party affairs. He was a delegate to the Democratic National Convention in 1864 and actively backed George B. McClellan's unsuccessful presidential bid. He subsequently attended his party's national conventions in 1872, 1876, and 1880.[18] But on occasion Fuller put aside partisan considerations. Following the assassination of Lincoln, he was appointed to a committee of one hundred prominent Chicago citizens who escorted the president's remains to Springfield.[19]

The personal characteristics that enabled Fuller to make friends across party lines facilitated his rise at the Chicago bar and his selection as chief justice. He excelled in establishing harmonious personal relations with people of diverse legal and political views. Fuller was of a genial nature, with an urbane sense of humor and unfailing courtesy. He combined a scholarly manner and quick mind with generous impulses. In his law practice Fuller exemplified the virtues of loyalty, integrity, and diligence. One contemporary recalled that in court Fuller was always "a gentleman and a scholar."[20]

Fuller's striking appearance was also impressive. He was of modest height, standing five feet six inches, but his rugged face, alert eyes, win-

---

15. *Ibid.*, 728–729.
16. *People ex rel Harless v. Hatch*, 33 Ill. 9 (1863).
17. For Fuller's decision to abandon a political career and concentrate on the practice of law see Keith R. Schlesinger, *The Power That Governs: The Evolution of Judicial Activism in a Midwestern State, 1840–1890* (New York: Garland, 1990), 122–125.
18. King, *Fuller*, 59–60, 77.
19. J. Seymour Currey, *Chicago: Its History and Its Builders*, vol. 2 (Chicago: S. J. Clarke, 1912), 155.
20. Palmer, *Bench and Bar of Illinois*, vol. 2, 646.

ning smile, and distinctive mustache gave him a graphic visage. Fuller dressed neatly but did not follow fashions. His whole bearing was reminiscent of that of a patriarchal figure.[21] With his clear voice and good command of language, Fuller developed a forceful oratorial style.

Fuller's financial and professional status was substantially aided by each of his two marriages. In June 1858 he married Calista Ophelia Reynolds. Her father, then deceased, had owned a meat packing plant and land on Dearborn Street in Chicago. Although their union evidently was not entirely happy, Fuller and his wife had two daughters. Calista never recovered from the birth of their second child in January 1864. She died of tuberculosis the following November, leaving Fuller with the young children. Fuller inherited the Dearborn Street property from his late wife and in 1865 erected the Reynolds Building, a large office building, on the site. He moved his office to the Reynolds Building and also received a sizeable rental income from this property.

After a whirlwind courtship Fuller, then thirty-three, married twenty-one-year-old Mary Ellen Coolbaugh in May 1866. Fuller later described his relationship with Mary Ellen as "a love match."[22] Her father, William F. Coolbaugh, was a wealthy banker and president of Union National Bank, the largest financial institution in Chicago. The couple honeymooned for months in Europe. In May 1867 Mary Ellen gave birth to a daughter, the first of eight children. In addition, she raised the two daughters from Fuller's first marriage.

In 1869 the Fullers moved into an elegant mansion on Lake Avenue given to Mary Ellen by her father. The residence was surrounded by large lawns, and there was a greenhouse on the property. The couple collected paintings and maintained an extensive library. Domestic by nature, Fuller delighted in his large family and enjoyed quiet evenings reading at home.

During the 1870s several misfortunes shattered Fuller's domestic tranquility. In October 1871 the great Chicago fire destroyed much of the city. Although Fuller's home was spared, the Reynolds Building was consumed by the blaze. His law office, books, and papers were entirely lost. Fuller relocated his office in temporary quarters, then borrowed money and constructed the Fuller Building, a store and office complex, on the Dearborn Street site.[23] Tragedy struck again in 1874 when Fuller's first son, Melville, died as the result of burns from a hot stove. Three years

---

21. *Chicago Tribune*, May 1, 1888.
22. King, *Fuller*, 65–73.
23. *Ibid.*, 74.

later his father-in-law, Coolbaugh, with whom Fuller had a close relationship, committed suicide.

Notwithstanding these disastrous occurrences, Fuller prospered professionally. Aided by his father-in-law's contacts, after 1866 he developed a large and successful practice focused on real estate and corporate law. He began to represent the Union National Bank and frequently appeared on behalf of other Illinois banks. Fuller also represented prominent business figures, such as Marshall Field, the merchant, and Philip D. Armour, the meat packer. Other clients included Jesse Hoyt, a railroad stockholder and grain elevator owner, and Erskine M. Phelps, a leading entrepreneur. Fuller defended the Chicago, Burlington and Quincy Railroad and the Illinois Central Railroad in personal injury litigation arising out of railroad accidents. He was also the attorney for the Chicago Gaslight and Coke Company in a contract dispute with another gas company.[24]

Although Fuller increasingly appeared on behalf of Chicago's business elite, he also served as counsel for municipal bodies. He became the attorney for the South Park Commissioners in 1882 and tried many eminent domain cases. He handled various legal matters for the City of Chicago, including a suit to enforce a municipal ordinance requiring inspection of flour sold in the city.[25] Fuller's most noteworthy case for the city involved a parcel of land with frontage along Lake Michigan. The Illinois Central Railroad claimed ownership of the disputed land by virtue of an 1869 act, which was subsequently repealed by the Illinois legislature. The railroad argued that the repeal measure was an unconstitutional impairment of the obligation of contract. In 1888, shortly before his elevation to the bench, Fuller secured a declaration from the Seventh Circuit Court of the United States that title to the land remained with the city.[26] This decision was later affirmed by the Supreme Court of the United States after Fuller's appointment as chief justice. He, of course, recused himself from the deliberations.

Fuller's most famous case was his defense of Rev. Charles E. Cheney in prolonged litigation that raised delicate issues of church-state relations. The case arose from a dispute between "low church" clergy, who urged modernization of the Episcopal liturgy, and their "high church"

---

24. *Ibid.*, 94. Stressing Fuller's extensive representation of corporate clients, one historian concluded that he "was one of the busiest and best-paid corporation attorneys in Chicago." Gustavus Myers, *History of the Supreme Court of the United States* (Chicago: Charles H. Kerr, 1912), 589.

25. Palmer, *Bench and Bar of Illinois*, vol. 1, 562; *City of Chicago v. Quinby*, 38 Ill. 274 (1865).

26. *State of Illinois v. Illinois Central Railroad Company*, 33 Fed. Cases 730 (1888).

bishop. Cheney, the popular rector of Christ Church in Chicago, regularly altered the prescribed baptism service by omitting the statement that a baptized child was "regenerate." In June 1869 the bishop of Illinois instituted disciplinary proceedings against Cheney, alleging both canonical disobedience with respect to the administration of baptism and the violation of ordination vows. Arguing that the ecclesiastical court was composed of "high church" clergy prejudiced against him, Cheney questioned whether the tribunal was legally constituted. When these objections were overruled, Fuller obtained a temporary injunction from the Superior Court of Chicago restraining the ecclesiastical court from proceeding with Cheney's trial. Fuller contended that a clergyman had a vested property right in his office. Consequently, he maintained, secular courts could properly examine the sufficiency of the charges before a church tribunal deprived an individual of his property.[27]

Despite Fuller's argument, in January 1871 the Supreme Court of Illinois ordered that the injunction be dissolved. The court ruled that the ecclesiastical courts were the final authority as to offenses against church discipline and that the secular courts could not adjudicate ecclesiastical concerns. Further, the court held that a rector did not have such a property right in his office as to authorize the intervention of the civil courts.[28] The ecclesiastical court reconvened in February 1871 and found Cheney guilty. The bishop then suspended Cheney from the ministry.

The case, however, did not end there. With the support of his vestry and congregation Cheney continued to serve as the rector of Christ Church. In May 1872 three pewholders of Christ Church began a new round of litigation by seeking to enjoin Cheney from officiating in the church building and from receiving any income from the parish. At issue were the ownership and control of Christ Church. Fuller again represented Cheney, contending that the title to the church property was vested in the congregation and was independent of any ecclesiastical governing body. This time Fuller's arguments found their mark. In 1879 the Supreme Court of Illinois ruled that the property belonged to the congregation and was not held in trust for the Episcopal Church as a denomination.[29] Throughout the controversy Fuller demonstrated an im-

---

27. A. T. Andreas, *History of Chicago,* vol. 2 (Chicago, A. T. Andreas, 1891, reprint New York: Arno Press, 1975), 412–413.
28. *Chase v. Cheney,* 58 Ill. 509 (1871).
29. *Calkins v. Cheney,* 92 Ill. 463 (1879).

pressive mastery of ecclesiastical doctrine, and he gained a degree of national recognition for his able representation of Cheney.[30]

In time Fuller became one of the busiest attorneys in Chicago; he tried approximately twenty-five hundred cases during his career. It was a reflection of his stature at the bar that Fuller was sometimes retained by other attorneys to handle difficult litigation. He was a skillful appellate advocate and appeared regularly before the Supreme Court of Illinois. He also participated often in jury trials. In 1871 Fuller handled his first appeal to the Supreme Court of the United States. The matter, however, was submitted on briefs without oral argument.[31] He was admitted to practice before the Court on February 29, 1872, and shortly thereafter argued a bankruptcy case.[32] Two years later he unsuccessfully represented the Merchants National Bank in a challenge to an Illinois tax on national bank stock.[33] Over the ensuing years Fuller's practice frequently took him before the Supreme Court. By the time of his appointment Fuller was well experienced in Supreme Court advocacy.

Fuller's extensive and diversified practice reached many fields of law. He dealt with a range of real property legal issues including evictions, foreclosures, leasehold obligations, homestead exemptions, and a party wall dispute. He also handled contractual litigation, tort cases, actions on promissory notes, challenges to municipal taxes and assessments, and a trademark case. In addition, Fuller participated in the preliminary stages of a celebrated Chicago divorce case.[34] Upon his Supreme Court appointment *Harper's Weekly* perceptively declared that Fuller "goes to the bench with probably a wider experience of all branches of law than has been enjoyed at the bar by any member of the Court."[35]

Fuller received several offers to become permanent counsel for corporations, but he preferred the independence of private practice. Although he often represented corporate interests and wealthy individuals, Fuller would not commit himself to serve a single client. As Fuller moved steadily to the top of the Chicago bar, he gained greater financial success. By the mid-1880s he was earning about thirty thousand dollars annually

---

30. When Fuller was nominated as chief justice Cheney wrote to him, "I have never ceased to be grateful to you for the enthusiasm with which you threw your ability and legal attainments into my case at a time when I sorely needed efficient aid and wise counsel." Charles E. Cheney to Fuller, May 1, 1888, Fuller Papers, LC.

31. *Dows v. City of Chicago*, 78 U.S. 108 (1871).

32. *Traders' Bank v. Campbell*, 81 U.S. 87 (1872).

33. *Tappan v. Merchant's National Bank*, 86 U.S. 490 (1873).

34. King, *Fuller*, 96.

35. *Harper's Weekly*, May 12, 1888, p. 340.

from his law practice, a figure that placed him among the most highly compensated Chicago attorneys. This was augmented by rental income from his real estate investments. In addition to financial security, Fuller won professional recognition from the members of the bar. He was elected president of the Chicago Law Institute in 1874 and president of the Illinois State Bar Association in 1886. In his 1887 presidential address Fuller urged passage of a bill to create intermediate federal appellate courts to relieve the overcrowded United States Supreme Court docket. He further recommended increased compensation for state and federal judges.[36]

Despite the demands of his active practice, Fuller found time to pursue his literary and other academic interests. He loved attending the theater. In 1878 he was chosen for membership in the Chicago Literary Club. This elite group met regularly to hear scholarly papers presented by members. Fuller also became a regular contributor to the *Dial*, a literary magazine started in 1880.[37] It is noteworthy that he devoted his energy to the world of literature and biography rather than to legal scholarship. In addition, Fuller maintained close ties to Bowdoin College, becoming an overseer of the college in 1875 and serving as a trustee from 1894 until his death in 1910.

Fuller's addresses, essays, and reviews give valuable insight into the political philosophy that he would bring to the bench. He wholeheartedly endorsed the Jeffersonian credo. "The fundamental principle of the Democratic party," he observed, "has always been that the Constitution of the United States should be strictly construed." Fuller pictured the Federalist Party and its successors as believing that "government should exercise the functions belonging to Divine Providence, and should regulate the profits of labor and the value of property by direct legislation."[38] Fuller adopted the Jeffersonian maxim that the best government is the least government. "Paternalism," he declared, "with its constant intermeddling with individual freedom, has no place in a system which rests for its strength upon the self-reliant energies of the people."[39]

As a corollary of his Jeffersonian faith, Fuller championed hard-money policies. One of his heroes was Senator Thomas H. Benton, whom he hailed for supporting metal currency and opposing govern-

---

36. Annual Address, *Proceedings of the Illinois State Bar Association* (1887), 59–68.
37. King, *Fuller*, 90.
38. *Dial*, vol. 6 (1885), 11; *Dial*, vol. 4 (1883), 4.
39. *Dial*, vol. 1 (1880), 103.

mental intervention in the economy.[40] On a more contemporary issue, Fuller criticized the Supreme Court's decision in *Julliard v. Greenman* (1884), which upheld the power of Congress to issue peacetime legal tender notes. Adopting a strict construction of congressional authority, he reasoned that "Congress can exercise no power by virtue of any supposed inherent sovereignty in the general government."[41]

Another theme advanced by Fuller was the preservation of states' rights. He advocated the Jeffersonian view that "all power, not expressly and clearly delegated to the general government, remains with the states and with the people." In 1883 he wrote that it was "perhaps time for the pendulum to swing" in the direction of the states.[42]

Fuller directly considered the question of economic regulation, which would occupy so much of his time while he was chief justice, in an 1879 memorial address honoring Judge Sidney Breese of the Illinois Supreme Court. This afforded Fuller an opportunity to comment upon *Munn v. Illinois* (1877), in which Breese had written an opinion for the Illinois court upholding state regulatory authority in broad terms. The Breese opinion was ultimately affirmed by the Supreme Court of the United States.[43] Pointing out that laws regulating prices had been enacted prior to the Declaration of Independence, Fuller framed the crucial inquiry as "how far can they be justified in this country since that event, and how far are they reconcilable with liberty?" In a departure from his usual insistence upon limited government, Fuller was somewhat ambivalent about the outcome in *Munn*. Although he quoted Breese's opinion at length with seeming approval, Fuller guardedly concluded that the views of Breese "will . . . be always referred to as presenting persuasive argument upon one side of the controversy."[44]

Notwithstanding his defined views, Fuller also recognized that constitutional doctrines ultimately rested upon popular support. He aptly noted that "constitutional theories, whatever their merits in the abstract, cannot prevail in the long run against the judgment of a majority of those for whom the Constitution was framed."[45] He understood that there was a political dimension to constitutionalism. Indeed, he con-

---

40. *Dial*, vol. 8 (1887), 11–15.
41. *Julliard v. Greenman*, 110 U.S. 421 (1884); "Constitutional Construction at the Ballot-Box," *Proceedings of the Illinois State Bar Association* (1886), 79.
42. *Dial*, vol. 4 (1883), 5.
43. *Munn v. Illinois*, 94 U.S. 113 (1877).
44. "Sidney Breese," 11 *Chicago Legal News*, January 25, 1879, 157–58.
45. *Dial*, vol. 3 (1882), 52.

tended that debates over constitutional interpretation could appropriately be part of political contests and placed before the general public.[46]

Throughout his long career Fuller remained steadfast to the political convictions he had forged in his early days. The core values that shaped them—limited government, aversion to paternalism, and respect for state authority—would be hallmarks of his constitutional jurisprudence. Fuller's success in the practice of law reinforced his ready acceptance of such principles. Historians have suggested that the tenets of Jacksonian democracy provided an intellectual basis for the emergence of laissez-faire constitutionalism late in the nineteenth century.[47] Fuller's legal thought vividly demonstrates the continuing vitality of the Jacksonian legacy in fashioning constitutional doctrine. His practical experience before the Supreme Court of Illinois, moreover, may have contributed to another strain of his jurisprudence. During the 1880s the Illinois court began actively reviewing the reasonableness of state economic regulations. Fuller was therefore accustomed to a judicial style that stressed a broad role for courts in the supervision of economic legislation.[48]

The sudden death of Chief Justice Morrison R. Waite on March 23, 1888, opened the door for Fuller's surprise appointment to the nation's top judicial post. After the Civil War, the Republican Party long dominated the national government, effectively depriving Fuller of any opportunity for public service at the federal level. This changed with the 1884 election of Grover Cleveland, a Democrat, to the presidency. As is commonly the case, political factors played a major role in Cleveland's decision making with respect to the chief justiceship. He sought a Democrat who shared his conservative economic philosophy.[49] Two practical considerations guided the selection process. First, a presidential election was only months away, and the canvass was generally expected to be very close. Cleveland could not afford to delay in making a choice. Second, the Senate was under Republican control by the narrow margin of 39 to 37. It was therefore essential to name a candidate who could attract some GOP support.

---

46. "Constitutional Construction at the Ballot-Box," *Proceedings of the Illinois State Bar Association* (1886), 83.
47. Michael Les Benedict, "Laissez-Faire and Liberty: A Re-Evaluation of the Meaning and Origins of Laissez-Faire Constitutionalism," 3 *Law and History Review* 318–331 (1985).
48. Schlesinger, *The Power That Governs*, 204–206.
49. Henry J. Abraham, *Justices and Presidents: A Political History of Appointments to the Supreme Court*, 3rd ed. (New York: Oxford University Press, 1992), 142–143.

Mindful of these political realities, Cleveland considered a large field of possible candidates.[50] Senator George F. Edmunds, chairman of the Judiciary Committee, urged the nomination of Edward J. Phelps, a fellow Vermonter, who was then the ambassador to Great Britain. After a close look, however, Cleveland decided against Phelps. The ambassador was unpopular with the Irish-American community and was thus a potential political liability for Cleveland. Moreover, there was already a justice from New England, Horace Gray. Another serious candidate was Senator George Gray of Delaware, but his nomination would cost the Democrats a valuable Senate seat. Several members of the Court recommended that Justice Stephen J. Field should be elevated to the chief justiceship. But no president had promoted an associate justice to the chief position. Adhering to this tradition, Cleveland wished to select a chief justice from outside the existing Court membership. Field, who wanted the post, was acutely disappointed and harbored bitter feeling toward Cleveland.[51]

Eventually Cleveland determined that the new chief justice should come from the West. He based this decision partly on the need for a representative of the Seventh Circuit (Illinois, Indiana, and Wisconsin) on the Supreme Court. The structure of the federal judicial system reinforced Cleveland's decision to name a justice from this area. Established by the Judiciary Act of 1789, the circuit courts were the principal federal courts of general jurisdiction. Supreme Court justices spent much of their time sitting on these circuit courts and adjudicating legal matters at this level. Traditionally presidents tended to select nominees from the various circuits. Yet the Seventh Circuit had been without such representation since 1877. Illinois could make a particularly strong claim for the appointment because the state produced more Supreme Court litigation than any jurisdiction except New York. Cleveland may have also hoped that he would strengthen his prospects for renomination and reelection by naming a candidate from Illinois. The president first approached Judge John Scholfield of the Illinois Supreme Court, but Scholfield declined consideration on grounds that he did not want to live in Washington.

---

50. King, *Fuller*, 104–110; John P. Frank, "Supreme Court Appointments: II," 1941 *Wisconsin Law Review* 351–353.

51. [George C. Gorham], *Biographical Notice of Stephen J. Field* [Washington, D.C., 1892], 107–108; Carl Brent Swisher, *Stephen J. Field: Craftsman of the Law* (Washington: Brookings Institution, 1930, reprint Chicago: University of Chicago Press, 1969), 319. See also Malcolm Clark, Jr., ed., *Pharisee Among the Philistines: The Diary of Judge Matthew P. Deady* (Portland: Oregon Historical Society, 1975), vol. 2, 536.

Scholfield's refusal opened the door for Cleveland to nominate Fuller as chief justice. Cleveland first met Fuller shortly after his inauguration. Fuller was an enthusiastic backer of the Cleveland administration and shared the president's commitment to frugal government, a hard-money policy, and tariff reduction. The president was impressed with Fuller's ability, and the two began a frequent correspondence. Cleveland consulted Fuller on the distribution of political patronage in Illinois. In 1885 Cleveland offered to name Fuller chairman of the Civil Service Commission. Civil service reform was a major goal of the Cleveland administration, and the chairmanship was a crucial position. Citing family needs, Fuller refused the appointment. A year later Cleveland tried again, asking Fuller to accept the post of solicitor general. Once more Fuller declined to enter public service. He also turned down the president's request to serve as one of three United States Pacific Railway commissioners to investigate alleged financial scandals. Despite Fuller's repeated rejection of federal positions, he and Cleveland remained fast friends. The president's visit to Chicago in October 1887 only cemented his high regard for Fuller.[52]

Given the close relationship between the two men and the president's need to select an Illinois candidate, Cleveland naturally turned to Fuller as his choice for the next chief justice. Chicago newspapers and Fuller's friends also put forth his name. Having decided upon Fuller, Cleveland took steps to secure the necessary GOP support. He sounded out Senator Shelby M. Cullom, an Illinois Republican, for his reaction to a Fuller nomination. Cullom ranked Fuller among the five best Democratic lawyers in Illinois. He described Fuller as "not only a good lawyer, but a scholarly man, a gentleman who would grace the position."[53]

On April 29 Cleveland's secretary wired Fuller in Chicago, "The President has determined on you and will act tomorrow unless you object."[54] The president brushed aside Fuller's request for time to consider and formally nominated him on April 30. Five days later Fuller wrote the president and explained his reluctance to accept the position. "My home ties are so strong," he observed, "my personal ambitions so slight, and the conservation of my business interests so very important to my large family, that I hope you will not misconceive me and think me ungracious if I say that I would be glad still to remain in what has been a very happy

52. Cleveland to Fuller, July 19, 1886, Fuller Papers, LC; Allan Nevins, *Grover Cleveland: A Study in Courage* (New York: Dodd, Mead, 1933), 250, 445–446; King, *Fuller*, 98–102.
53. Shelby M. Cullom, *Fifty Years of Public Service,* 2nd ed. (Chicago: A. C. McClurg, 1911), 237–238.
54. Telegram Daniel S. Lamont to Fuller, April 28, 1888, telegram Cleveland to Fuller, April 30, 1888, Fuller papers, LC.

retirement." Nonetheless, Fuller did not wish to embarrass the president or avoid public duty. He therefore accepted the nomination, "trusting that the country will never have cause to regret your calling me to it, and earnestly hoping that God will give me strength equal to the exalted responsibilities imposed."[55]

Fuller's hesitancy underscores the fact that he did not seek the appointment. Aside from his customary modesty, Fuller was understandably reluctant to disrupt his family and leave his stately Chicago home.[56] Financial considerations no doubt also played a part in his thinking. The salary of the chief justice was $10,500 a year, and Fuller would experience a substantial loss of professional income by taking the position. He did, of course, enjoy some independent income from investments and land, but this would hardly offset the reduction in salary.

News of Fuller's nomination was received with jubilation in Chicago.[57] Well-wishers mobbed Fuller at his club and his office. Republicans and Democrats alike applauded the appointment. Recommendations for the nominee streamed in from attorneys, judges, and business leaders. Of special significance was the endorsement of Robert T. Lincoln, the son of the late president, an active Republican and a member of the Chicago bar. The *Chicago Tribune* was also a strong Fuller backer. Illinois's two Republican senators were counted on to promote Fuller's candidacy in the Senate.

Reaction elsewhere to the president's move was more guarded. Although Fuller was a successful lawyer, he was not widely known outside Chicago. Moreover, he was the first appointee to the position of chief justice who had not previously held a federal office. Consequently, some eastern newspapers expressed disappointment at the choice. The *New York Herald* complained that Fuller was "so unknown that his name does not appear in the latest standard works of contemporary biography." The *Utica Herald* declared that "proof is required that Mr. Fuller possesses a single qualification for Chief Justice above ten thousand other lawyers scattered through the Northwest."[58] But most press comment was supportive and stressed Fuller's impressive professional record. *Harper's Weekly*, for instance, observed, "Character, ability, learning, temperament, age, locality—all the demands which are made by the great

---

55. Fuller to Cleveland, May 5, 1888, Cleveland Papers, LC.

56. Fuller wrote to his wife, "My heart is not in this appointment" and declared that he could not contemplate "such a thing without serious misgiving." Fuller to Mrs. Fuller, April 21, April 23, 1888, Fuller Papers, LC.

57. *Chicago Tribune*, May 1, 1888.

58. *New York Herald*, May 1, 1888. Newspaper reaction to the nomination of Fuller is collected in *Public Opinion*, vol. 5, May 5, 1888.

office have been apparently satisfied in the gentleman selected."[59] Likewise, the *Nation* concluded that Fuller's professional success, "conjoined to very engaging personal qualities, to wide scholarship, to rare modesty, and to a character without reproach, gives abundant promise that Mr. Fuller will be equal to the position to which he has been unexpectedly called."[60] The *Indianapolis Sentinel* optimistically predicted that Fuller would "make one of the greatest Chief Justices the country has had."[61]

Despite forecasts of rapid confirmation, Fuller's path to Senate approval was rocky. Disappointed that Cleveland had not appointed his friend Phelps, Senator Edmunds actively opposed Fuller's confirmation from the outset. He delayed Judiciary Committee action and launched an exacting search of Fuller's record. This investigation raised questions with respect to Fuller's brief political career, his opposition to the issuance of legal tender notes, and his professional conduct. Fuller's political activities during the Civil War furnished ample ammunition for his critics. They circulated a pamphlet, *The War Record of Melville W. Fuller,* which reviewed his speeches and voting pattern at the 1863 "peace" legislature. The pamphlet charged that Fuller was a copperhead—a northern sympathizer with the South—and concluded that "the records of the Illinois legislature of 1863 are black with Mr. Fuller's unworthy and unpatriotic conduct."[62] Similarly, the *New York Tribune* branded Fuller "a Copperhead of the most pronounced type." The *Tribune* predicted that many Republican senators would hesitate to confirm a nominee with such sentiments.[63]

Prominent Illinois Republicans rallied to Fuller's defense. They discounted Fuller's Civil War stand as the product of youthful folly and misplaced party loyalty. They stressed that Fuller had favored prosecution of the war and never joined treasonable secret societies. The support of President Lincoln's son was instrumental in dispelling the intimations of wartime disloyalty. Although some Republicans continued to harp on the issue, it proved difficult to make the allegations of copperheadism stick.[64]

The sharp debate over Gilded Age currency policy posed yet another snare for Fuller. Like Cleveland, Fuller supported the gold standard and opposed soft money. His views reflected the position of eastern bankers

---

59. *Harper's Weekly,* May 12, 1888, p. 330. See also *Richmond Daily Tribune,* May 1, 1888.
60. *Nation,* May 3, 1888.
61. *Public Opinion,* vol. 5, May 5, 1888.
62. *The War Record of Melville W. Fuller,* Correspondence and Reports Relating to the Nomination of Melville W. Fuller, National Archives.
63. *New York Tribune,* May 8, 1888.
64. *Chicago Tribune,* May 10, 1888.

and capitalists. As discussed earlier, Fuller had attacked the *Julliard* decision in which the Supreme Court sustained the issuance of legal tender notes in peacetime. Opponents of Fuller hinted that, as chief justice, he might be inclined to reverse *Julliard*. Fuller's backers responded that, whatever his personal opinion, he would accept the *Julliard* precedent and not seek to reopen the legal tender question.[65]

Finally, two Chicago residents questioned Fuller's character. They made shadowy charges of professional misconduct concerning Fuller's handling of certain legal matters in which they had an interest. One set of objections, raised by John C. Dunlevy, a Chicago lawyer, related to two eminent domain proceedings. Dunlevy alleged that in one case Fuller pocketed part of an inflated condemnation award. He further charged that in another case Fuller used his position as jury commissioner to select jurors favorable to his clients and thereby personally profited at Dunlevy's expense.[66] Similarly, Jacob Forsyth complained that Fuller, as opposing counsel in the case of *Forsyth v. Doolittle* (1887), appeared before a jury selected while he was jury commissioner.[67]

Edmunds exhaustively investigated these accusations but could not produce any credible evidence of impropriety on Fuller's part. He even wrote Fuller outlining the charges but without giving the names of the complainants. Edmunds maintained that Senate rules prevented such disclosure. This tactic backfired. Fuller promptly responded that he could not "consent to reply to anonymous aspersions of the character referred to" and requested permission to publish the correspondence. Having secured Edmunds's consent, Fuller released the correspondence and declared that "publication will dispose of these fabrications without subjecting me to the humiliation of having to notice them."[68] The attorneys who participated in these cases submitted affidavits exonerating Fuller of any wrongdoing and emphasizing his high professional standing. For instance, Forsyth's attorney, William H. King, wrote that his client's allegations were unfounded. Moreover, the federal judge who conducted the eminent domain trials promptly issued a statement reject-

---

65. *Chicago Tribune*, May 30, 1888.
66. Frank, "Supreme Court Appointments: II," 355–357; *Chicago Tribune*, June 12, 1888.
67. *Forsyth v. Doolittle*, 120 U.S. 73 (1887); Frank, "Supreme Court Appointments: II," 357–359.
68. Edmunds to Fuller, June 11, 1888, Fuller Papers, LC; telegrams Fuller to Edmunds, June 13 and June 15, 1888, Correspondence and Reports Relating to Nomination of Melville W. Fuller, National Archives. The *Nation* asserted on June 21, 1888, that "Mr. Fuller's dignified treatment of the matter will do much to strengthen the impression that he is worthy of the office for which he has been nominated."

ing the allegations.[69] Upon investigation, then, the charges against Fuller's character evaporated, and the complainants appeared to be disgruntled litigants seeking revenge.

Still the Judiciary Committee did not take action on Fuller's nomination. It appeared that Edmunds hoped to stave off any report until after the upcoming presidential election. But political considerations cut against this delay strategy. Illinois Republicans feared that an unjustified refusal to confirm Fuller would hurt the GOP's chances of carrying Illinois. Eventually Cullom pressed the committee to report the nomination, and in early July Fuller's name was sent to the Senate without any committee recommendation.[70] Unhappy with Fuller's Civil War record, Republican committee members refused to support a favorable recommendation, and thus the committee's action represented a compromise.

On July 20 Fuller's nomination came before an executive session of the Senate. Edmunds led the fight against confirmation. Reviewing Fuller's wartime speeches and legislative votes, Edmunds argued that he could not be trusted to interpret the Reconstruction amendments in the proper spirit. "How long will the results of the Civil War be safe if the President may fill up the Supreme Court with disloyalists," he asked.[71] Senator William M. Evarts of New York covered much of the same ground. He stressed the need to preserve the constitutional outcome of the Civil War and expressed doubt about the soundness of Fuller's constitutional views. Senator William M. Stewart of Nevada bitterly assailed Fuller as a copperhead and attacked his stand for a hard-money policy.[72]

Proponents of Fuller rallied to urge his confirmation. Senator Charles B. Farwell of Illinois defended Fuller's conduct during the war and strongly endorsed him as a man of high personal character. In a sharply worded address Cullom rebuked the Judiciary Committee for entertaining vague and malicious charges against Fuller. He then turned the tables on Edmunds by questioning the sincerity of his objections to Fuller's wartime record. To demonstrate his point, Cullom read a strongly anti-Lincoln speech delivered by Ambassador Phelps, Edmunds's personal choice for the chief justiceship. He contended that Edmunds was applying a double standard to Fuller.[73] This tactic effectively silenced Fuller's critics. Delighted to watch the Republicans fight among themselves, the Democratic senators took no active part in the debate.

---

69. *Nation,* June 21, 1888.

70. Cullom, *Fifty Years of Public Service,* 238–239; *Chicago Tribune,* July 3, 1888.

71. As quoted in King, *Fuller,* 120.

72. For the Senate debate on Fuller see *Chicago Tribune,* July 21, 1888.

73. *Ibid.;* Cullom, *Fifty Years of Public Service,* 239.

Following three hours of discussion the Senate voted to confirm Fuller's appointment by a margin of 41 to 20. Ten GOP senators, headed by Cullom and Farwell, joined the Democrats in support of the nominee. Particularly noteworthy was the backing of Senator Matthew S. Quay of Pennsylvania, chairman of the Republican National Committee. The two Republican senators from Maine, Fuller's native state, also voted for his confirmation.[74]

Although some press comment continued to deprecate Fuller, newspapers generally applauded his confirmation.[75] Several papers, however, criticized the partisan overtones of the confirmation process. The *Chicago Tribune,* for example, described the Republican hope of delaying confirmation until the presidential election as "both unwise and dangerous." Reflecting regional pride in Fuller's appointment, the *Tribune* admonished "a narrow, provincial feeling" among some easterners that Fuller was not sufficiently prominent to be chief justice.[76] *Harper's Weekly* attacked Edmunds's intimation that no Democrat could be trusted to interpret the Constitution. The *Weekly* also expressed reservations about the Senate's handling of the nomination:

> The President nominated for the most important office in his gift a gentleman not generally known to the country. The immediate and unanimous testimony from the State and city in which he lived, however, was in the highest degree favorable. But party spirit, on the eve of a Presidential election, sought every means to discredit him. His whole personal, professional, and political career was searched with electric lights. Months were devoted to the scrutiny, but even party spirit could find nothing substantial enough on which to base a rejection of the nomination, and it was grudgingly reported to the Senate without a recommendation.[77]

In a similar vein, the *New York Times* sharply criticized the Judiciary Committee for "the contemptible partisan policy" of delaying consideration of Fuller while hunting for "something against the character of the President's nominee."[78]

Fuller's distinctive white mustache sparked a light-hearted debate while he was awaiting confirmation. No prior chief justice had worn a

---

74. *Journal of the Executive Proceedings of the Senate,* 1887–1889, vol. 26, 313.

75. Southern newspapers hailed the confirmation of Fuller's appointment. *Atlanta Constitution,* July 21, 1888; *Richmond Dispatch,* July 22, 1888.

76. *Chicago Tribune,* July 21, 1888.

77. *Harper's Weekly,* August 4, 1888, 566–567.

78. *New York Times,* July 21, 1888.

mustache, and some speculated that Fuller would remove it in deference to tradition. Other commentators insisted that Fuller should assert his individuality and keep his mustache.[79] In the end Fuller retained the mustache, and it became an endearing trademark. Several years after Fuller became chief justice the *New York Sun* drolly observed that "Chief Justice Fuller is allowed to keep his flowing mustachios, because there would be too little left of him if they were cut off."[80]

The ensuing weeks were busy for Fuller and his family. Promptly after the Senate vote Fuller wrote Cullom to thank him for his vigorous support. "I hope that you will never have cause to regret your action," he observed. "I can't tell you how pleased I am that Maine and Illinois, both so dear to me, stood by me."[81] In late July Fuller and his wife journeyed to Washington, where he paid a courtesy call on President Cleveland and looked for suitable housing. Cleveland asked Fuller to take the oath of office as soon as possible, but Fuller preferred to wait until the Supreme Court convened in October. There was, he explained to Cleveland, "really no emergency requiring me to qualify." Moreover, one of his first duties as chief justice would be to allot himself a circuit court, and this raised the possibility of reassigning all the justices. Although the chief was authorized to assign circuit duties when the Court was not in session, Fuller wisely wished not to offend his associates by taking any unilateral action.[82]

On October 8, 1888, fifty-five-year-old Melville Fuller took the oath in open court, swearing to "administer justice without respect to persons, and do equal right to the poor and to the rich." In keeping with congressional legislation, Fuller was the first person to be formally commissioned "Chief Justice of the United States."[83] He immediately began to preside over the Supreme Court's deliberations. Professional success and political fortune had combined to catapult Fuller from a relatively unknown law practice to the highest judicial post in the nation. He now faced the daunting task of establishing himself as a force on the Court and defining his judicial philosophy.

---

79. *Harper's Weekly,* May 12, 1888, 331; *Richmond Daily Times,* May 8, 1888.
80. *New York Sun,* July 22, 1892.
81. Cullom, *Fifty Years of Public Service,* 240.
82. Fuller to Cleveland, August 6, 1888, Cleveland Papers, LC.
83. Robert J. Steamer, *Chief Justice: Leadership and the Supreme Court* (Columbia, S.C.: University of South Carolina Press 1986), 5.

2

Never a Better Administrator

When Fuller took his seat in October 1888, his initial task was to exert leadership over his colleagues. This was a daunting assignment for a new chief justice who had only limited experience in public life. Although Fuller had appeared as counsel before the Supreme Court on a number of occasions, he was hardly a known quantity to the associate justices. Several of his colleagues harbored doubts that Fuller had sufficient stature for the chief's position. Justice Joseph P. Bradley, for instance, lamented that although Fuller was "a very estimable man and a successful practitioner, [this] hardly fills the public expectation for the place of Chief Justice of the United States." He observed that Fuller might "by happy accident turn out to be an admirable appointment" but cautioned that "an appointment to this place ought not to depend for its success on accident and good fortune."[1] Little wonder that Fuller was somewhat apprehensive about establishing himself with the sitting justices. "No rising sun for me," he mused in 1890, "with these old luminaries blazing away with all their ancient fires."[2]

COLLEGIAL RELATIONSHIPS

A likeable man, Fuller excelled in establishing warm collegial relations. He needed his skills as a mediator, because the Supreme Court, at least during the early years of his tenure, was composed of diverse and strong-willed individuals. Perhaps the biggest prima donna was Justice Stephen J. Field. Appointed by President Abraham Lincoln, Field pioneered a

---

1. As quoted in Irving Schiffman, "Melville Fuller" in Leon Friedman and Fred L. Israel, eds., *The Justices of the United States Supreme Court, 1789–1978* (New York: Chelsea House, 1980), vol. 2, 1479.
2. Fuller to Bancroft Davis, January 18, 1890, Bancroft Davis Papers, LC.

broad reading of the due process clause of the Fourteenth Amendment to protect private property from state regulation. Field was the most influential justice during the Gilded Age, and his property-conscious views gained ascendancy during Fuller's chief justiceship.[3] Also cantankerous and vindictive, he had coveted the chief's position for himself. When Fuller's nomination was announced, a Chicago attorney predicted that Field would "eat him in one bite."[4]

Field was often a vexation to his colleagues. In 1892 a frustrated Justice Horace Gray complained that Field "this term seems to be behaving more like a wild bull than before."[5] Field's overbearing nature is vividly illustrated by his sustained campaign challenging the accuracy of a headnote prepared by court reporter John Chandler Bancroft Davis for the case of *O'Neil v. Vermont* (1892).[6] For weeks Field futilely badgered his fellow justices and Davis in an effort to change the headnote. Fuller sided with the reporter, advising Field that his complaint "greatly surprises and pains me." Field even declared that he would make the headnote dispute public, but he never carried out his threat.[7]

Despite Field's irascible temperament, Fuller managed to achieve a friendship with him through a combination of tact and deference. In a conciliatory gesture, Fuller asked Field to speak for the Court at the 1890 centennial celebration in New York of the organization of the federal judiciary.[8] Fuller then profusely praised Field's address, a step which doubtless pleased the self-assured Field. Fuller's accommodation with Field was eased by their common allegiance to the Democratic Party and by the fact that Fuller shared Field's economic views.

Fuller's close affinity with Field was demonstrated in December 1893 when the latter was ill and effectively gave Fuller his proxy to vote at the conference of the justices. Field wrote to the chief, "You can cast my vote

---

3. See Carl Brent Swisher, *Stephen J. Field: Craftsman of the Law* (Washington: Brookings Institution, 1930, reprint Chicago: University of Chicago Press, 1969); Robert G. McCloskey, *American Conservatism in the Age of Enterprise, 1865–1910* (Cambridge, Mass.: Harvard University Press, 1951), 72–126; John E. Semonche, *Charting the Future: The Supreme Court Responds to a Changing Society, 1890–1920* (Westport, Conn.: Greenwood Press, 1978), 102–104.

4. As quoted in Willard L. King, *Melville Weston Fuller, 1888–1910* (New York, Macmillan, 1950, reprint Chicago: University of Chicago Press, 1967), 128.

5. Gray to Fuller, May 8, 1892, Fuller Papers, LC.

6. *O'Neil v. Vermont,* 144 U.S. 323 (1892).

7. Alan F. Westin, "Stephen J. Field and the Headnote to O'Neil v. Vermont: A Snapshot of the Fuller Court at Work," 67 *Yale Law Journal* 363 (1958).

8. Centennial Celebration of the Organization of the Federal Judiciary, February 4, 1890, 134 U.S. 711 (1890).

in all the cases with your own, with the exception of the case of the Northern Pacific. In all others I believe your opinion corresponds with my own."[9]

Another imposing figure on the Court was Samuel F. Miller, a Republican from Iowa who had written some major opinions. Miller, who had been sharply critical of Fuller's predecessor, Morrison R. Waite, was often disputatious and a source of irritation to his fellow justices. But in time he also succumbed to Fuller's charm. Senator Cullom reported, "Justice Miller told me on-one occasion that Fuller was the best presiding judge that the Supreme Court had had within his time; and in addition he was a most lovable, congenial man."[10]

Fuller also gained the affection of Bradley, who had favored the selection of Field and was unenthusiastic about Fuller's appointment. Bradley was an able jurist who had served with Miller on the 1877 electoral commission, which resolved the disputed presidential election between Rutherford B. Hayes and Samuel J. Tilden. Fuller won Bradley's support by the simple expedient of seeking his counsel and deferring to his suggestions. Bradley responded warmly and soon took the new chief justice under his wing. Although Bradley served for only three years with Fuller, they became close friends.[11]

Justice Horace Gray of Massachusetts was the most scholarly member of the Court. He was an acknowledged expert on legal history and had a prodigious knowledge of English constitutional developments. Gray was a stickler for judicial etiquette. Even in an age of formality he stood out as a martinet on courtroom dress and procedure. Although Fuller and Gray clashed on a number of issues, they maintained a good working relationship. A former chief justice in Massachusetts, Gray admired Fuller's diplomatic management of the judicial conference. Fuller often relied on Gray's scholarship in preparing opinions.[12]

Fuller's relations with Justice John Marshall Harlan warrant particular comment. In 1877 Fuller, together with other Chicago attorneys, had opposed Harlan's appointment to the Supreme Court. Fuller's primary

---

9. Field to Fuller, December 16, 1893, Fuller Papers, LC.

10. Charles Fairman, *Mr. Justice Miller and the Supreme Court, 1862–1890* (Cambridge: Mass.: Harvard University Press, 1939), 349, 373, 409; Shelby M. Cullom, *Fifty Years of Public Service,* 2nd ed. (Chicago: A. C. McClurg, 1911), 241.

11. King, *Fuller,* 129–131. See generally Charles Fairman, "What Makes A Great Justice? Mr. Justice Bradley and the Supreme Court, 1870–1892," 30 *Boston University Law Review* 49 (1950).

12. King, *Fuller,* 132–134; see generally Robert M. Spector, "Legal Historian on the United States Supreme Court: Justice Horace Gray, Jr., and the Historical Method," 12 *American Journal of Legal History* 181 (1968).

concern was geographic representation on the Court. He was troubled by the prospect of having Harlan, who was from Kentucky, sit for the Seventh Circuit, which was composed of Illinois, Indiana, and Wisconsin. Fuller felt strongly that there should be a justice appointed from within the Seventh Circuit, and he urged consideration of a federal judge from Chicago. Harlan's qualifications were also suspect to Fuller, who termed his nomination "a disagreeable surprise." Fuller was contemptuously dismissive of Harlan, commenting that "there seems positively no reason for this circuit justice. It accomplished nothing except to reward a Louisiana Commissioner, a personal and secondary consideration. I hope the nomination will fail of confirmation."[13]

Despite Fuller's reservations about Harlan, the two had become friends before Fuller's appointment as chief justice. Fuller appeared before Harlan several times when he presided at the circuit court for the Seventh Circuit. Harlan's son James studied law in Fuller's office, and the Fullers sometimes stayed at Harlan's home when they were in Washington. After Fuller became chief justice, James Harlan served briefly as his secretary and then organized a law firm that succeeded to Fuller's Chicago practice.

A colorful individualist, Harlan was the justice least comfortable with the jurisprudence of the Fuller years. Confident of his moral rectitude, he was inclined to lecture his colleagues during conferences. This was not an endearing trait and sometimes generated friction among the justices. Harlan became known for his spirited delivery of dissenting opinions. But he did not personalize differences over legal principles, and he was a lighthearted comrade off the bench. Notwithstanding their divergent views, Fuller and Harlan remained on good personal terms until Fuller's death.[14]

Fuller's desire to win the friendship and support of his colleagues was complicated by frequent changes in the composition of the Supreme Court. Eleven new justices appointed by five presidents joined the Court during Fuller's twenty-two-year tenure. The decade of the 1890s produced an unusually large fluctuation in the Court's membership. Five of the justices sitting when Fuller joined the Court died by 1893, and Justice Field resigned in 1897. Several of the newly appointed justices, such as Howell E. Jackson and William T. Moody, served for just a brief period and left little mark. Of the justices sitting when Fuller took his seat, only

---

13. As quoted in John P. Frank, "The Appointment of Supreme Court Justices: Prestige, Principles and Politics," 1941 *Wisconsin Law Review* 207–208. See also "Document: The Appointment of Mr. Justice Harlan," 29 *Indiana Law Journal* 46, 58–59 (1953).
14. King, *Fuller,* 131–132; Loren P. Beth, *John Marshall Harlan: The Last Whig Justice* (Lexington: University Press of Kentucky, 1992), 157–158.

Harlan remained on the Court throughout Fuller's tenure. A high turn-over rate on the Court is potentially disruptive because it reduces the opportunity for individual justices to become socialized into a cohesive group.

Fortunately for Fuller, the incoming justices proved to be agreeable colleagues who worked well together. Justices Brewer and Henry Billings Brown, for instance, were personable individuals who cheerfully carried their share of the Court's work.[15] The jovial Brewer was particularly close to Fuller, and the two were often in agreement on the issues before the Court. In 1891 Fuller informed his wife, "Brewer is a great favorite with me. He is a genuine man."[16] Likewise, Fuller commanded the respect and affection of George Shiras, Jr. Although he was retiring by nature, Shiras had an even temper and a well-developed sense of humor. Fuller appreciated Shiras's ability to remain calm in heated conference-room debates. Following his retirement in February 1903, Shiras regularly corresponded with Fuller until the chief's death.[17]

During his second term President Cleveland appointed two conservative Democrats to the Supreme Court. One of them, Rufus W. Peckham, strongly resembled Fuller in appearance and shared many of the chief's political values and constitutional ideas. Fuller and Peckham had known each other for years through their activities on behalf of the Democratic Party, and they became fast friends as well as judicial allies.[18] Fuller also established a good relationship with Edward Douglas White, who joined the Court in 1893. Possessed of a forceful personality and independent mind, White was an industrious worker whose opinion output was behind only those of Fuller and Brewer.[19] He succeeded Fuller as chief justice in 1910, the first associate justice elevated to the center chair.

The nomination of Joseph McKenna to the Supreme Court in 1897

---

15. See Robert J. Glennon, Jr., "Justice Henry Billings Brown: Values in Tension," 44 *University of Colorado Law Review* 553 (1973); Michael J. Brodhead, *David J. Brewer: The Life of a Supreme Court Justice, 1837–1910* (Carbondale, Ill.: Southern Illinois University Press, 1994); Robert E. Gamer, "Justice Brewer and Substantive Due Process: A Conservative Court Revisited," 18 *Vanderbilt Law Review* 615 (1965); Francis Bergan, "Mr. Justice Brewer: Perspective of A Century," 25 *Albany Law Review* 191 (1961); J. Gordon Hylton, "David Brewer and the Rights of Property: A Conservative Justice Reconsidered," unpublished paper.

16. As quoted in King, *Fuller,* 155.

17. George Shiras III, *Justice George Shiras, Jr., of Pittsburgh* (Pittsburgh: University of Pittsburgh Press, 1953), 123–126, 212–213.

18. King, *Fuller,* 191. See also "Mr. Justice Peckham," 30 *American Law Review* 100 (1896).

19. See Robert B. Highsaw, *Edward Douglass White: Defender of the Conservative Faith* (Baton Rouge: Louisiana State University Press, 1981).

put Fuller in an awkward position. McKenna had served for five years as a circuit judge on the Ninth Circuit before becoming attorney general under President William McKinley. Fuller received several letters from federal judges asserting that McKenna had poor legal training, was an undistinguished judge, and lacked the qualifications for a seat on the Supreme Court. After investigating these allegations, Fuller took the unusual step of raising the matter with President McKinley and attempting to prevent the appointment.[20] The president, however, stuck by his choice, and McKenna was confirmed a month later. In contrast to his normal practice, Fuller spent little time seeking to gain McKenna's favor. Although McKenna was honest and diligent, he never achieved the confidence of his colleagues. Fuller assigned him the easier cases, and their relationship was always somewhat distant.[21]

In contrast to his lack of enthusiasm for McKenna, Fuller was pleased when Oliver Wendell Holmes joined the Supreme Court in 1902. Holmes formed few close friendships among his colleagues on the bench. Despite differences in temperament, however, Fuller and Holmes soon became intimate friends.[22] Fuller was delighted with Holmes's prompt preparation of opinions but sometimes expressed concern that Holmes's detached attitude caused resentment by other justices. After the death of Fuller's wife in 1904, Holmes made regular Sunday calls on Fuller in Washington.[23] This cemented a personal bond between the aging chief and Holmes. By 1905 Holmes noted his "affectionate relations" with Fuller.[24]

Fuller was a masterful social leader of the Court. He successfully directed the talents of his diverse and independent-minded associates. Despite sharp divisions in some important cases, Fuller prevented destructive personal feuds from erupting and damaging a collegial working environment. Indeed, by modern standards the justices stood together to a remarkable degree. Throughout Fuller's service as chief, the

---

20. Charles B. Bellinger to Fuller, September 11, 1897, Judge C. H. Hanford to Fuller, October 7, 1897, Fuller Papers, LC; King, *Fuller*, 228–230. See also Matthew McDevitt, *Joseph McKenna: Associate Justice of the United States* (Washington: Catholic University of America Press, 1946, reprint New York: Da Capo Press 1974), 103–105.

21. Semonche, *Charting the Future*, 105, 108–109.

22. King, *Fuller*, 289–301. The affinity between Fuller and Holmes is examined in G. Edward White, *Justice Oliver Wendell Holmes: Law and Inner Self* (New York: Oxford University Press, 1993), 315–318.

23. Mark DeWolfe Howe, ed., *Holmes-Pollock Letters: The Correspondence of Mr. Justice Holmes and Sir Frederick Pollock, 1874–1932*, 2nd ed. (Cambridge, Mass.: Harvard University Press, 1961), vol. 1, pp. 144, 148, 152, 155; Liva Baker, *The Justice from Beacon Hill: The Life and Times of Oliver Wendell Holmes* (New York: HarperCollins, 1991), 436.

24. As quoted in Baker, *The Justice from Beacon Hill*, 408.

Supreme Court was staffed by a Republican majority. Yet under his leadership the justices almost never divided along party lines. Justices appointed by Republican and Democratic presidents commonly voted together, and partisan affiliation was not a determining factor in deciding cases. The historian Charles Warren cogently observed that "the slight importance . . . which was to be attached to the party designations of the Judges upon the Court was never better illustrated than during Fuller's Chief Justiceship."[25] The conservative economic views of Democrats Fuller and Peckham, for instance, easily blended with the Republican policy of defending entrepreneurial liberty. Thus the major rulings of the Fuller years were supported by justices named by both Republican and Democratic presidents. Even the politically charged series of cases known as the Insular Cases did not produce a split on straight partisan lines. Nor did Fuller hesitate in *Pollock v. Farmers' Loan & Trust Company* (1895) to strike down the 1894 income tax supported by a Democratic Congress and President Cleveland. This record underscores Justice Brown's observation that he had "never known partisan considerations to enter into the disposition of cases."[26]

Early in his term as chief justice, Fuller had an opportunity to solidify his position with his fellow justices and the general public. To mark the centennial of the inauguration of President George Washington, Congress invited Fuller to deliver an address before a joint session on December 11, 1889. The president and much of official Washington attended the commemoration services. Fuller's remarks were well received; he was repeatedly applauded during his presentation. The Washington commemoration was an auspicious beginning for Fuller and immeasurably enhanced his standing with both his colleagues and the nation. Justice Bradley, for instance, lavishly praised a draft of Fuller's remarks as "admirable in conception & execution."[27] Justice Harlan wrote Fuller's wife, "The address has *fixed* the position of the Chief Justice before the country and will add greatly to the power and prestige of the Court in the popular mind."[28] At Justice Miller's suggestion, the justices decided to publish Fuller's speech in the Supreme Court reports. The *New York Times* reported that Fuller's oration "was at once a surprise and a delight to the

25. Charles Warren, *The Supreme Court in United States History,* rev. ed. (Boston: Little, Brown, 1926), vol. 2, p. 721; John B. Gates, *The Supreme Court and Partisan Realignment* (Boulder, Colo.: Westview Press, 1992), 58–90.

26. Charles A. Kent, *Memoir of Henry Billings Brown* (New York: Duffield, 1915), 30–31.

27. *New York Times,* December 12, 1889; Bradley to Fuller, December 5, 1889, Fuller Papers, LC.

28. As quoted in King, *Fuller,* 132.

vast audience that heard it" and that it won "hearty praise" even from senatorial opponents.[29]

Aside from gaining Fuller collegial and popular acclaim, the address gave him a chance to speak in general terms about some of the fundamental constitutional issues of the day. It contains important clues to his approach to these questions. One of the issues Fuller discussed was the balance between the states and the federal government. Although he noted the increased power of the federal government, Fuller stressed the vital importance of the states. In his view, the Civil War preserved the Union "without the loss of distinct and individual existence or of the right of self-government by the States." Fuller also addressed the place of property rights in the constitutional scheme. He guardedly approved legislative steps to alleviate inequality of conditions but warned that "when man allows his beliefs, his family, his property, his labor, each of his acts, to be subjected to the omnipotence of the State, or is unmindful of the fact that it is the duty of the people to support the government and not of the government to support the people, such a surrender of independence involves the cessation of such progress in its largest sense." This indicates Fuller's basic commitment to the tenets of laissez-faire constitutionalism. He then probed the interplay between the rights of property owners and economic regulation, observing that

> while the rights to life, to use one's faculties in all lawful ways, and to acquire and enjoy property are morally fundamental rights antecedent to constitutions, which do not create but secure and protect them, yet it is within the power of the State to promote the health, peace, morals, education, and good order of the people by legislation to that end, and to regulate the use of property in which the public has such an interest as to be entitled to a certain control.

Further, Fuller hailed the provisions of the Constitution "which inhibit the subversion of individual freedom, the impairment of the obligation of contracts, and the confiscation of property."[30]

Such language is revealing as to Fuller's constitutional priorities. Evidently influenced by natural law theory, Fuller concluded that private property existed before the creation of political authority and that a principal purpose of government was to protect property rights. He identified property ownership with the preservation of individual liberty.

---

29. Fuller to Bancroft Davis, January 18, 1890, Bancroft Davis Papers, LC; "Address in Commemoration of the Inauguration of George Washington, December 11, 1889," 132 U.S. 706 (1889). For contemporary reaction see *New York Times,* December 12, 1889.
30. "Address in Commemoration of the Inauguration of George Washington," 132 U.S. 728, 732.

Last, while not closing the door on growth of federal authority or any economic regulations, Fuller clearly signaled the central place of states' rights and private property in his understanding of the constitutional order.

ADMINISTRATIVE RESPONSIBILITIES

In addition to winning the support of his colleagues, Fuller skillfully managed the Supreme Court's business. The leadership ability of the chief justice is a vital force in the operations of the Court. In many respects the chief justice has no greater authority than any of the associate justices, but the role of the chief encompasses managerial responsibilities. Consequently, an effective chief can use a variety of techniques to guide the justices and influence the direction of judicial doctrine. Fuller has deservedly received high marks for his administrative leadership.[31] Felix Frankfurter later observed that "there never was a better administrator on the Court than Fuller."[32]

Fuller soon demonstrated his influence on the working of the Court. He expedited the Court's business and presided with dignity over public sessions and oral arguments. Although Fuller's chair on the bench had to be raised several inches to compensate for his short stature, his presence and sense of decorum dominated the courtroom. Attentive and patient, Fuller was particularly considerate of fledgling counsel. He once permitted the attorney general of Hawaii, who was appearing before the Court for the first time, to begin his oral argument again after the inexperienced attorney had wasted much of his allotted time on irrelevant background information.[33] Frankfurter, who argued before Fuller, recalled that "he presided with great gentle firmness. You couldn't but catch his own mood of courtesy. Counselors too sometimes lose their tempers, or, in the heat of argument, say things, and there was a subduing effect about Fuller."[34] Former Attorney General Richard Olney declared that under Fuller "the court at Washington has been universally acclaimed as the most agreeable tribunal in the country to appear before."[35]

---

31. Robert J. Steamer, *Chief Justice: Leadership and the Supreme Court* (Columbia, S.C.: University of South Carolina Press, 1986), 123, 134–135; Schiffman, "Melville W. Fuller," 1479–1480.

32. Felix Frankfurter, "Chief Justices I Have Known," 39 *Virginia Law Review* 884, 890 (1953).

33. Charles Henry Butler, *A Century at the Bar of the Supreme Court of the United States* (New York: G. P. Putnam's Sons, 1942) 162–163.

34. Frankfurter, "Chief Justices I Have Known," 889.

35. *Proceedings of the Bar and Officers of the Supreme Court of the United States in Memory of Melville Weston Fuller,* December 10, 1910 (Washington, 1911), 9.

Despite his gentle nature, Fuller's patience was sometimes strained during oral arguments. Charles Henry Butler, the court reporter, recalled one incident in 1905 that involved a young Kansas attorney who appeared before the justices "in a yellow tweed suit—no vest, flowing necktie, pink shirt and tan shoes." He represented a drugstore operator who had been arrested for selling liquor to an "allottee" Indian. In the course of argument Justice Brewer asked, "What do you think the status of an allottee is?" The attorney responded, "If you fellows up there don't know, how do you think us fellows down here should know?" Butler reported the stunned reaction of the justices: "The shocked expression on the face of dear Chief Justice Fuller will never be forgotten. Justice Holmes, shaking with laughter, buried his face in his arms on the Bench to hide his amusement, and there was a sort of dazed expression on the features of the other members of the Court."[36] Notwithstanding this amusing gaffe, the Supreme Court decided the case in favor of the attorney's druggist client.

Presiding at the conferences of the justices posed another challenge for Fuller. Justice Brewer colorfully described the atmosphere that often prevailed in the conference room during the early Fuller years: "When they all get settled the tug of war commences. They are all strong men, and do not waste a word. They lock horns and the fight is stubborn; arguments are hurled against each other, the discussion grows animated and continues for hours. But we always think that justice is triumphant—except the dissenters."[37] Fuller's easy manners and genial temperament served him well in managing judicial conferences. Samuel Williston, the law secretary of Justice Gray, remembered that Fuller "soon acquired reputation as an excellent presiding officer, not only when the court was sitting, but at its consultations on Saturday morning." Gray reported that the conferences "became not infrequently somewhat heated, and a calm moderator, of pleasant manners, was helpful."[38] Fuller softened differences among the justices with lubricating humor. He could sharply disagree with colleagues and still maintain personal friendships.

One incident illustrates Fuller's use of humor to dispel tension in the conference room. Justice Harlan was explaining his view of a pending case when Holmes interrupted and declared, "But that just won't wash." Harlan was furious, but Fuller promptly interceded to prevent a quarrel. With a smile Fuller began a washboard motion with his hands and said,

---

36. Butler, *A Century at the Bar,* 74–75. For a contemporary account of this incident see *New York Tribune,* January 11, 1905. See *Matter of Heff,* 197 U.S. 488 (1905).

37. As quoted in Fairman, "What Makes A Great Justice?," 75–76

38. Samuel Williston, *Life and Law: An Autobiography* (Boston: Little, Brown, 1940), 95.

"But I just keep scrubbing away, scrubbing away." The justices laughed and the matter was closed.[39] As part of his effort to foster harmonious working relations among the justices, Fuller introduced the practice of requiring each justice to shake hands with the other justices each morning in the conference room.[40] He hoped that this custom, which has endured to the present, would minimize permanent rifts among the justices.

As chief justice Fuller was responsible for assigning the preparation of opinions when he was in the majority. Fuller generally voted with the majority, and thus he assigned most of the opinions during his service on the Court. Throughout the Court's history, many chief justices have chosen to write the decision in cases of greatest interest.[41] Early in his tenure Fuller kept some of the major opinions, such as *Pollock v. Farmers' Loan & Trust Company* (1895) and *United States v. E. C. Knight Co.* (1895), for himself. Thereafter, at considerable cost to his historical reputation, he generally assigned significant cases to others. One exception to this rule was *Loewe v. Lawlor* (1908), in which Fuller spoke for a unanimous Court.

Fuller established this assignment pattern at the outset of his service. Shortly after Fuller took the center chair, Justice Lucius Q. C. Lamar urged him to write for the Court in the Bell Telephone patent case, which had received widespread public attention. "The case is one on which you will have a good opportunity to make your first exposition of national law in your character as Chief Justice," Lamar explained. "I do not think you should give it away."[42] Characteristically, however, Fuller assigned the opinion to another.

Fuller's behavior in this regard has led some historians to speculate that he was uncomfortable with public law issues.[43] This seems unlikely. Fuller held firm convictions about the Constitution and the powers of government. He was not reticent to express his views on controversial cases forcefully at judicial conferences and in written opinions. More likely this assignment policy reflected Fuller's self-effacing nature as well as his desire to promote judicial harmony. Fuller was not one to put himself forward at the expense of his colleagues.

---

39. Frankfurter, "Chief Justices I Have Known," 888–889.
40. King, *Fuller,* 134.
41. Steamer, *Chief Justice,* 29.
42. As quoted in King, *Fuller,* 136; *United States v. American Bell Telephone Co.,* 128 U.S. 315 (1888).
43. Schiffman, "Melville W. Fuller," 1479–1480; Jeffrey B. Morris, "The Era of Melville Weston Fuller," *Yearbook 1981 Supreme Court Historical Society,* 43.

The use of assignment power by the chief has sometimes generated resentment among his colleagues. Fuller largely avoided this problem by following an eminently fair and even-handed approach to assignment decisions. There is no evidence that he used assignments to reward or punish colleagues for their views. Such a policy would have undermined Fuller's effort to foster good will among the justices. "In the assignment of decisions to the different judges," Holmes later observed, "his grounds were not always obvious, but I know how serious and solid they were and how remote was any partiality from his choice."[44]

Of course, some justices received more significant decisions than others. Fuller was guided in part by a justice's dispatch in writing opinions and his expertise in particular fields of law.[45] Thus he usually assigned patent and admiralty cases to Justices Samuel Blatchford and Henry Billings Brown and opinions involving mining law to Field. Fuller also considered a justice's ability to hold a majority together. One historian has suggested, for instance, that he selected Justice Blatchford to write for the Court in *Chicago, Milwaukee and St. Paul Railway Company v. Minnesota* (1890) because Blatchford was a consensus builder who could attract majority support for a pivotal decision that restricted state regulatory authority.[46] Fuller was influenced too by his assessment of his colleagues' capability. As noted earlier, he usually assigned cases of slight importance to McKenna because he doubted McKenna's legal acumen. By the mid-1890s Fuller recognized that Field was increasingly senile and incapable of handling a full load. Consequently, he gave Field only a handful of decisions during the 1894 and 1895 terms.[47]

There were occasional flashes of anger at Fuller's choices. In 1898 Justice Harlan complained to Fuller, "Two Saturdays in succession you have not assigned to me any case but have assigned cases and important ones to Justice Gray. I was in the majority in each case assigned to him."[48] Such an outcry, however, was rare under Fuller's leadership.

An indefatigable worker, Fuller shouldered far more than his share of opinions for the Court. He authored 840 majority opinions, writing for the Court more often than any other justice during his period of service. According to one calculation, Fuller was the fifth most productive opin-

---

44. As quoted in King, *Fuller*, 334.
45. Kent, *Memoir of Henry Billings Brown*, 30–31.
46. Semonche, *Charting the Future*, 19.
47. King, *Fuller*, 224.
48. As quoted in *Ibid.*

ion writer in the Court's history.[49] Fuller was especially active during his first decade on the Court, preparing 45 opinions in his first term, 65 in the 1893 term, and 69 in the 1894 term. His output noticeably declined in his last five years. He wrote just 14 opinions during the 1908 term and 18 in his last term.

Because he assigned most major cases to others, Fuller tended to write unglamorous opinions dealing with jurisdictional and procedural matters or commercial transactions. Few of these rulings had a long-term impact on the evolution of legal doctrine. Yet Fuller's influence cannot be measured only by the decisions he authored. Reflecting the prevalent laissez-faire philosophy, he led the Supreme Court in a new direction, toward greater protection of property ownership and the free flow of interstate commerce.

Fuller's judicial opinions conspicuously lacked the grace that characterized his addresses and extrajudicial writings. Somehow Fuller's literary qualities eluded him when he authored opinions. Perhaps his heavy workload, coupled with the other duties of the chief justice, resulted in the hasty execution of opinions. His prose style, like the styles of many of his colleagues, was verbose and diffuse. His opinions were clogged with excessive quotations from other decisions. He rarely turned a witty or memorable phrase. As Frankfurter aptly commented, Fuller was "not an opinion writer whom you read for literary enjoyment."[50] His prolix manner of expression also tended to diminish Fuller's influence on later jurisprudence.

Since the time of John Marshall, chief justices had consistently endeavored to discourage public expression of dissenting views. They stressed the desirability of presenting the Supreme Court to the public as a united institution, notwithstanding private disagreements.[51] As a consequence, there was no tradition of frequent dissent on the Court. Ideally, dissenting opinions were reserved for situations in which justices had strongly-held convictions in major decisions. Like his predecessors, Fuller sought to curtail dissenting opinions. He preferred to engineer a compromise through conciliation and diplomacy. Leading by example, Fuller wrote just 30 dissents during his twenty-two years as chief.[52] He dissented without opinion in another 112 cases, maintaining a low dis-

49. *Ibid.*, 339; Albert P. Blaustein and Roy M. Mersky, *The First One Hundred Justices: Statistical Studies on the Supreme Court of the United States* (Hamden, Conn.: Archon, 1978), 99.
50. Frankfurter, "Chief Justices I Have Known," 889.
51. Steamer, *Chief Justice*, 24–25.
52. King, *Fuller*, 340.

sent rate of 2.3 percent.[53] By rarely dissenting, Fuller retained greater control over the assignment of opinions. There is no evidence, however, that he ever altered his personal views to enable him to join the majority and thereby assign particular opinions.

Fuller's own dissent behavior reinforced the consensual norms of the Court. By today's standards Fuller was remarkably successful in achieving unanimity in the decision-making process. The dissent rate during Fuller's tenure was uniformly low, never exceeding 20 percent in any year.[54] In some years there was only a handful of dissenting opinions. Despite Fuller's skillful efforts, unanimity often escaped him in major constitutional cases. Reflecting divisions within American society as a whole, the number of closely divided cases increased. Under Fuller there were 71 decisions rendered by a 5 to 4 or 4 to 3 vote of the Court.[55] This figure included several prominent cases, such as *Pollock, Champion v. Ames* (1903), *Lochner v. New York* (1905), and *Employers' Liability Cases* (1908). Moreover, the Insular Cases split the justices into cohesive voting blocs, with Fuller usually in dissent. But the sharp division in these highly visible cases does not detract from the fact that Fuller was able to build a consensus on most issues presented to the Court. During his service the Court obtained unanimity in such path-breaking decisions as *In re Debs* (1895), *Smyth v. Ames* (1898),[56] *Allgeyer v. Louisiana* (1897), and *Loewe*. His record in eliminating expressed dissent contrasts markedly with that of the chief justices serving after 1941. Indeed, the number of 5 to 4 decisions significantly jumped in the years following World War II and currently remains at a high level.[57]

---

53. Thomas G. Walker, Lee Epstein, and William J. Dixon, "On the Mysterious Demise of Consensual Norms in the United States Supreme Court," 50 *Journal of Politics* 383 (1988). For a slightly different calculation of Fuller's dissent rate see Table 4.2, Dissent Rates, Fuller Court, in Sheldon Goldman, *Constitutional Law and Supreme Court Decision-Making* (New York: Harper and Row, 1982), 174.

54. Walker, Epstein, and Dixon, "On the Mysterious Demise of Consensual Norms," 363 (Figure 1).

55. Note, "Judgments of the Supreme Court Rendered by a Majority of One," 24 *Georgetown Law Review* 984 (1936).

56. Fuller took no part in the *Smyth* decision but was doubtless sympathetic to the outcome.

57. See Walker, Epstein, and Dixon, "On the Mysterious Demise of Consensual Norms." In two recent years the number of 5 to 4 rulings by the Supreme Court exceeded the total of 5 to 4 decisions while Fuller was chief justice. During the 1988 term of the Supreme Court there were 33 decisions rendered by a 5 to 4 vote, and during the 1989 term, 39 such decisions. "The Supreme Court, 1988 Term," 103 *Harvard Law Review* 397 (1989); "The Supreme Court, 1989 Term," 104 *Harvard Law Review* 362 (1990).

The most prolific dissenter during Fuller's tenure was Harlan, who authored 79 dissenting opinions and dissented without opinion in 208 other cases.[58] Some of Harlan's dissents came in landmark cases, including *Pollock* and *Plessy v. Ferguson* (1896). Partly out of step with his contemporaries, Harlan has been seen by modern scholars as a precursor of liberal judicial attitudes.[59] Brewer and Brown were also inclined to express their individual views, writing 42 and 39 dissents respectively.[60] Holmes, whose historical reputation rests largely upon his dissents, rarely filed separate opinions while Fuller was chief. Although Holmes's dissenting opinion in *Lochner* was well received by Progressives, he generally adhered to the no-dissent policy. In keeping with this custom, Holmes declared in 1904, "I think it useless and undesirable, as a rule, to express dissent."[61] Holmes was in fact among the justices most in agreement with Fuller in the disposition of cases.[62] He began to dissent more frequently, however, during the later portion of his Supreme Court career.

The physical facilities of the Supreme Court posed another challenge for Fuller's administrative skills. During his tenure the Court met in the historic old Senate chamber in the south wing of the Capitol. Despite some attractive decor, these quarters became increasingly inadequate for the efficient conduct of judicial business. The robing room, in actuality a private sitting room, was across a hall from the courtroom. Thus the justices had to parade across a public corridor to enter and leave the courtroom. There were no chambers for the justices, so they maintained offices in their homes. Although Congress provided a conference room, the facilities were not suitable, and the Saturday conferences of the justices were often held at Fuller's home.[63]

58. King, *Fuller*, 340–341. For a discussion of Harlan's dissent behavior see Karl M. Zo-Bell, "Division of Opinion in the Supreme Court: A History of Judicial Disintegration," 44 *Cornell Law Quarterly* 199–201 (1959) and Goldman, *Constitutional Law and Supreme Court Decision-Making*, 174–175.

59. Beth, *John Marshall Harlan*, 269–271; G. Edward White, "John Marshall Harlan I: The Precursor," 19 *American Journal of Legal History* 1 (1975).

60. Brewer often withheld his support from majority opinions without preparing a dissent. He once explained to Fuller, "I do not care to write any dissent in those cases, but even if alone I want to be marked as dissenting." Brewer to Fuller, January 9, 1899, Fuller Papers, LC. For an analysis of Brewer's dissent behavior see Brodhead, *David J. Brewer*, 167.

61. Baker, *Justice from Beacon Hill*, 400–401. See also ZoBell, "Division of Opinion in the Supreme Court," 201–203; *Northern Securities Company v. United States*, 193 U.S. 197, 400 (1904).

62. Goldman, *Constitutional Law and Supreme Court Decision-Making*, 175.

63. Fuller's correspondence contains evidence of frequent evening meetings at his home. See, for example, Field to Fuller, May 22, 1897, Fuller to Gray, May 21, 1898, Fuller Papers, LC. King, *Fuller*, 152.

CIRCUIT COURT DUTIES

When Fuller became chief justice, the operations of the Supreme Court were hampered by an antiquated federal court structure and an unwieldy caseload. The federal court system was basically unchanged since the Judiciary Act of 1789, which divided the country into judicial circuits. In addition to attending sessions of the Supreme Court from October to May, justices were required to hold circuit court in their respective circuits. This necessitated extensive travel away from Washington during the summer. Constituting a second tier in the federal judicial system, these circuit courts conducted trials involving the most important civil cases and exercised a limited appellate jurisdiction over the district courts. As a further complication, there was no intermediate court of appeals; matters appealed from the circuit courts went directly to the Supreme Court as a matter of right. Accordingly, Fuller early turned his attention to winning congressional approval of court reform.

Under an 1867 statute the Supreme Court was required to assign each justice to a particular circuit court. One of Fuller's first administrative tasks, therefore, concerned the allotment of circuits. Usually a justice was assigned to a circuit in which he had once lived or with which he had some connection. Under long-settled practice, however, the chief justice presided over the Fourth Circuit (Maryland, Virginia, West Virginia, North Carolina, and South Carolina). In view of his professional ties to Chicago and his real estate interests there, Fuller strongly preferred to sit in the Seventh Circuit. He also expressed concern that his designation to the Fourth Circuit might not be well received in the South.[64] Even before accepting the appointment as chief justice, Fuller explored Justice Harlan's willingness to give up his Seventh Circuit post. Harlan reluctantly agreed, but he stressed the advantages of having the Fourth Circuit assigned to Fuller. He observed that "in reference to my taking another circuit, the usage has been for the Chief Justice to take the Va. Circuit. After a little while the Chief Justice must be settled there and he is convenient to the Va. Circuit. There is very little to do. . . . If your comfort as Chief Justice is to depend *in any degree* upon your having the Chicago Circuit, you shall have no difficulty about it so far as I am concerned."[65] Perhaps hesitant to displace Harlan, Fuller never pressed his desire to preside in the Seventh Circuit. When circuit assignments were made in December

---

64. Fuller to Cleveland, August 6, 1888, Cleveland Papers, LC.
65. Harlan to Fuller, May 3, 1888, Fuller Papers, LC. For Harlan's reluctance to change circuits see Beth, *John Marshall Harlan,* 158.

1888, he was allotted to the Fourth Circuit, a position he retained until his death.[66]

An account of the litigation heard by Fuller as circuit court justice casts light on several aspects of his chief justiceship. First, it illustrates the variety and nature of the cases brought before the circuit courts. Further, it underscores the onerous nature of circuit court duty and the pressing need for reform to relieve Supreme Court justices of this task.

The first term of the Supreme Court under Fuller's leadership ended in mid-May 1889. Fuller promptly journeyed to Charleston, South Carolina, to conduct circuit court trials and to hear appeals from the federal district courts. His initial circuit court opinion, *Lee v. Simpson* (1889), concerned the execution of a testamentary power of appointment by Anna M. Clemson in favor of her husband, who in turn devised the land at issue to the state.[67] Fuller's decision upholding the exercise of the power was therefore instrumental in the creation of Clemson University.

Until the reform of the circuit court system in 1891, Fuller visited the circuit annually and conducted court in various of its districts. As a practical matter, it was impossible for Fuller to handle any significant amount of circuit court business during the summer months. Given the size of the circuit, moreover, his attendance at particular districts was inevitably sporadic. In addition to his work in the Fourth Circuit, Fuller also held a circuit court session in Chicago in August 1889.[68]

Fuller authored at least four decisions while performing his circuit court duties. None treated significant issues of public law, but they give some clues as to the type of litigation that claimed Fuller's attention. He considered the removability to federal circuit court of an action in state court alleging that corporate directors were defrauding stockholders and a motion to enjoin a public works project. In an 1891 opinion Fuller rejected the contention that a statutory grant of the right to mine phosphate rock was perpetual. In so doing, he applied the well-settled doctrine "that the grant is to be construed strictly in favor of the state and against the grantee."[69] These cases underscore the incongruity of

---

66. Assignment to Circuits, December 17, 1889, 128 U.S. 701.
67. *Lee v. Simpson*, 39 F. Rep. 235 (Cir. Ct., D.S.C., 1889).
68. *Union Steam-Boat Co. v. City of Chicago*, 39 F. Rep. 723 (Cir. Ct., N.D. Ill., 1889).
69. *Union Steam-Boat Co. v. City of Chicago*, 39 F. Rep. 723 (Cir. Ct., N.D. Ill., 1889); *Wilder v. Virginia, Tennessee & Carolina Steel & Iron Co.*, 46 F. Rep. 676 (Cir. Ct., W.D. Va., 1891); *State ex rel. Tillman v. Coosaw Mining Co.*, 47 F. Rep. 225 (Cir. Ct., S.D.S.C., 1891). The issue presented in the *Coosaw Mining* case was previewed for Fuller by the circuit judge for the Fourth Circuit. Hugh L. Bond to Fuller, May 25, 1891, Fuller Papers, LC.

having Supreme Court justices spend their time deciding routine matters on circuit.

Active circuit duty exacerbated the problem of a swelling Supreme Court docket. Reflecting industrial growth, territorial expansion, and the impact of the Fourteenth Amendment, the workload of the Court increased steadily during the Gilded Age. Most cases reached the Supreme Court on a writ of error that was available to all litigants whose suits came within the Court's appellate jurisdiction. The 1884 term began with 1,315 appellate cases on the docket. By 1888 this total reached 1,563, and in 1890 the number was 1,800.[70] Patent cases and private law matters involving state law under diversity of citizenship jurisdiction composed much of the increased flow of appeals. This burden rendered impossible the prompt and efficient administration of justice. There was a three-year backlog in the disposition of cases. During the 1880s members of the Supreme Court, as well as leaders of the bar, repeatedly urged Congress to ease the pressure on the Court. Many, including Fuller in 1887, the year before his appointment, called for a judicial reorganization and the creation of intermediate appellate tribunals. Sectional and political differences, however, stymied all reform proposals.

In 1890 Senator William M. Evarts of New York, an outspoken opponent of Fuller's confirmation, led the fight to establish federal courts of appeal. Evarts proposed to retain much of the traditional court structure but also to divert appeals from the Supreme Court.[71] Acutely aware of the necessity of reducing the Supreme Court's docket, Fuller maneuvered skillfully to assist the reform effort. In January 1890 he gave a dinner party in honor of the newly appointed Justice Brewer. The guests included key members of the Senate Judiciary Committee, such as Evarts and George F. Edmunds of Vermont. Following this hospitable gesture, the committee sent all pending legislation for Supreme Court relief to Fuller and indicated that the committee was open "to receive . . . the views of the Justices." Fuller asked Justice Gray to prepare a report on behalf of the justices. As expected, this report strongly recommended a series of reform measures. The most important was the establishment of intermediate courts of appeals, but the justices also called for creation of a court of patent appeals and the transfer of current cases on the Su-

70. Felix Frankfurter and James M. Landis, *The Business of the Supreme Court: A Study in the Federal Judicial System* (New York: Macmillan, 1928), 86.

71. *Ibid.*, 97–101; Charles L. Barrows, *William M. Evarts: Lawyer, Diplomat, Statesman* (Chapel Hill, N.C.: University of North Carolina Press, 1941), 479–483.

preme Court docket to the new tribunals.[72] Hence Fuller mounted a campaign to lobby Congress for legislation reforming the federal judicial system.[73]

Despite their complaints about circuit court duty, the justices did not seek abolition of this responsibility. This concession was likely dictated by tactical considerations. The justices realized that many senators were attached to the traditional concept of circuit attendance and that to reopen this issue might well jeopardize any legislative relief.

As it was enacted in March 1891, the Evarts Act (Circuit Court of Appeals Act) granted substantial relief to the overworked Supreme Court but fell short of mandating all the reforms suggested by the justices.[74] The measure established nine new circuit courts of appeals and curtailed appeals to the Supreme Court. Decisions of the circuit courts of appeals arising under diversity jurisdiction or involving patent, revenue, or admiralty law were reviewable only by a discretionary writ of certiorari. The Court could thus refuse to hear cases not deemed to be of sufficient importance. On the other hand, Congress did not permit the transfer of pending Supreme Court cases to the new courts, and it failed to create a specialized court for patent litigation. Nor did the Evarts Act abolish the existing circuit courts. To Fuller's consternation, the act inadvertently enlarged the right of direct appeal to the Supreme Court in federal criminal cases. This produced a sharp jump in the number of criminal appeals,[75] and the justices became increasingly involved in reviewing the criminal work of the lower federal courts.

Its limitations notwithstanding, the Evarts Act did afford substantial relief to the Supreme Court. The justices secured greater control of their docket, and new business dropped remarkably. Another effect of the Evarts Act was to shrink the number of private law cases argued before the Court, thereby accelerating the Court's shift toward concentration on public law issues. Despite this reform, however, the Court continued to hear many private lawsuits turning upon common law doctrines. The expansion of criminal appeals, moreover, brought numerous unimportant cases before the Court and produced a clamor for additional reform.

---

72. King, *Fuller*, 150; Answer of the Justices of the Supreme Court, March 12, 1890, Records of the Senate Committee on the Judiciary, 51st Congress, National Archives.

73. Steamer, *Chief Justice*, 134.

74. Frankfurter and Landis, *Business of the Supreme Court*, 101–102. See also Edwin C. Surrency, *History of the Federal Courts* (New York: Oceana Publications, 1987), 50–51.

75. Frankfurter and Landis, *Business of the Supreme Court*, 108–113; Surrency, *History of the Federal Courts*, 220–221.

Fuller again played an important role in closing the door to appeals in criminal cases. In February 1892 he wrote Senator Hoar that criminal appeals, "though often argued at great length, rarely present questions of law of particular difficulty." Fuller concluded that "some restriction" of appellate jurisdiction in noncapital cases "is necessary to enable the court to perform duties of paramount importance to the public." After years of delay, Congress finally curtailed Supreme Court review of criminal cases in 1897.[76]

Under the Evarts Act the justices of the Supreme Court were "competent to sit as judges of the Circuit Court of Appeals within their respective circuits." This provision was a gesture to tradition, and it is unclear to what extent the justices were expected to attend the Circuit Court of Appeals. Fuller's experience, however, indicates that some justices took circuit duty seriously. On June 16, 1891, Fuller presided at the ceremonial opening of the Court of Appeals for the Fourth Circuit in Richmond, Virginia.[77] Between April 1892 and January 1909 he participated in at least 42 cases heard by the Circuit Court of Appeals for the Fourth Circuit and wrote 12 opinions in his capacity as circuit justice. Most of this activity was clustered in the years before 1898, suggesting that other commitments gradually reduced the time he had available for circuit attendance. For instance, Fuller made only one Fourth Circuit Court of Appeals appearance between 1902 and 1907. Nonetheless, he presided at 4 appeals in 1908 and wrote his last opinion for the Fourth Circuit in 1909. Fuller also regularly visited Chicago during the summer and occasionally presided over the Court of Appeals for the Seventh Circuit. He participated in at least 5 appeals before the Seventh Circuit in 1893 and 1894, writing 2 opinions. Although he was able to handle only a small amount of business in the circuit courts, Fuller's work in them should dispel casual assumptions that such practice abruptly disappeared after 1891.

As circuit justice Fuller heard a wide variety of civil actions. He decided several admiralty cases involving the collision of vessels or personal injury.[78] Another group of cases involved bankruptcy, the priority of claims against an insolvent corporation, and the allocation of the pro-

76. Fuller to George F. Hoar, February 1, 1892, 23 Cong. Rec. 3285–3286. Frankfurter and Landis, *Business of the Supreme Court,* 113–114.

77. Peter G. Fish, "A New Court Opens: The United States Court of Appeals for the Fourth Circuit," 2 *Georgia Journal of Southern Legal History* 171 (1993).

78. For example, *The Lepanto,* 50 F. 234 (4th Cir. 1892); *Steam Tug Luckenbach,* 50 F. 129 (4th Cir. 1892); *The William Branfoot,* 52 F. 390 (4th Cir. 1892).

ceeds of foreclosure sale.[79] Fuller sat on 2 appeals concerning patent infringement.[80] Railroad accidents generated a large number of appeals. Rejecting a contributory negligence defense, he joined a decision affirming a tort judgment for an injured passenger against a railroad and decided that an action by an employee alleging negligence on the part of a railroad presented a question of fact for the jury.[81] Fuller was less generous in another case involving injured railroad employees. He ruled that acceptance of benefits paid by the railroad prevented the employees from maintaining an action for damages.[82] Fuller also considered issues pertaining to property. He passed upon a foreclosure of a mortgage on railroad property, a bill to set aside a tax sale of land, an action to quiet title, and the authority of a married woman to mortgage her separate estate. Reasoning that the insured failed to comply with policy terms, Fuller denied recovery on a fire insurance policy protecting cotton bales.[83] In addition, he adjudicated many procedural and jurisdictional matters.

Fuller's most important decision as circuit justice arose from the national controversy over opening the 1893 World's Columbian Exposition in Chicago on Sundays.[84] While the fair was in the process of being organized, religious groups campaigned heavily against its being open on Sundays. In 1892 Congress appropriated funds to help defray the cost of completing the fair. The legislation declared that all appropriations "are made upon the condition that the said exposition shall not be opened to the public" on Sunday.[85] In an age when a six-day week was common, however, many workers were unable to see the fair on any other day. Despite the sharp disapproval of Sabbatarians, in May 1893 the directors voted to open the exhibition on Sunday. Meanwhile, at the behest of a stockholder in the fair exposition company, the Superior Court for Cook

---

79. *Thomas v. Blythe*, 55 F. 961 (4th Cir. 1893); *Hoffman v. Knox*, 50 F. 484 (4th Cir. 1892); *Finance Co. of Pennsylvania v. Charleston, Cincinnati, and Chicago Railroad*, 62 F. 205 (4th Cir. 1894).

80. *Western Electric Co. v. Sperry Electric Co.*, 58 F. 186 (7th Cir. 1893); rehearing den. 59 F. 295 (7th Cir. 1894); *Dodge Manufacturing Co. v. Collins*, 106 F. 935 (4th Cir. 1901).

81. *Baltimore & Ohio & Chicago Railroad v. Meyers*, 62 F. 367 (7th Cir. 1894); *Patton v. Southern Railway Co.*, 82 F. 979 (4th Cir. 1897).

82. *Atlantic Coast Line Railroad Co. v. Dunning*, 166 F. 850 (4th Cir. 1908).

83. *Bound v. South Carolina Railway Co.*, 58 F. 473 (4th Cir. 1893); *Harman v. Stead*, 59 F. 962 (4th Cir. 1894); *Holladay v. Land & River Improvement Co.*, 57 F. 775 (4th Cir. 1893); *Aetna Insurance Co. v. People's Bank of Greenville*, 62 F. 222 (4th Cir. 1894).

84. Rossiter Johnson, ed., *A History of the World's Columbian Exposition* (New York: D. Appleton, 1897), vol. 1, 359–367.

85. Act of August 5, 1892, ch. 381, sec. 4, 28 Stat. 389, 390.

County enjoined the directors from closing the exposition on Sunday.[86] At this point Attorney General Richard Olney instructed the United States district attorney to institute proceedings to halt Sunday operations. The government argued that the courts should enjoin a breach of the express condition in the congressional appropriation. On June 8 the federal circuit court ruled that the state court action was no bar to the federal proceeding and granted a preliminary injunction.[87] Caught between conflicting judicial rulings, the fair directors immediately appealed to the Seventh Circuit Court of Appeals.

With Justice Harlan abroad as an American representative for the Bering Sea arbitration, Fuller was temporarily presiding as circuit justice for the Seventh Circuit. It was initially thought that Fuller might decline to participate with his colleagues in hearing the appeal, but he promptly took center stage in the controversy and suspended the operation of the circuit court injunction. "I had hoped to avoid sitting in this case," he declared, "but now will have to, though it is excessively disagreeable to me." To eliminate any appearance of conflict of interest, Fuller gave away his stock shares in the fair exposition company. He and two other judges then heard two days of argument during which Fuller repeatedly asked counsel pointed questions. Recognizing the need for a resolution of the Sunday closing issue, all parties publicly agreed that there would be no appeal to the Supreme Court.[88]

On June 17, before a crowded courtroom, Fuller announced a decision reversing the circuit court order and denying the requested injunction.[89] Relying on traditional equitable principles, he emphasized that there was no showing of irreparable injury to the government or allegation that the remedy at law was inadequate. Accordingly, the court could not grant equitable relief to prevent a contractual violation. Moreover, Fuller rejected the contention that the congressional appropriation constituted a charitable trust that equity should enforce. Emphasizing adherence to precedent, Fuller concluded, "It is not for courts of justice, in the exercise of an unregulated discretion, to remove the settled landmarks of the law."[90]

86. David F. Burg, *Chicago's White City of 1893* (Lexington: University Press of Kentucky, 1976), 89–91; Johnson, *A History of the World's Columbian Exposition,* 362.

87. *United States v. World's Columbian Exposition,* 56 F. 630 (Cir. Ct., N.D. Ill., 1893).

88. *Chicago Tribune,* June 11, 16, 17, 1893.

89. *World's Columbian Exposition v. United States,* 56 F. 654 (7th Cir. 1893).

90. *Ibid.* at 675. For an analysis of the federal government's attempt to enjoin Sunday opening along the lines adopted by Fuller see 27 *American Law Review* 571 (1893).

His decision affirmed the authority of the directors to control the exhibition and permitted them to open the fair on Sunday.

The ruling was warmly received in Chicago. The *Chicago Tribune* urged a reduced rate for Sunday attendance "so that the poor workingman can do what Chief Justice Fuller said he had a right to do—go to the Exposition on the one day of the week which is peculiarly his own." Sabbatarians, on the other hand, were outraged. The *Advance*, a religious newspaper, compared Fuller's ruling to the *Dred Scott* case and accused the chief justice of permitting the exposition company to repudiate the conditions of the congressional appropriation.[91]

The Fuller ruling was instrumental in resolving the issue, but it was not the final chapter. Sunday attendance proved disappointing, and in July the directors voted to close the exhibition on that day for business reasons. Cited for contempt of state court order, they eventually opened the fair on Sunday for the rest of the season.[92]

The Sunday closing controversy reflected uncertainty about the appropriate role of Christianity in American society. To many, closing the fair on Sunday constituted a symbolic reaffirmation of the religious dimension in life.[93] Although it was predicated on equitable grounds, the Columbian Exposition ruling demonstrated Fuller's lack of sympathy with Sunday closing laws. In a sense it can properly be seen as a step toward religious freedom and a new understanding about the place of religion in a changing society.

MISCELLANEOUS RESPONSIBILITIES

Still other difficulties tested Fuller's executive ability. One was the question of how to deal with aging colleagues, an issue that can pose particular problems for the Supreme Court. There is no formal mechanism to remove justices who are no longer able to discharge their duties. By the mid-1890s age was catching up with Justice Field. He alternated between periods of lucidity and periods of senility, and his colleagues grew increasingly worried about the situation. Field's feeble condition posed a vexing challenge for Fuller's leadership. Unfortunately, Field showed no inclination to resign. Deprived of the chief justiceship by President

---

91. *Chicago Tribune*, June 18, 1893; *Advance*, June 22, 1893.

92. Reid Badger, *The Great American Fair: The World's Columbian Exposition & American Culture* (Chicago: Nelson Hall, 1979), 93–94.

93. Robert T. Handy, *Undermined Establishment: Church-State Relations in America, 1880–1920* (Princeton, N.J.: Princeton University Press, 1991), 71–74.

Cleveland's appointment of Fuller, Field was determined not to leave the bench while Cleveland was chief executive.[94] Moreover, he hoped to set a new record for longevity of service. Fuller attempted tactfully to persuade Field to resign. Concerned about the older man's declining mental state, Fuller stopped giving Field opinions after the 1895 term. In March 1896 Field complained to Fuller, "I do not know and shall not ask the reason that no cases have been assigned to me within the past six months."[95]

Additional pressure was clearly needed to convince Field to step down. In consultation with his colleagues, Fuller fashioned a more direct strategy, for which he drew on the 1869 example of Justice Robert C. Grier. A delegation of justices, including Field, had convinced the failing Grier to leave the bench. Late in 1896 Harlan was deputized to remind Field of this incident. Arousing Field from a state near sleep in the robing room, Harlan gingerly raised the Grier matter. Grasping the import of Harlan's hint, Field heatedly replied, "Yes! And a dirtier day's work I never did in my life!" This effort to secure Field's resignation ended in failure.[96]

By early 1897 a resolution of the Field matter became imperative. Fuller and Justice Brewer, Field's nephew, renewed their push to effect his resignation. During the process of negotiation Field asked for some assurance that he would be replaced by a Californian. President-elect McKinley, through Justice Brewer, gave informal assurances that he would name McKenna, thus satisfying Field's wish. Fuller and Brewer enlisted the help of Reverend Henry Field, the justice's brother. In April 1897 Reverend Field delivered his brother's letter of resignation to Fuller. Without any public announcement, the chief justice set December 1 as the effective termination date and promptly presented the letter to President McKinley.[97] But even this step did not finally resolve the problem. By August, Field was feeling better and was talking privately of serving on the bench for another year. A frustrated Fuller confided to his

---

94. Swisher, *Stephen J. Field*, 442–444; Arthur Wallace Dunn, *From Harrison to Harding* (New York: G. P. Putnam's Sons, 1922), 149.

95. Field to Fuller, March 7, 1896, Fuller Papers, LC.

96. As quoted in Swisher, *Stephen J. Field*, 444. For a study casting doubt on standard accounts of this incident see Charles Alan Wright, "Authenticity of 'A Dirtier Day's Work' Quote in Question," 13 *Supreme Court Historical Society Quarterly* 6 (1990).

97. Field to the president, April 24, 1897, Field to Fuller, May 6, 1897, Fuller Papers, LC. See also Swisher, *Stephen J. Field*, 224–226.

wife, "Judge Field bothers me a good deal." When the 1897 term began in October, however, Field's resignation was publicly announced.[98]

Fuller took appropriate steps to deal sensitively but firmly with Field's condition. The need to induce a colleague to leave the bench has plagued subsequent chief justices. Fuller set a sound example for the conscientious handling of such delicate problems in the future.

Only a few years after Field's resignation, Fuller faced a similar situation with respect to John Chandler Bancroft Davis, the Supreme Court's reporter. After serving as a diplomat and a court of claims judge, Davis was named reporter in 1883. Perhaps because of his earlier prominence he was rather patronizing and never established a good working relationship with the members of the Court. There were recurring difficulties with the publication of Court opinions. Concerned with accuracy, Fuller frequently wrote Davis, correcting his punctuation. Davis, however, often neglected to make proposed changes in the proofs of court opinions. This upset even the patient Fuller. In 1896 he wrote to Davis concerning certain corrections and pointedly added, "I have called your attention to this before."[99] Preparation of headnotes was another source of friction. Displaying little confidence in Davis, Fuller even wrote some headnotes for his own opinions.[100] Increasingly inattentive to detail, Davis generated many headnotes in the late 1890s that were vague or misleading.[101] By 1902 the associate justices were urging Fuller to replace him.[102] Fuller tactfully but directly suggested that the eighty-year-old Davis consider resigning and forthwith secured his resignation.[103]

In December 1902 Fuller announced that Charles Henry Butler, a member of New York bar, had been appointed court reporter. Butler had been suggested to Fuller by one of Fuller's Bowdoin College classmates.[104] Thereafter Butler worked closely with Fuller and discharged his duties in a satisfactory manner for the remainder of the chief's tenure on the Court.

Other responsibilities also claimed Fuller's time. Two examples illustrate the wide range of his official activities. In 1893, following the death

---

98. Brewer to Fuller, August 21, 1897, Fuller to Mrs. Fuller, October 4, 1897, Fuller Papers, LC; Correspondence Between Mr. Justice Field and the Other Members of the Court With Regard to His Retiring From the Bench, 168 U.S. 713–718 (1897).

99. As quoted in King, *Fuller*, 230.

100. *Ibid.*, 142, 231–232.

101. Samuel Blatchford to Fuller, September 11, 1891, Fuller Papers, LC.

102. For Harlan's unhappiness with Davis see Beth, *John Marshall Harlan*, 164–165. Harlan was pleased when Davis resigned. Harlan to Fuller, September 18, 1902, Fuller Papers, LC.

103. Fuller to Davis, September 10, 1902; Davis to Fuller, September 11, 1902, Fuller Papers, LC.

104. Butler, *A Century at the Bar*, 64, 71.

of Justice Blatchford, Fuller used his authority to allot circuit assignments out of term by naming Justice Gray to the Second Circuit.[105] In 1905 Fuller administered the required oath to the members of the Senate sitting in the impeachment trial of Judge Charles H. Swayne.[106]

At times the diverse demands of the chief justiceship almost overwhelmed Fuller. "I am so weary I can hardly sit up," he confided to Davis in May 1890.[107] Yet for twenty-two years Fuller ran the Supreme Court with efficiency, courtesy, and good judgment. His administrative achievements did not receive much public attention, but they had a major impact on the working of the Court. He was the first chief justice to push for judicial reform legislation and systematically to use the formal powers attached to his office. Certainly his colleagues greatly appreciated Fuller's accomplishments and always spoke of him in the highest terms. Holmes, in his assessment of Fuller, cogently observed,

> I think the public will not realize what a great man it has lost. Of course, the position of the Chief Justice differs from that of the other judges only on the administrative side; but on that I think he was extraordinary. He had the business of the court at his fingers' ends; he was perfectly courageous, prompt, decided. He turned off the matters that daily call for action easily, swiftly, with the least possible friction, with imperturbable good-humor, and with a humor that relieved any tension with a laugh.[108]

EXTRAJUDICIAL DUTIES

In addition to his administrative responsibilities and circuit duties, extrajudicial activities claimed a good deal of Fuller's time. He maintained a close relationship with President Grover Cleveland, and the two corresponded regularly for years.[109] Fuller was depressed by Cleveland's defeat for reelection in November 1888, just three weeks after Fuller took his oath as chief justice. He urged Cleveland to seek reelection in 1892 and hailed his firm stand against the unlimited coinage of silver. Straining the bounds of judicial propriety, during the spring of 1892 Fuller

---

105. Fuller to Cleveland, July 16, 1893, Cleveland Papers, LC.
106. Thirty-ninth Cong. Rec. 1289 (1905).
107. As quoted in King, *Fuller,* 149.
108. Holmes to Judge William L. Putnam, July 12, 1910, "Judge Putnam's Recollections of Chief Justice Fuller," 22 *Green Bag* 529 (1910).
109. See generally collection of correspondence from Cleveland to Fuller, Fuller Papers, LC.

tried to win an endorsement of Cleveland by the *Chicago Times*.[110] Despite the chief justice's steadfast support of Cleveland, some of Fuller's friends proposed him as the Democratic nominee instead of Cleveland. Fuller discouraged such suggestions; he wrote Cleveland in May 1892, "You must not suppose that I talk or write politics—I don't—but I must say that my conviction that you are the only nominee absolutely certain of success remains unshaken & I entreat you not to be of any other opinion."[111]

Fuller's political sympathy with Cleveland was of no comfort, however, during the former president's only Supreme Court argument, which took place in October 1890. At issue was a claim against the city of New Orleans arising from an abandoned drainage project. Nervously preparing his argument, Cleveland wrote Fuller inquiring when the justices would likely reach the case.[112] Cleveland did not receive special treatment by the Court when the case was heard. Fuller always insisted upon a prompt adjournment of the Court, even if counsel was in the middle of an argument. Concluding his remarks, Cleveland noted that it was nearly adjournment time and that he would detain the justices only a few more minutes to finish his argument. The Chief Justice courteously responded, "Mr. Cleveland, we will hear you tomorrow morning."[113] The Supreme Court eventually ruled against Cleveland's client, but Fuller joined two other justices in dissent. Cleveland expressed to Fuller his acute disappointment and his doubt over whether he should represent clients before the Court.[114]

Fuller was jubilant about Cleveland's reelection in November 1892. He was completely surprised when Cleveland asked him to resign from the Court and become secretary of state. After several days of consideration, Fuller declined the president-elect's offer. Although stressing his "earnest desire for the success of your Administration," Fuller maintained, "I am convinced that the effect of the resignation of the Chief Justice under such circumstances would be distinctly injurious to the court. The surrender of the highest judicial office in the world for a political position, even though so eminent, would tend to detract from the dignity and weight of the tribunal. We cannot afford this." Significantly, Fuller added, "I am fond of the work of the Chief Justiceship. It is arduous but

---

110. King, *Fuller,* 163–164.
111. Henry W. Scott to Fuller, June 30, 1891, Fuller Papers, LC; Fuller to Cleveland, May 4, 1892, Cleveland Papers, LC.
112. Cleveland to Fuller, February 28, 1890, Fuller Papers, LC; *Peake v. New Orleans,* 139 U.S. 342 (1890).
113. Butler, *A Century at the Bar,* 122–123.
114. Cleveland to Fuller, March 10, 1891, Fuller Papers, LC.

nothing is truer than that 'the labor we delight in physics pain.' "[115] Fuller's refusal to leave the center chair, even for such an important political post, has been pictured as enhancing the Supreme Court's prestige.[116]

Fuller remained keenly interested in national political developments. He was upset when the 1896 Democratic convention repudiated his hero Cleveland and nominated William Jennings Bryan. To compound Fuller's distress, the Democrats adopted a platform calling for the free coinage of silver and criticizing Fuller's opinions in the *Pollock* case, which invalidated the income tax. Consistently a champion of sound money, Fuller called the free silver agitation "simply an attack upon property."[117] He worried about the security of his Chicago bank account in the event of Bryan's election. Like many conservative Democrats, Fuller was privately relieved when McKinley was elected president.[118]

Fuller's relationship with President Theodore Roosevelt was uncomfortable. The source of the difficulty was Roosevelt's earnest efforts to place his friend William Howard Taft on the Supreme Court. Beginning in 1903 Roosevelt tried to pressure Fuller to resign to make room for Taft. The president repeatedly instigated rumors in the press that Fuller was about to step down. Fuller, who was nearly seventy years old when the initial reports appeared, deeply resented Roosevelt's actions. "I am not," Fuller advised Holmes, "to be 'paragraphed' out of my place."[119] Fuller erroneously laid some of the blame for these persistent rumors on Taft. To be sure, Taft had his eyes firmly on the chief justiceship. "The Chief Justice," he complained to his wife in 1904, "is as tough as a knot so that if he does not go by resignation, I shall have to whistle for his place."[120] But Taft evidently played no role in Roosevelt's maneuvering. Fuller's friends and colleagues grew alarmed at the published reports of his imminent retirement. In 1906, following another spate of rumors, Fuller replied to Holmes, "Dear Holmes, thank you very much for your expressions yesterday of the hope that I would not yield to newspaper paragraphs & retire—Of course I won't—But I am glad to be assured that my brethren see no particular reason why I should."[121] Roosevelt's

115. Fuller to Cleveland, January 2, 1893, Correspondence of President Cleveland to Melville W. Fuller, 3 *American Scholar* 245, 248 (1934).

116. Frankfurter, "Chief Justices I Have Known," 889.

117. Fuller to Hugh C. Wallace, June 18, 1896, Fuller Papers (microfilm), CHS.

118. King, *Fuller*, 235.

119. *Ibid.*, 302–309; *Holmes-Pollock Letters*, vol. 2, 161.

120. As quoted in Henry F. Pringle, *The Life and Times of William Howard Taft* (New York: Farrar & Rinehart, 1939), vol. 1, 265.

121. As quoted in King, *Fuller*, 307.

attempts to induce Fuller's resignation may have backfired, prompting the chief justice to stay at his post longer than he might have otherwise. In an ironic turn of fate, Fuller administered the oath of office when Taft became president in March 1909. By this time, however, the chief justice was showing unmistakable signs of frailty.

Fuller's most extensive extrajudicial activities arose from his interest in settling international disputes through arbitration. In the early years of the new republic chief justices John Jay and Oliver Ellsworth represented the United States on diplomatic assignments abroad. Fuller revived this tradition of diplomatic service by participating as a judge on international tribunals. He was also a vice-president and active member of the American Society of International Law.

In 1897 Fuller, along with Justice Brewer, became an arbitrator to settle the long-standing boundary dispute between Venezuela and British Guiana. This controversy was an international cause célèbre. Threatening to invoke the Monroe Doctrine, President Cleveland had pressured the British to accept arbitration. Under the terms of the arbitration treaty the president of Venezuela designated Fuller as one of the five arbitrators. Fuller reluctantly accepted the appointment from a sense of duty, and the delay in convening the tribunal convinced him that his participation was a mistake. Following lengthy preparations, the hearing was further postponed to avoid a conflict with the Supreme Court's calendar. The arbitration panel finally convened in Paris in summer 1899. After hearing fifty-five days of tedious arguments and digesting thirty volumes of materials, Fuller no doubt wished that he had refused the appointment. Despite some misgiving by Fuller and Brewer, the arbitrators unanimously awarded most of the disputed territory to Great Britain.[122]

While the Venezuela boundary arbitration was pending, President McKinley approached Fuller about participating in the peace commission to end the Spanish-American War. Clearly influenced by his experience with the Venezuela matter, Fuller turned down McKinley's request. He explained to the president that, given his other duties, the chief justice "should not take on any additional burden." Speaking in general terms, Fuller added, "I think moreover that considering the nature of the office it is far wiser that the Chief Justice should not participate in public affairs."[123] As things developed, Fuller's decision was the prudent course.

---

122. Memorial Note, "Melville Weston Fuller," 4 *American Journal of International Law* 909, 912–914 (1910); King, *Fuller,* 249–261.

123. Fuller to McKinley, August 19, 1898, Fuller Papers, LC.

The peace treaty came before the Court in the Insular Cases, and Fuller would likely have felt compelled to recuse himself.

When the Permanent Court of Arbitration was established at the Hague in 1899, President McKinley named Fuller as one of the four American representatives to the Court. Over the next ten years Fuller was asked to serve as an arbitrator on three occasions, but he accepted only one assignment. In October 1904 he was selected by the British government to serve on a tribunal of arbitration in the case of the Muscat *Dhows*. This controversy concerned the right of France to grant the protection of its flag to vessels belonging to the subjects of the sultan of Muscat. Fuller spent part of the summer of 1905 in the Hague and joined in a decision that defined the authority of a nation to grant the privilege of its flag.[124]

Washington social life placed additional demands on Fuller's time and energy. In the late nineteenth century the justices of the Supreme Court were not cloistered from Washington society, and they participated fully in official dinners and receptions. Being of a retiring nature, Fuller found the social dimensions of the chief justiceship an unpleasant chore, and he declined as many social engagements as possible. Fortunately, Mrs. Fuller was a charming hostess who entertained graciously. Fuller made a practice of giving a dinner for each new justice appointed to the Court. After the death of his wife in 1904 Fuller largely withdrew from formal social activities. One scholar has suggested that in so doing, he initiated the process that eliminated the Supreme Court justices from Washington society.[125]

Notwithstanding his aversion to official social functions, Fuller jealously safeguarded the dignity of the Supreme Court. In an era when correct etiquette was of utmost importance, he insisted upon the precedence of the Supreme Court justices at formal ceremonies. This led to an embarrassing incident at a presidential reception for the judiciary in 1907. As the result of a mix-up, the diplomatic corps was permitted to precede the justices in the procession. The usually modest Fuller protested this slight. Justice Harlan was even more incensed, later maintaining that "the little whippersnapper" of an aide "actually and violently assaulted the Chief Justice" to prevent him from leading the procession. The justices considered leaving the reception but remained to greet President Roosevelt. Fuller and Harlan called on the president the next

---

124. Memorial Note, "Melville Weston Fuller," 914–915; George Grafton Wilson, comp., *The Hague Arbitration Cases* (Boston: Ginn and Company, 1915, reprint Littleton, Colo.: Fred B. Rothman Co., 1990), 64–81; "The Muscat Dhows," 23 *Law Review Quarterly* 83 (1907).

125. Morris, "The Era of Melville Weston Fuller," n. 73.

morning and were assured that the problem would not occur again.[126] Nonetheless, matters of ceremony continued to rankle Fuller. In May 1910, just before his death, he complained about the seating arrangements for the justices at the memorial service for King Edward VII.[127] To modern eyes Fuller's reaction to these episodes appears rather peevish, but it underscores his determination to preserve public respect for the Court.

Fuller found time in his demanding schedule for various incidental activities. For example, he was deeply interested in the Smithsonian Institution. By virtue of his appointment as chief justice, Fuller became an ex officio member of the Smithsonian's board of regents. He was elected its chancellor in January 1889 and held that post until his death, regularly presiding over meetings of the board and advising the secretary on legal matters and pending legislation. At his last board meeting, in February 1910, Fuller presented the Smithsonian's Langley Medal to Wilbur and Orville Wright.[128] He also served as a trustee of the Peabody Education Fund, a charitable trust that supported educational endeavors in the South.[129] In addition, Fuller was an ex officio member of the Foundation for the Promotion of Industrial Peace. Established by an act of Congress in 1907 and funded by President Roosevelt's Nobel Prize award, the Foundation sought to encourage better relations between employers and employees. Shortly before his death in 1910 Fuller also edited a collection of essays entitled *The Professions* and designed to interest readers in medicine, law, and the ministry.[130]

An eloquent speaker, Fuller was frequently invited to give addresses at special exercises and to civic organizations.[131] For instance, in February 1901 he was a featured speaker at the memorial observance of the hundredth anniversary of Chief Justice John Marshall's appointment.[132] In 1894 Fuller delivered an address to commemorate the centennial of his

---

126. Butler, *A Century at the Bar,* 126–129.

127. Philander Chase Knox to Fuller, May 31, 1910, Fuller Papers (microfilm), CHS.

128. Charles D. Wolcott, "Melville Weston Fuller, 1833–1910," *Annual Reports of The Board of Regents of the Smithsonian Institution* [1910], 113–123. For presentation of Langley Medal see *Ibid.,* 22–23.

129. J. L. M. Curry, *A Brief Sketch of George Peabody and a History of the Peabody Education Fund* (Cambridge, Mass.: University Press, 1898), 102.

130. Melville Weston Fuller, ed., *The Professions* (Boston: Hall and Loche, 1911).

131. For example, Fuller, "The Supreme Court," speech at annual dinner of New England Society of Pennsylvania, December 22, 1888, in Thomas B. Reed, ed., *Modern Eloquence,* vol. 2 (Philadelphia: J. D. Morris, 1900), 513–517.

132. "Remarks of Chief Justice Fuller," the Marshall Centennial, February 4, 1901, in 180 U.S. 645 (1901).

alma mater, Bowdoin College.[133] Fittingly, he was a featured speaker at the 1909 memorial exercises for President Cleveland, and one participant praised Fuller's address as "the gem of the occasion."[134] Fuller rarely, however, used these public addresses as an opportunity to defend or explain decisions of the Court.

Since the role of chief justice encompasses many duties beyond participation in the decision making of the Court, an evaluation of Fuller as chief should not be based solely on the influence of his opinions but must consider how he shaped the Court as an institution. In several respects Fuller's tenure marked a watershed in Supreme Court history. As was exemplified by his part in securing passage of the Evarts Act and his preservation of harmonious relations among the diverse members of the Court, Fuller significantly helped to define the modern office of chief justice. His substantive achievements were also considerable. Under Fuller's predecessor, Chief Justice Morrison R. Waite, the Supreme Court had been largely deferential to the exercise of state police power and resistant to a broad construction of the Fourteenth Amendment. This changed with Fuller in the center chair. Somewhat overshadowed by more prominent colleagues, Fuller successfully harnessed their talents and guided the Court to a more activist role in American life.

In retrospect it can be said that Cleveland's selection of Fuller as chief over any of the sitting justices was a wise move. With his patient nature and flair for administration, Fuller proved to be adept both at managing the Court's internal relations and at representing the Court in its increasingly significant relationship with the public and other branches of government.

---

133. "Anniversary Address" by Melville Weston Fuller, June 28, 1894, in *Addresses and Poem on the Occasion of the One Hundredth Anniversary of . . . Bowdoin College* (Brunswick, Maine, 1894).

134. Richard Olney to Fuller, March 20, 1909, Fuller Papers (microfilm), CHS.

3

CONSERVATIVE JURISPRUDENCE IN THE AGE OF ENTERPRISE

When Fuller became chief justice in 1888 the United States was experiencing sweeping social and economic change. This transformation generated a variety of novel and vexing issues that eventually found their way to the Supreme Court.

A NATION TRANSFORMED

The most conspicuous change in the country during this period was the swift growth of industry and large-scale corporate enterprise. Industrial productivity and national wealth rose markedly in the decades following the Civil War. Manufacturing eclipsed agriculture as the primary source of wealth. By 1900 the United States had become the foremost industrial nation in the world. Railroads, America's first big business, forged a national market for goods, tied farming communities and small towns to urban centers, and drew farmers into the market economy. This spectacular economic spurt was fueled largely by private investment capital, not government aid.[1] A steady flow of investment capital was essential to finance industrial development. Much of the necessary capital was provided by European investors. Banks and insurance companies were another important source of capital. Corporate profitability, of course, was the key to attracting these investment funds.

The consequences of this economic change were far-reaching. With the stimulus of industrialization, rapid urban growth ensued. People relentlessly migrated from farm to city, joining new immigrants in the pursuit of greater economic opportunities. The urban share of the

---

1. Morton Keller, *Affairs of State: Public Life in Late Nineteenth Century America* (Cambridge, Mass.: Harvard University Press, 1977), 372. I have relied on Keller's excellent work here and elsewhere in this chapter.

population climbed steadily during the late nineteenth century. In Chicago, for instance, the population trebled between 1880 and 1900. Such pell-mell growth caused overcrowded housing and public health problems. City leaders struggled to provide housing, public works, and water and sewer services to the burgeoning urban population. Yet effective municipal government was often hampered by ethnic and class divisions among the residents. As urban areas grew, the cultural gap between city and country increased markedly.

The distribution of wealth generated by the new industrial order was also a concern. Although many Americans prospered during the late nineteenth century and property ownership was widespread, there were fears about an increasing economic disparity. Historians have debated whether the proportionate income of the wealthy actually grew during the Gilded Age,[2] but reformers charged that there was an undue concentration of money and power in the hands of the rich. The federal government was financed almost entirely by excise taxes and customs duties. Yet pressure would build in the early 1890s for an income tax as a means of reducing the tariff and redistributing wealth.

As business became larger, employment relations were fundamentally altered. Corporate employees frequently worked in an impersonal environment and had little bargaining power to improve their working conditions. Relatively few employees were members of labor unions, and thus employers could effectively dictate wages and other terms of employment. A ten-hour workday was common. Workplace safety, too, became an issue. Early factories were often dangerous, and many workers were injured on the job. Work on railroads was particularly hazardous. Fixing responsibility for the costs of accidents posed a major challenge for the legal system. The victims of industrial and railroad accidents instituted numerous lawsuits for negligence, but common-law doctrines limited employer liability. As a consequence, many injured employees received no compensation.

In addition to economic changes, the United States experienced massive immigration in the late nineteenth century. To the consternation of many old-stock Americans, the majority of the new immigrants came from southern and eastern Europe. A growing number of Americans questioned the traditional policy of open immigration. Critics linked unrestricted immigration with radicalism, crime, and a host of social ills. Organized labor feared the loss of jobs and a declining wage level as a

---

2. Lee C. Soltow, "Evidence on Income Inequality in the United States, 1866–1965," 29 *Journal of Economic History* 279–286 (1969).

result of competition with newcomers. In response to these concerns, Congress gradually tightened the laws governing immigration.

Immigrants from China and Japan were particularly resented. There was a persistent clamor to halt further Chinese immigration and restrict the Chinese already living in the country. In 1882 and again in 1892 Congress passed Chinese exclusion acts. Congress also created procedures to expel Chinese laborers unless they obtained special certificates of residence. Japanese immigration was similarly restricted.[3]

Sectionalism remained a potent force in shaping American life. Recovering slowly from the ravages of the Civil War, an impoverished South continued to occupy a distinctive place in the polity. Southerners were ambivalent about the new economic order. Proponents of a New South hoped to lure northern entrepreneurs with tax exemptions and subsidies. Indeed, southern railroad mileage expanded, and industrial activity in textiles, tobacco, and iron and steel grew markedly. At the same time, many southern leaders looked askance at northern domination of the southern regional economy. In the 1890s southern Populists stridently attacked railroad companies and federal courts as agents of Yankee economic control. Despite some economic development, the South generally lagged behind other regions of the country in industrialization and personal income. Throughout the Gilded Age much of the South was plagued by widespread and persistent rural poverty.[4]

There were still other problems associated with the South in the late nineteenth century. Debt-laden states and cities repudiated or scaled down their bonded obligations. Repudiationist policies, which sharply divided southerners, threatened future credit and were a fertile source of lawsuits.[5]

The restoration of white rule was another notable feature of the southern experience. As public opinion in the North abandoned Reconstruction, white supremacist sentiments gained ascendancy in southern politics. With the acquiescence of northerners, southern Democrats restricted black suffrage and imposed formal racial segregation on many social institutions. An outbreak of lynching swept across the South in the 1890s, reflecting bitter racial animosity. Racist social policies were widely accepted in the United States by 1900, but the South stood out with its

---

3. Keller, *Affairs of State,* 443–447.
4. Harry N. Scheiber, "Federalism, the Southern Regional Economy, and Public Policy Since 1865," in David J. Bodenhamer and James W. Ely, Jr., eds., *Ambivalent Legacy: A Legal History of the South* (Jackson: University Press of Mississippi, 1984), 69–105.
5. John V. Orth, *The Judicial Power of the United States: The Eleventh Amendment in American History* (New York: Oxford University Press, 1987), 58–89.

insistence on a legalized color line to separate whites and blacks.[6] Southern leaders relied on the doctrine of states' rights to provide legitimacy to their system of racial control. Seeking largely to be left alone, they were quick to defend state autonomy against perceived national encroachment.

The Spanish-American War in 1898, which marked the debut of the United States as a world power, brought other important changes in the American polity. As a result of the war, the United States acquired the noncontiguous territories of the Philippines and Puerto Rico. This imperialistic step sparked a sharp debate over the constitutional status of these annexed lands. Imperialists contended that the United States could govern its overseas territories without the extension of constitutional guarantees or promise of eventual statehood. Anti-imperialists countered that to rule foreign peoples without their consent contradicted a fundamental tenet of American constitutionalism.

The new economic and social order touched every aspect of American life. The central question in the late nineteenth century was how the nation should respond to the rapid and often bewildering changes. Optimistic and enterprising Americans embraced the new economy, stressing the increasing wealth and power of the United States and pointing to a future of boundless growth. They identified corporate enterprise with technological advance and high wages, and they generally favored private economic ordering. Others were less sanguine. Critics dwelt upon the social problems of industrialization—class conflict, frightening corporate power, and urban slums. They called for governmental intervention that would restore the older values of a preindustrial society.

Tension between old values and the new conditions of American life hampered effective policy making at both the federal and state levels. Several political factors—localism, persistent distrust of active government, widespread resistance to higher taxes—frustrated legislative attempts to deal with the unsettling consequences of industrialization. Notwithstanding the adoption of a number of policies designed to promote economic growth, there was no broad expectation that the federal government should play a larger part in governing American society. Neither the Republicans nor the Democrats seriously questioned the laissez-faire norms or offered a comprehensive program of reform. Leaders of both major parties espoused limited government and respect for private property. The prevailing political sentiment was forcefully expressed by Democratic Governor Roswell P. Flower of New York. Rejecting a request for public projects to combat unemployment during the depression of 1893, Flower de-

---

6. Lawrence M. Friedman, *A History of American Law,* 2nd ed. (New York: Simon and Schuster, 1985), 504–508.

clared, "In America the people support the government; it is not the province of the government to support the people. Once recognize the principle that the government must supply public work for the unemployed, and there will be no end of official paternalism."[7]

As a result of this widely shared commitment to a free market, the response of the federal and state governments to the new economy was halting. The two major pieces of federal economic legislation, the Interstate Commerce Act of 1887, which attempted to regulate railroads, and the Sherman Anti-Trust Act of 1890, reflected the public's ambivalence toward corporate enterprise. These laws proved difficult to enforce and did not have much impact on the economy until after 1900. It was the states, acting under their police power to protect the health, safety, and morals of their citizens, that took the lead in seeking to mitigate the negative consequences of industrialization. State legislatures increasingly passed laws regulating the conditions of labor. Such legislation imposed workplace safety and health standards and placed a ceiling on working hours. In addition, state legislatures and commissions sought to control the rates charged by railroads and grain elevators. States also set requirements that restricted entry into certain occupations. The states were especially vigorous when public health and morals appeared to be at issue. For instance, lawmakers in several states prohibited the manufacture and sale of alcoholic beverages and banned adulterated food products.

Such state attempts to deal with economic change raised a number of troublesome issues. Labor regulations necessarily curtailed contractual freedom and the right of owners to use their property. Further, experience soon demonstrated that the states could not effectively control the operations of businesses, such as railroads, that transcended state boundaries. Last, piecemeal state regulations threatened to interfere with interstate commerce and the emerging national market. Given the limited nature of federal regulation and the inadequacy of state supervision, the federal courts had ample room to influence direction of public policy with respect to the new economic order.

NEW PATTERNS IN CONSTITUTIONAL THOUGHT

Constitutional thought in the late nineteenth century was shaped by broad intellectual trends that disparaged government intervention in the economy. The emergence of laissez-faire constitutionalism provided a legal counterpoint to the economic and social transformation of the nation.

---

7. As quoted in Richard L. McCormick, *From Realignment to Reform: Political Change in New York State, 1893–1910* (Ithaca, N.Y.: Cornell University Press, 1981), 57.

Central to the innovations in constitutional thought was an expansive interpretation of the Fourteenth Amendment. This amendment, adopted in 1868, potentially altered the balance between the federal government and the states by opening new possibilities for federal supervision of the states. Legal battles over the reach of the Fourteenth Amendment focused largely on the provision that no state should "deprive any person of life, liberty, or property, without due process of law."

The concept of due process had deep roots in Anglo-American legal history. The due process guarantee was commonly associated with procedural regularity. It required that the government must follow settled procedures and provide an impartial hearing before any person could be deprived of his or her rights. Scholars have reached different conclusions as to whether due process was understood to incorporate substantive rights as well.[8] Substantive due process rested on the belief that there existed certain fundamental liberties, in addition to those specifically enumerated in the Constitution, that government could not arbitrarily abridge. The due process clause placed substantive limitations on legislative authority. Statutes that invaded property or other personal rights were not, by their nature, valid laws, and enforcement of such laws therefore violated due process.[9]

State courts had been wrestling with substantive interpretations of due process throughout the nineteenth century.[10] In *Wynehamer v. People* (1856), the first important application of the doctrine, the New York Court of Appeals struck down a state law outlawing the sale of liquor. The court found that the statute was a deprivation of property without due process as applied to liquor already acquired when the law took effect. This trend accelerated after the Civil War. In 1885 the New York Court of Appeals invalidated a statute restricting the manufacture of cigars in tenement houses on grounds that it deprived cigar makers of liberty and property. Similarly, the Supreme Court of California invoked

---

8. See Robert E. Riggs, "Substantive Due Process in 1791," 1990 *Wisconsin Law Review* 941, 943–947.

9. Stephen A. Siegel, "*Lochner* Era Jurisprudence and the American Constitutional Tradition," 70 *North Carolina Law Review* 2, 58–61 (1991).

10. Riggs, "Substantive Due Process," 977–984; Siegel, "*Lochner* Era Jurisprudence," 52–57; William M. Wiecek, "State Protection of Personal Liberty: Remembering the Future," in Paul Finkelman and Stephen E. Gottlieb, *Toward a Usable Past: Liberty Under State Constitutions* (Athens: University of Georgia Press, 1991), 380–383.

substantive due process in 1890 to declare that the water rates fixed by a municipal body amounted to confiscation of property.[11]

As the state courts groped toward a substantive interpretation of due process, trends in legal thought emphasized due process as a limit on legislative authority. Thomas M. Cooley, the leading constitutional theorist of the Gilded Age, paved the way for a broad reading of the Fourteenth Amendment. Cooley's influential *Treatise on the Constitutional Limitations Which Rest upon the Legislative Power of the States* (1868) was instrumental in fashioning the due process clause into a substantive restraint on state power to regulate economic rights.[12] As is suggested by the title of his treatise, Cooley's primary goal was to impose limits on arbitrary legislative action. He maintained that due process went beyond mere procedure and shielded individuals from interference with their private property. Further, Cooley fused the Jacksonian principles of equal rights and hostility to special economic privilege with due process protection of property. He sharply questioned the constitutionality of class legislation, laws that benefited one segment of society at the expense of another. Arguing for equality of rights, Cooley asserted, "The State, it is to be presumed, has no favors to bestow, and designs to inflict no arbitrary deprivation of rights. Special privileges are obnoxious, and discriminations against persons or classes are still more so, and as a rule of construction are always to be leaned against as probably not contemplated or designed."[13] Widely used by attorneys, Cooley's treatise provided a rationale for more exacting judicial scrutiny of the legislative branch.

Another significant laissez-faire theorist, Christopher G. Tiedeman, amplified Cooley's views. In *A Treatise on the Limitations of Police Power in the United States* (1886), Tiedeman advanced a narrow concept of the police power. He asserted that states should use their police power only to "provide for the public order and personal security by the prevention and

---

11. *In re Jacobs,* 98 N.Y. 98 (1885). See Katha G. Hartley, "Spring Valley Water Works v. San Francisco: Defining Economic Rights in San Francisco," 3 *Western Legal History* 287–308 (1990).

12. Benjamin R. Twiss, *Lawyers and the Constitution: How Laissez-Faire Came to the Supreme Court* (Princeton, N.J.: Princeton University, 1942), 18–41; Michael Les Benedict, "Laissez-Faire and Liberty: A Re-Evaluation of the Meaning and Origins of Laissez-Faire Constitutionalism," 3 *Law and History Review* 330–331 (1985). For the continuing importance of Jacksonian doctrines in shaping judicial sympathy for free markets see Howard Gillman, *The Constitution Besieged: The Rise and Demise of Lochner Era Jurisprudence* (Durham, N.C.: Duke University Press, 1993), 33–60.

13. Thomas M. Cooley, *A Treatise on the Constitutional Limitations Which Rest upon the Legislative Power of the States* (Boston: Little, Brown, 1868, reprint New York: Da Capo Press, 1972), 393.

punishment of crimes and trespasses."[14] Tiedeman condemned most governmental intervention in the economy and urged judicial protection of free market principles. He also maintained that the freedom to enter contracts was a property right not subject to general state regulation.

Although Cooley and Tiedeman gave impetus to acceptance of laissez-faire constitutionalism, the Supreme Court was initially reluctant to adopt a broad reading of the Fourteenth Amendment. In the *Slaughterhouse Cases* (1873) the Court, by a 5 to 4 margin, rejected a challenge to a state-conferred monopoly of the slaughtering business in New Orleans. Placing a circumscribed construction on the Fourteenth Amendment, the justices declared that a contrary ruling would "constitute this court a perpetual censor upon all legislation of the States on the civil rights of their own citizens." Justices Stephen J. Field and Joseph P. Bradley filed spirited dissents. Anticipating substantive due process, Justice Bradley stated that "a law which prohibits a large class of citizens from adopting a lawful employment . . . does deprive them of liberty as well as property without due process."[15]

The justices also denied due process arguments in *Munn v. Illinois* (1877). At issue was an Illinois statute that set the charges for storing grain in Chicago elevators. Speaking for the Court, Chief Justice Morrison R. Waite sidestepped the Fourteenth Amendment issue and affirmed state regulatory authority over private property "devoted to a public use." Justice Field, the most forceful champion of substantive due process, dissented. In an opinion that anticipated the future direction of the Court, he maintained that the due process clause afforded substantive protection to owners in the use of and income from their property.

During the 1880s judicial attitudes began to change, and Field's views gradually gained ascendancy.[16] Armed with the ideas of Cooley and Tiedeman, attorneys for business interests repeatedly pressed the contention that the due process clause limited state police power. Influenced by the principles of laissez-faire constitutionalism, the justices gradually formulated doctrines that enlarged the scope of economic liberty. In *Mugler v. Kansas* (1887) the Supreme Court moved toward a substantive interpretation of the due process clause to safeguard fundamental

---

14. Christopher G. Tiedeman, *A Treatise on the Limitations of Police Power in the United States* (St. Louis: F. H. Thomas, 1886), 150. See also David N. Mayer, "The Jurisprudence of Christopher G. Tiedeman: A Study in the Failure of Laissez-Faire Constitutionalism," 93 *Missouri Law Review* 93–161 (1990).

15. *Slaughterhouse Cases,* 83 U.S. 36, 78, 122 (1873).

16. James W. Ely, Jr., *The Guardian of Every Other Right: A Constitutional History of Property Rights* (New York: Oxford University Press, 1992), 87–89.

property rights. A brewer attacked the constitutionality of a Kansas prohibition statute as a deprivation of property without due process. Although the justices upheld the prohibition measure as a valid use of the state police power to protect health and morals, Justice Harlan, speaking for the Court, emphasized that courts could scrutinize the purpose behind state regulation as well as the means employed to achieve the stated ends. The Court, Justice Harlan cautioned, need not accept a legislative exercise of the police power at face value. Rather, he declared that courts were under a duty to "look at the substance of things" and ascertain whether the provisions of the statute bore any real relationship to its ostensible purpose. Further, Harlan insisted that there were "limits beyond which legislation cannot rightfully go."[17] Under *Mugler,* laws that purported to protect health, safety, or morals might in fact unreasonably deprive an owner of property without due process. The effect of this decision was to assert far-reaching federal judicial supervision of state economic legislation.

With *Mugler* the Supreme Court seemingly recognized substantive due process. But the justices had yet to apply the doctrine to invalidate any state legislation. Hence Fuller's appointment as chief justice in 1888 occurred at a pivotal point in the evolution of due process. Although he was no constitutional theorist, Fuller played a central role in securing judicial acceptance of the emerging due process guarantees. In short order substantive due process became the principal vehicle by which the Supreme Court would vindicate the principles of laissez-faire constitutionalism.

SOCIAL UNREST AND REFORM MOVEMENTS

Despite misgivings about the power of large corporations, most Americans came to terms with the dramatic changes sweeping the nation during the late nineteenth century. An expanding urban middle class enjoyed an improved standard of living. But an economic expansion of such magnitude as occurred during this period inevitably produced social dislocation. Many farmers and industrial workers felt vulnerable in an increasingly urban and corporation-dominated society. Their grievances fueled a culture of militant political protest.

An agricultural depression gripped the Great Plains in the early 1890s. Confronted with falling crop prices and drought, farmers struggled under a burden of debt. Frustrated by indebtedness and per-

---

17. *Mugler v. Kansas,* 123 U.S. 623, 661 (1887).

sonal hardships, western farmers lashed out at the new economic order.[18] Railroads, as the most visible symbol of economic change, received
the brunt of their attacks. Evidence indicates that freight rates were
stable, but farm organizations accused the railroads of oppressive
charges that took the farmers' profits. Impoverished southern farmers
shared many of these complaints and were also ripe for radical political
action.

This profound agrarian disenchantment with the consequences of
economic development formed the basis for the Populist movement of
the 1890s. The Populists vainly hoped to preserve an agrarian social order in the face of an industrializing economy. They repudiated both the
prevailing laissez-faire ideology and the existing political structure. See-
ing economic issues in a moralistic light, they blamed economic distress
on large corporations and concentrated wealth. Populist leaders angrily
charged that American society was being divided between the rich and
the poor.

In 1892 Populist discontent coalesced into a third political party, the
People's Party. Warning that a "vast conspiracy against mankind has been
organized on two continents," the People's Party platform darkly pictured "a nation brought to verge of moral, political and material ruin."
Flying in the face of laissez-faire norms, the Populists asserted that "the
powers of the government—in other words, of the people—should be
expanded" to the end that "oppression, injustice and poverty, shall eventually cease in the land." To achieve their objective the Populists called for
government ownership of the railroads, a graduated income tax, currency policies to help debtors, restrictions on immigration, and shorter
working hours.[19] Many of these proposals were decades old, and there is
room to doubt that any of them really addressed the underlying causes
of agrarian discontent. Nonetheless, Populism was the first important attempt in American history to insist that the government curb private economic power and assist the disadvantaged.

Elements of the radical Populist program were gradually absorbed by
the major parties and enacted into law at the federal or state level. As the
Supreme Court under Fuller handed down a series of decisions sympathetic to railroads, invalidated the income tax, and limited the reach of
antitrust laws, frustrated Populist leaders bitterly condemned the justices
as tools of corporate power. One scholar has aptly noted that "the protest

---

18. Keller, *Affairs of State,* 571–580.
19. People's Party Platform of 1892, in Kirk H. Porter and Donald Bruce Johnson,
comps., *National Party Platforms 1840–1956* (Urbana: University of Illinois Press, 1956), 89–
91.

groups were faced with a Supreme Court concept of property rights which ran directly counter to their reform programs, as well as a general conservative bias in the federal judiciary which was beyond their ability to affect by popular processes."[20] The intense antagonism toward the Supreme Court reached a climax in the Democratic Party platform of 1896. Under the strong influence of Populist sentiment, the Democrats assailed the Supreme Court for striking down the income tax and denounced the Debs labor injunction decision. The course of the Supreme Court became a major issue in the 1896 presidential election.[21] The victory of Republican William McKinley, however, quelled the anti-Court agitation for the time being.

Although industrial workers were not generally attracted to the rural-based Populist movement, they too had many grievances with respect to the new economic order. Lack of job security was a major concern. Industrial employment was subject to downturns in the business cycle. The depression of 1893–97 left more than 18 percent of the work force unemployed. In 1894 Joseph Coxey led an "army" of the unemployed to Washington to demand that Congress create public works projects.

The growth of large-scale industrial enterprise and the changing nature of the labor force produced many labor-management disputes. Strikes increased in frequency and violence during the Gilded Age, occurring in the railroad industry, coal mines, and steel factories. On occasion strikes precipitated riots. There were furious clashes between strikers and the police in various places. The great Pullman strike of 1894 in Chicago was the most severe of those disturbances. Most of this strike activity was defensive in character. Strikes were typically triggered by employer efforts to reduce wages, not employee attempts to improve working conditions. Consequently, strikers sometimes enjoyed a high level of public support.

Unions were not a significant power in American life. The American Federation of Labor, formed in 1886, pushed for legal recognition of unions and protective legislation for workers. But less than 10 percent of the industrial work force was unionized in the late nineteenth century. Despite the modest size of unions, many middle-class Americans feared the violence associated with the labor movement and regarded unions as a threat to social stability. Lawmakers were of two minds in handling the new developments in the labor market. On one hand, state legislatures

---

20. Alan Furman Westin, "The Supreme Court, The Populist Movement and the Campaign of 1896," 15 *Journal of Politics* 20 (1953).
21. *Ibid.,* 30–39.

tried to ameliorate the worst excesses of industrial work. States outlawed the payment of workers in script and restricted the hours of work in hazardous occupations such as mining. Some states also began to curtail the use of child labor and limit the length of the workday for women. On the other hand, lawmakers passed antiunion statutes that banned boycotts and restricted picketing. In the same vein, federal and state judges issued injunctions against strikes and boycotts. Union leaders increasingly perceived the federal courts as hostile to their interests.[22]

After 1900 a broad-based reform movement known as Progressivism emerged as a significant force in American public life.[23] The objectives of the Progressive coalition were diverse and to some extent worked at cross-purposes. The Progressives borrowed ideas from the Populists and the labor movement. Unlike these groups, however, they were largely middle-class in social background and held centralist political opinions. Progressivism appealed strongly to urban professionals, who were anxious about their place in a society dominated by large business enterprises.

The primary goal of the Progressives was to correct the imbalance of economic power associated with the new industrial order.[24] At the heart of the reform program lay the Progressive insistence on a more active role for both state and federal governments in regulating the economy and meeting social needs. Accordingly, Progressives renewed the attack on railroads and successfully pushed to enlarge the power of the Interstate Commerce Commission (ICC) to fix railroad charges. They also favored strengthening the antitrust laws to prevent predatory price-fixing and safeguard small businesses from consolidation. Progressives persuaded state legislators to enact a wide range of statutes protecting employees in the workplace. They were instrumental in establishing workmen's compensation and limiting child labor. The Progressive movement advocated an expansive understanding of state police power to provide a constitutional basis for the protective legislation they had helped to bring about.

Progressives placed great confidence in the ability of social science to solve social and economic ills. To implement reforms they championed

---

22. Kermit L. Hall, *The Magic Mirror: Law in American History* (New York: Oxford University Press, 1989), 200. For criticism of the federal judiciary by organized labor see Christopher L. Tomlins, *The State and the Unions: Labor Relations, Law, and the Organized Labor Movement in America, 1880–1960* (Cambridge: Cambridge University Press, 1985), 61–67.
23. Hall, *The Magic Mirror,* 196–197.
24. Melvin I. Urofsky, *A March of Liberty: A Constitutional History of the United States* (New York: Alfred A. Knopf, 1988), 543–545.

the creation of administrative agencies to regulate aspects of the economy. As envisioned by reformers, independent regulatory agencies composed of nonpolitical experts would exercise sound judgment in carrying out legislative policy. Regulation by means of administrative agencies, as they saw it, offered the advantages of expertise and flexibility and promised a rational method of managing business activity.

In retrospect this faith in administrative regulation seems naive. Many regulations were driven as much by the self-interest of organized groups as by any concern for the public welfare. As a practical matter, political considerations could rarely be divorced from agency decisions on economic issues. Indeed, it is doubtful that the regulatory agencies ever lived up to the expectations of reformers. Legislation in the early twentieth century strengthening the ICC's control of railroad rates, for instance, has long been hailed by historians as a hallmark of Progressive reform. But revisionist scholarship presents a very different view of the ICC. Albro Martin has forcefully argued that the agency's heavy-handed regulations virtually destroyed the railroad industry, discouraged technological innovation, and utterly failed to encourage a stable national transportation system.[25]

Fuller's tenure as chief justice coincided with the early years of the Progressive era. Progressivism reached fruition under the presidency of Woodrow Wilson, who took office nearly three years after Fuller's death. In the early twentieth century Progressive reformers were more or less disenchanted with the direction of the Supreme Court under Fuller. Accordingly, they leveled a barrage of complaints against the Court and the doctrine of laissez-faire constitutionalism. Theodore Roosevelt, seeking the presidency in 1912, charged that the Court had placed "well-nigh or altogether insurmountable obstacles in the path of needed social reform."[26] Such overblown charges have too often received uncritical acceptance and thus served to perpetuate the old image of the Supreme Court as a servant of business interests.

THE FULLER COURT

Historians have long designated eras of Supreme Court history by the names of chief justices. For instance, scholars commonly speak of a Marshall Court and a Taney Court. This practice is employed as a convenient means of focusing on chronological segments of the Court's past, but it is

---

25. Albro Martin, *Railroads Triumphant: The Growth, Rejection, and Rebirth of a Vital American Force* (New York: Oxford University Press, 1992), 367.

26. Theodore Roosevelt, "Judges and Progress," 100 *Outlook* 42 (January 6, 1912).

potentially misleading in several respects. It implies that there is sharp break in the direction of the Court when a new chief justice takes office, which is not necessarily the case; there is frequently a good deal of continuity from one chief justice's tenure to the next. Further, describing the Court in terms of the chief suggests a degree of domination over the justices that most chiefs have never achieved. Few of John Marshall's successors have ever matched his unique personal influence over his colleagues.[27]

Notwithstanding Fuller's accomplishments as a judicial administrator, he never gained intellectual ascendancy over his associates. Fuller did not lead the Court by the force of his ideas, and he delivered few significant opinions. Like other chief justices, he certainly did not prevail on all the important legal issues that divided the Court. Thus Fuller could not persuade his colleagues to ameliorate the fellow servant rule (under which an employer was not liable for injury to an employee caused by a fellow worker), to halt the summary deportation of Chinese aliens, to strike down state restrictions on the sale of colored oleomargarine, or to extend full constitutional protections to the insular possessions. In this limited sense, then, there was no Fuller Court. The fact that Fuller's views did not win out in some major cases indicates a lack of intellectual leadership and underscores Fuller's instinctive determination to guide the Court through skillful administration, moderating tensions, and building coalitions among the justices. Fuller had a solid core of associate justices who shared many of his constitutional values. He could therefore be an effective leader by forging working majorities and using the talents of his colleagues.

Fuller's appointment as chief justice brought to fruition a gradual shift in the formulation of constitutional doctrine. The Supreme Court under his predecessor, Morrison R. Waite, had been largely deferential to state regulation of economic activities. In this regard the Fuller Court and the Waite Court differed markedly. The most important change in constitutional law during the Fuller period concerned the Supreme Court's willingness to invalidate state and federal economic legislation. Relying in part on an expanded reading of the due process clause of the Fourteenth Amendment, the Fuller Court assumed an activist role in defending the rights of property owners from legislative infringement. As a corollary to this development, the Court restricted the scope of state police power. In the notable case of *Chicago, Milwaukee & St. Paul Railway Co. v. Minnesota*

---

27. G. Edward White, *The American Judicial Tradition: Profiles of Leading American Judges* (New York: Oxford University Press, 1976), 201.

(1890), decided early in Fuller's tenure, the justices made clear their new emphasis on property rights and distrust of regulatory policy.[28]

To be sure, defense of property rights was hardly a novel theme in American constitutionalism. In this respect there was a marked continuity between the jurisprudence of the Fuller years and prior constitutional developments.[29] From the time of John Marshall the protection of the rights of property owners had been a major concern of the Supreme Court. "Fuller's Court," one scholar has pointed out, "acted faithfully in accordance with that concept."[30] But the Fuller Court did more: it pursued this objective with heightened zeal, striking down both federal and state legislation in the process. A profound commitment to property and private economic ordering gave a distinct cast to the jurisprudence of the Fuller years. The upshot was a vastly enlarged range of judicial authority that, during Fuller's tenure, served conservative interests.

In other fields of law, however, the Fuller Court was less active. It offered slight comfort to racial minorities and criminal defendants. Following settled practice, the Court largely upheld state authority over race relations, the administration of criminal justice, and public morals. Likewise, the justices sustained congressional control of immigration and insular territories. They were disinclined to challenge popularly held views except for those situations in which economic liberty was at issue, and even here they adhered closely to dominant public sentiment. Because of its passive record in many areas of law, the historical reputation of the Fuller Court is closely linked with property rights and commerce.

Under the lingering influence of the Progressives, much historical scholarship has cast the work of the Supreme Court under Fuller in an unfavorable light. For decades historians have pictured the justices as re-

---

28. James W. Ely, Jr., "The Railroad Question Revisited: *Chicago, Milwaukee & St. Paul Railway v. Minnesota* and Constitutional Limits on State Regulations," 12 *Great Plains Quarterly* 121 (1992). See also Richard C. Cortner, *The Iron Horse and the Constitution: The Railroads and the Transformation of the Fourteenth Amendment* (Westport, Conn.: Greenwood Press, 1993), 110–113.

29. Gillman, *The Constitution Besieged*, 199; Morton J. Horwitz, *The Transformation of American Law, 1870–1960: The Crisis of Legal Orthodoxy* (New York: Oxford University Press, 1992), 7.

30. Leo Pfeffer, *This Honorable Court: A History of the United States Supreme Court* (Boston: Beacon Press, 1965), 213.

actionary, particularly with respect to economic regulations.[31] Unsympathetic to the Fuller Court's conservative bent and free market orientation, they have often given a skewed account of judicial behavior in the late nineteenth century. Historians have devised several hypotheses to explain the jurisprudence of the era. Although each of these explanations has some merit, none provides a satisfactory assessment of Fuller and his colleagues. Each theory is inconsistent with the thesis offered here.

One common assertion is that the Supreme Court adopted legal formalism as a theory of judicial decision making.[32] Although scholars are not in full agreement on the characteristics of formalism, it can be said that the concept encompassed both a mode of legal thought and a style of writing judicial opinions. Formalism treated law as an intellectually coherent and self-contained system based upon immutable principles. A formalist approach separated law from politics and tended to detach judicial decision making from policy considerations. It relied on deductive reasoning rather than a consideration of the actual results of decisions. In short, legal formalism involved mechanical reliance on precedent and logic to determine the outcome of cases. Such jurisprudence exalted judicial authority over legislative bodies by emphasizing the technical dimensions of the law that only judges could master and apply.[33]

Formalism in the late nineteenth century has been associated with laissez-faire ideology and the defense of property rights. Historians have charged that formalism served the interests of the elite by camouflaging the conservative economic and political values that actually impelled judicial decisions. Thus one prominent scholar has argued that "legal formalism, as the paradigm of conservative jurisprudence in the last quarter of the nineteenth century came to be called, not only made law work for those in power, but also supplied moral and intellectual arguments for denying its benefits to the powerless. Workers, blacks, immigrants, and

---

31. Alan Dawley, *Struggles for Justice: Social Responsibility and the Liberal State* (Cambridge, Mass.: Harvard University Press, 1991), 26; Pfeffer, *This Honorable Court,* 210–216; John P. Roche, "Entrepreneurial Liberty and the Fourteenth Amendment," in John P. Roche, *Sentenced to Life* (New York: Macmillan, 1974), 205–236; Gustavus Myers, *History of the Supreme Court of the United States* (Chicago: Charles H. Kerr, 1912), 578–694; William M. Wiecek, *Liberty Under Law: The Supreme Court in American Life* (Baltimore: Johns Hopkins University Press, 1988), 121–126.

32. Urofsky, *A March of Liberty,* 494–495.

33. Hall, *The Magic Mirror,* 221–222; Friedman, *A History of American Law,* 381–384. For a discussion of legal thought in the late nineteenth century see Horwitz, *The Transformation of American Law, 1870–1960,* 9–31.

women need not apply—or so read the hegemonic message of American jurisprudence in the Gilded Age."[34]

According to many historians, the style of legal writing generally was also influenced by the emergence of formalism. Judicial opinions became diffuse and overloaded with citations. The quality of judicial craftsmanship supposedly fell below that of antebellum judges. There is undeniably some truth in this complaint about a changing style of judicial rhetoric. But with respect to the Supreme Court, the explanation is obvious. The greatly increased docket took a heavy toll on the preparation of opinions. As Lawrence M. Friedman has aptly noted, "Marshall's court had more time to ponder, to compose, to discuss, to polish its work than Fuller's."[35] In the late nineteenth century the justices were required to churn out a large number of opinions. Judicial craftsmanship inevitably suffered. Furthermore, it is not clear that formalism is an accurate way of characterizing the literary style of Fuller and his colleagues. Walter F. Pratt, Jr., has demonstrated that there were several styles of writing opinions on the Supreme Court in the Fuller years and a wide variation among the justices. Allegations of a uniform commitment to a formalist style are wide of the mark.[36]

There remains, however, an even more fundamental problem with the formalist thesis. Copious evidence suggests that the Supreme Court under Fuller was not a bastion of legal formalism.[37] On the contrary, the Fuller era witnessed a burst of creativity in both constitutional and private law adjudication. The justices adopted a substantive interpretation of the Fourteenth Amendment, fashioned the liberty of contract doctrine, and sustained a ground-breaking injunction against interference by strikers with interstate commerce. Likewise, the Court in *Ex Parte Young* (1908) established a significant new doctrine to circumvent the Eleventh Amendment and vindicate federally protected rights. The same dynamic pattern can be found in the Fuller Court's handling of diversity jurisdiction cases. The justices were highly instrumental in

---

34. R. Kent Newmyer, "Harvard Law School, New England Legal Culture, and the Antebellum Origins of American Jurisprudence," 74 *Journal of American History* 814 (1987).

35. Friedman, *A History of American Law,* 623.

36. Walter F. Pratt, "Rhetorical Styles on the Fuller Court," 24 *American Journal of Legal History* 189–220 (1980); Harry N. Scheiber, "Instrumentalism and Property Rights: A Reconsideration of American 'Styles of Judicial Reasoning' in the 19th Century," 1975 *Wisconsin Law Review* 1.

37. John E. Semonche, *Charting the Future: The Supreme Court Responds to a Changing Society, 1890–1920* (Westport, Conn.: Greenwood Press, 1978), 426–427; Richard S. Kay, "The Equal Protection Clause in the Supreme Court, 1873–1903," 29 *Buffalo Law Review* 723–724 (1980).

evaluating policy alternatives, molding legal rules to facilitate economic growth, encourage modern commercial practices, and provide an alternative forum to the state courts for business disputes.[38] Nor were the justices hesitant to overturn precedent. Perhaps the most dramatic illustration was *Pollock v. Farmers' Loan and Trust Co.* (1895), in which Fuller, for the Court, struck down an income tax despite earlier authority that seemingly sustained such a levy. It is wrong for critics to suggest that Fuller and his colleagues blindly invoked the policy of stare decisis or pursued a mechanical jurisprudence. Far from adhering to a static conception of law, they followed a bold and innovative path; they devised new substantive rules and vigorously asserted judicial authority.

A second line of criticism posits class bias as an explanation for the Supreme Court's behavior. Many studies charge that the Court under Fuller defended the wealthy and business corporations at the expense of the poor.[39] Judges drawn from the corporate bar were seen as unduly sympathetic to business interests. "By the end of the century," a noted scholar has insisted, "lawyers and judges had become almost totally identified in the public mind as allies of the corporate rich, reactionary, and antidemocratic."[40] This protection-of-business thesis echoes the fierce attacks of the Populists and Progressives upon the Supreme Court during the Fuller years. "It is no exaggeration," activist attorney Clarence Darrow declared, "to say that nine-tenths of the laws are made nowadays by the judges and that these are made in the interests of the rich and powerful to destroy the poor."[41]

The protection-of-business theory, however, oversimplifies a more complex story and does not offer an adequate interpretation of the Supreme Court under Fuller. In the first place, it impugns the integrity of Fuller and his colleagues on the basis of assertion rather than fact. There is no direct evidence that the justices were consciously protecting the interests of business and the affluent. Fuller's attitude toward the fellow servant rule is a case in point. As an attorney Fuller had represented railroad companies and raised the fellow servant rule as a defense in negligence actions. Yet as chief justice he consistently labored to modify the

---

38. Edward A. Purcell, Jr., *Litigation and Inequality: Federal Diversity Jurisdiction in Industrial America, 1870–1958* (New York: Oxford University Press, 1992), 253–254.

39. For example, William F. Swindler, *Court and Constitution in the Twentieth Century: The Old Legality, 1889–1932* (Indianapolis: Bobbs-Merrill, 1969), 28–38.

40. Urofsky, *A March of Liberty*, 514.

41. As quoted in Ray Ginger, *Altgeld's America: The Lincoln Ideal Versus Changing Realities* (New York: Funk & Wagnalls, 1958), 214.

harsh consequences of this doctrine, contrary to the interests of corporate defendants. Other justices also displayed a willingness to rule against corporate interests. For all his attachment to property rights, Justice David J. Brewer authored many decisions adverse to business litigants.[42]

Second, there was little unity among business leaders in the Gilded Age as to the appropriate role of government in determining economic policy. They had widely divergent economic interests. Some embraced laissez-faire theory, while others favored economic regulations that created entry restrictions and stifled competition. Notwithstanding laissez-faire ideology, large segments of the business community welcomed government promotion of economic activity. Since business was not of one mind about regulatory and promotional goals, slack generalizations about the Supreme Court as a patron of corporations and capitalists must be viewed with caution.

Third, the class bias hypothesis is inconsistent with the Court's record as a whole. Critics have focused on a handful of decisions, such as *Pollock* (1895) and *Lochner v. New York* (1905), to make their point. Yet even in this era of supposed laissez-faire constitutionalism, the Supreme Court sustained many more regulations than it overturned.[43] In a study of cases heard by the Fuller Court in which state action was challenged on Fourteenth Amendment, commerce clause, and contract clause grounds, J. Gordon Hylton demonstrates that the Court had a surprising tolerance of regulatory legislation. The justices overturned state legislation in just 17 percent of such cases.[44] As this record shows, the Court made no persistent attempt to shield business or the wealthy against legislative attempts to impose public controls.

Another thesis emphasizes the impact of Social Darwinism on the work of the Supreme Court. Derived from the evolutionary theory of Charles Darwin, Social Darwinism sought to apply Darwin's insights to society at large. Social Darwinists insisted that competition and survival of the fittest would enhance overall economic productivity. Consequently, government could do little to achieve social progress and should play only a minimal role in ordering the economy. Herbert Spencer, an

---

42. Michael J. Brodhead, *David J. Brewer: The Life of a Supreme Court Justice, 1837–1910* (Carbondale, Ill.: Southern Illinois University Press, 1994), 84–103; J. Gordon Hylton, "David Brewer and the Rights of Property: A Conservative Justice Reconsidered," unpublished paper.
43. Hall, *The Magic Mirror*, 238–246. See also Melvin I. Urofsky, "Myth and Reality: The Supreme Court and Protective Legislation in the Progressive Era," *Yearbook 1983 Supreme Court Historical Society*, 53–72.
44. Hylton, "David Brewer and the Rights of Property," Table 1.

English social philosopher, and William Graham Sumner, a Yale University professor, championed the doctrine of Social Darwinism in the United States. They found a receptive audience among some segments of American society in the late nineteenth century.[45]

It has become an article of faith among many scholars that the Supreme Court under Fuller was responsive to the tenets of Social Darwinism. By the 1890s, Robert Green McCloskey charged, the "curious mixture" of Darwinism and Spencerism "had now taken over the American constitutional tradition." Another scholar maintained that the Fuller Court was "'packed' with stalwart followers of Herbert Spencer."[46] Those who contend that Social Darwinism was a determining factor in shaping the Court's jurisprudence premise their argument on Justice Oliver Wendell Holmes's famous dissenting opinion in *Lochner.* Holmes's declaration that "the Fourteenth Amendment does not enact Mr. Herbert Spencer's Social Statics" implies that the majority proceeded on Darwinist assumptions about the appropriate role of government.[47] Yet a single dissent by Holmes is a slender foundation upon which to conclude that the justices were disciples of Social Darwinism. Indeed, there is a conspicuous dearth of evidence linking the Fuller Court to Darwinist ideology. Since the Supreme Court never formally endorsed or even cited the views of Herbert Spencer, the Social Darwinist thesis rests upon conjecture.

The actual influence of Social Darwinism upon judicial decision making, therefore, remains problematic. Undoubtedly Darwinism had a powerful impact on scientific thought at the end of the nineteenth century. The justices, as well as elite attorneys, would have been exposed to Darwinian writings. But other intellectual forces did more to shape the judicial outlook than the work of Darwin. Fuller, for instance, received his formal education long before Darwin's work was known in the United States. Nurtured in the Jacksonian faith, he was early committed to limited government, laissez-faire precepts, and respect for states' rights. Fuller was already a successful attorney and active conservative Democrat when Herbert Spencer toured the country in 1882. Social Darwin-

---

45. The classic study of Social Darwinism is Richard Hofstadter, *Social Darwinism in American Thought,* rev. ed. (New York: George Braziller, 1959). See also Roche, "Entrepreneurial Liberty and the Fourteenth Amendment," 210–211.

46. Robert Green McCloskey, *American Conservatism in the Age of Enterprise* (Cambridge, Mass.: Harvard University Press, 1951), 82; Alpheus Thomas Mason, book review of *Melville Weston Fuller* by Willard L. King, 36 *Cornell Law Quarterly* 606, 607 (1951).

47. *Lochner v. New York,* 198 U.S. 45, 75 (1905).

ism may have served to reinforce his mature economic and political convictions, but even this is uncertain. Revealingly, Fuller's private writings, judicial opinions, and public addresses contain no specific reference to Darwinism. A look at Justice Brewer, the Fuller Court's most outspoken champion of property rights, also calls into question the influence of Social Darwinism. Brewer was a deeply religious man who was committed to the protection of individual liberty. His opinions and speeches are couched in terms of biblical themes and natural law philosophy, not evolutionary language. Brewer was more in harmony with John Locke than with Darwin and Spencer.[48] As these examples suggest, the notion that the Fuller Court wrote Darwinism into the Constitution is highly suspect. Quite the opposite conclusion seems warranted. "The degree to which Darwinism and Social Darwinism *failed* to permeate the thinking of the Supreme Court in any way," Herbert Hovenkamp concluded, "is most amazing."[49]

Still another interpretation of the Fuller Court pictures property-minded justices as apprehensive of radicalism and majority rule. Critics have accused the Court of responding to a crisis atmosphere, which supposedly characterized the mid-1890s, by expanding judicial power to defend the property rights of the conservative minority from threatened spoliation by the majority.[50] Certainly the justices were aware of the social tensions present in late-nineteenth-century society. Seeking to arouse judicial anxiety, prominent counsel raised the specter of communism in arguments before the Court. For example, John W. Cary contended in 1890 that a Minnesota railroad rate regulation was "destructive of the rights of property and more to be feared than the inane ravings of the advocates of socialism and the commune."[51] Similarly, Joseph H. Choate described the 1894 income tax "as communistic in its purposes and ten-

---

48. Robert E. Garner, "Justice Brewer and Substantive Due Process: A Conservative Court Revisited," 18 *Vanderbilt Law Review* 631–632 (1965).

49. Herbert Hovenkamp, *Enterprise and American Law, 1836–1937* (Cambridge, Mass., Harvard University Press, 1991), 99–100. See also Joseph Frazier Wall, "Social Darwinism and Constitutional Law with Special Reference to *Lochner v. New York*," 33 *Annals of Science* 465 (1976). One scholar contended that Social Darwinism had less influence on American society in the late nineteenth century than has been supposed. Robert C. Bannister, *Social Darwinism: Science and Myth in Anglo-American Thought* (Philadelphia; Temple University Press, 1979).

50. For the leading presentation of this view see Arnold Paul, *Conservative Crisis and the Rule of Law: Attitudes of Bar and Bench, 1887–1895* (Ithaca, N.Y.: Cornell University Press, 1960).

51. As quoted in Ely, "The Railroad Question Revisited," 125.

dencies."[52] Before he joined the Court, Holmes gave support to this hypothesis of fearful behavior. He observed in 1897, "When socialism first began to be talked about, the comfortable classes of the community were a good deal frightened. I suspect that this fear has influenced judicial action both here and in England."[53] Following this line of analysis, one prominent scholar has explained Justice Field's impassioned support for property rights as a reaction to the Paris Commune and fear of communism.[54] In a like vein, another observer has insisted that the Fuller Court was "a body dominated by fear—the fear of populists, of socialists, of communists, of numbers, majorities and democracy."[55]

Although this argument has some force, it is ultimately overdrawn and unpersuasive. The depiction of this Court as fearful rests upon a skimpy factual basis. To be sure, occasional alarmist rhetoric by judges seemingly demonstrated worry over class conflict. Justice Field's vigorous concurring opinion in *Pollock* is often cited as evidence that the Supreme Court was responding to a perceived menace of radicalism. Field darkly warned, "The present assault upon capital is but the beginning. It will be but the stepping-stone to others, larger and more sweeping, till our political contests will become a war of the poor against the rich."[56] Rufus Peckham, while a member of the New York Court of Appeals in 1889, similarly denounced a grain warehouse rate regulation in class-laden terms: "To uphold legislation of this character is to provide the most frequent opportunity for arraying class against class; and, in addition to the ordinary competition that exists throughout all industries, a new competition will be introduced, that of competition for the possession of the government, so that legislative aid may be given to the class in possession thereof in its contests with rival classes or interests in all sections and corners of the industrial world." For good measure Peckham also characterized the law as "vicious in its nature, communistic in its tendency."[57]

But such observations fall short of establishing that the Court was motivated by fear. It should be pointed out that most of the justices never expressed such sentiments. Although he disliked the Populists, Fuller's letters show no trace of deep anxiety about the course of national events.

52. For Choate's argument in the *Pollock* case see Frederick C. Hicks, ed., *Arguments and Addresses of Joseph Hodges Choate* (St. Paul: West, 1926), 419, 422.

53. Oliver W. Holmes, "The Path of the Law," 10 *Harvard Law Review* 467–468 (1897).

54. Howard Jay Graham, "Justice Field and the Fourteenth Amendment," 52 *Yale Law Journal* 856–860 (1943).

55. Mason, book review, 607.

56. *Pollock v. Farmers' Loan & Trust Co.*, 157 U.S. 429, 607 (1895).

57. *People v. Budd*, 117 N.Y. 1, 68–69, 71 (1889) (Peckham, J., dissenting).

One could also question whether Field's remarks, made at the end of his long career, were truly representative of his views. But there is a more serious deficiency with the fearful-court hypothesis. The Fuller Court was the first to confront systematically the modern special interest state in which organized groups lobbied for legislative favors. Viewed in historical context, then, Field and Peckham were denouncing class legislation. They were following the Jacksonian political tradition, Thomas Cooley, and the dominant constitutional theory by attacking laws that aided special interests at the expense of others. Rather than responding to fear of the masses, Fuller and his colleagues were dubious that certain regulations actually served the broad public interest.

It is an exaggeration, moreover, for historians to assert that judicial conservatives were apprehensive about the stability of the social order. In an 1894 public address William Howard Taft, then a judge on the Sixth Circuit Court of Appeals, expressed concern about what he saw as unfair and misguided attacks on corporations. But Taft revealingly added, "I do not think the present state of social unrest is any ground for a pessimistic view of modern civilization. We are passing through an era of tremendous economic changes and the apparently alarming phenomena in the social horizon are only the necessary results of an adjustment to new conditions."[58] These temperate remarks do not suggest a judicial system consumed with fear.

The thesis presented here is that Fuller and his colleagues were genuinely devoted to the preservation of individual liberty in a changing society. Unlike modern liberals, the Fuller Court defined freedom largely in economic terms and highly valued individual choice in economic matters. As Stephen A. Siegel has cogently noted, "in nineteenth-century America, property was considered among the most important civil liberties."[59] In the eyes of the Fuller Court it was therefore essential to restrict the exercise of governmental power in order to preserve this concept of liberty. Jennifer Nedelsky has perceptively observed that "the notion that property and contract were essential ingredients of the liberty the Constitution was to protect, was common to Madison, Marshall, and the twentieth-century advocates of laissez-faire."[60] Since individual liberty had long been linked to private property in Anglo-American constitu-

---

58. William H. Taft, "The Right of Private Property," 3 *Michigan Law Journal* 231–232 (1894).

59. Siegel, "*Lochner* Era Jurisprudence," 33 n. 154. See also Semonche, *Charting The Future,* 102–103.

60. Jennifer Nedelsky, *Private Property and the Limits of American Constitutionalism: The Madisonian Framework and Its Legacy* (Chicago: Chicago University Press, 1990), 228.

tional thought,[61] respect for property ownership limited the bounds of legitimate governmental authority. "It should never be forgotten," Justice Field observed in 1890, "that protection to property and to persons cannot be separated. Where property is insecure, the rights of persons are unsafe."[62] As Field's comments indicate, constitutional thought in the late nineteenth century viewed the security of private property as a vital prerequisite for the enjoyment of individual liberties such as the freedom of speech.[63] Accordingly, the Fuller Court assumed the desirability of private economic ordering and looked with disfavor upon legislation that infringed upon the operations of the free market. Fuller and his colleagues were particularly concerned with laws that conferred special privileges, interfered with contractual relationships, or in effect transferred wealth from one group to another. This explains the Court's deep suspicion of regulatory agencies, the income tax, and rate-fixing for certain industries. In the final analysis, then, the Fuller Court strengthened private property as a primary personal right immune from government tampering. A preoccupation with economic liberty had more to do with the course of the Fuller Court than any hidden desire to safeguard the interests of business per se.

The Fuller Court was sensitive to the dangers that unchecked government could pose to individual liberties. This concern was forcefully expressed by Justice Brewer, a champion of both economic and personal freedom, when he declared in 1894 that "the paternal theory of government is to me odious. The utmost possible liberty to the individual, and the fullest possible protection to him and his property, is both the limitation and duty of government."[64] In an era of the welfare state Brewer's protestation is no longer widely accepted. But this should not obscure the sincerity of his commitment to limited government and the rights of the individual.[65]

At the same time, one must be careful not to attribute an elaborate judicial philosophy to the Fuller Court. In fact, the justices upheld a good deal of regulatory legislation that impinged on laissez-faire principles. Their defense of economic individualism was tempered by a commit-

61. Ely, *The Guardian of Every Other Right*, 10–41.

62. Stephen J. Field, "The Centenary of the Supreme Court," February 4, 1890, reprinted in 134 U.S. 729, 745.

63. Mark A. Graber, *Transforming Free Speech: The Ambiguous Legacy of Civil Libertarianism* (Berkeley: University of California Press, 1991), 20–26.

64. *Budd v. New York,* 143 U.S. 517, 551 (1892).

65. J. Gordon Hylton, "The Judge Who Abstained in *Plessy v. Ferguson:* Justice David Brewer and the Problem of Race," 61 *Mississippi Law Journal* 338–341 (1991).

ment to federalism and antagonism to monopoly. Reflecting a clash of contrary values, the pattern of decisions by the Fuller Court dealing with economic issues was hardly uniform. The justices invariably sustained legislation that they perceived as protecting the health, safety, or morals of the public. Indeed, the Court sometimes accepted fatuous justifications at face value to uphold special-interest legislation. Thus in 1894, over dissents by Fuller, Field, and Brewer, the Court ruled that Massachusetts could prohibit the sale of colored oleomargarine on grounds that such products might deceive the public.[66] As this record makes clear, the Fuller Court never launched a wholesale assault on state regulatory authority. It also gave the states wide latitude to tax corporate property and inherited wealth.

Nor it is easy to pigeonhole the individual justices into neat categories on the judicial spectrum. The property-conscious Justice Brewer wrote several libertarian opinions dealing with Chinese immigration.[67] Despite his liberal views on race relations and the income tax, Justice Harlan took the lead in scrutinizing state regulatory measures and was instrumental in formulating the liberty of contract doctrine. Justices Brown and Holmes moved between liberal and conservative positions. For instance, the moderate Brown voted to sustain the income tax and then authored the Court's opinion in *Plessy v. Ferguson* (1896) and joined the majority in *Lochner*. Notwithstanding a professed willingness to permit lawmakers great latitude in making policy, Holmes sometimes voted to strike down economic regulations under the due process or contract clause during Fuller's tenure.

Recognition that the Fuller Court acted to safeguard economic liberty rather than to serve some ulterior purpose does not absolve the justices from criticism. The central failing of the Fuller Court was its inability to comprehend the diminished significance of economic individualism in a national economy dominated by giant enterprises. This problem was particularly evident in employment relationships. As a practical matter, individuals often had no bargaining power and were compelled to accept whatever terms were offered by employers. Yet the Fuller Court was reluctant to sanction governmental intervention to strengthen the legal position of industrial workers and encourage the formation of labor unions.

Despite this conspicuous blind spot, there was a dynamic, forward-looking dimension to the Fuller Court's handling of economic issues. Put

---

66. *Plumley v. Massachusetts,* 155 U.S. 461 (1894).
67. Semonche, *Charting The Future,* 244–245; Brodhead, *David J. Brewer,* 105–108.

simply, the justices glimpsed the economic future of the United States more clearly than their Populist and Progressive critics. Suspicious of concentrated economic power, many Populists and Progressives yearned to restore an older America with an economy centered on small-scale and geographically limited enterprise. To achieve this end they called upon government to play a more active role in managing economic affairs. Yet the Progressive reforms proved no panacea to the conditions of the new industrial society and created other problems for the economy. Even Holmes, the darling of the Progressives, doubted the economic wisdom of antitrust laws and railroad rate regulations, both staples of the Progressive reform agenda.[68] Indeed, the regulatory movement itself would in due course come under sharp attack for hampering business efficiency, encouraging short-term political solutions to long-range economic problems, and harming the interests of consumers. In the last analysis, antitrust laws did not restrain the growth of large corporate enterprise. Time has made clear that the crusade against bigness, championed by leading Progressives such as Louis D. Brandeis, was a futile gesture. All of this evidence raises the possibility that the Fuller Court's skepticism about the regulatory movement proceeded from sound instincts.

In any event, the economic predilections of the Fuller Court ran counter to those of the liberal reformers. Although they were strongly opposed to monopoly, the justices identified with burgeoning industrial capitalism. Fuller, who had represented banks and railroads during his years at the bar, was comfortable with large corporations. Linking security of private property with economic development, the Court sought to protect capital formation and defend the national market from obstructive state laws. Protection of property rights therefore dovetailed with utilitarian considerations. As Morton Keller has perceptively observed, "an old concern for private rights and individual freedom coexisted with the desire to foster the development of a national economy."[69] The Supreme Court under Fuller was more receptive to the new realities of American economic life than many other sectors of the polity. This gulf between opposing conceptions of the economic future explains the bitter antagonism toward the Fuller Court from those whose values were rooted in preindustrial society.

---

68. Mark DeWolfe Howe, ed., *Holmes-Pollock Letters: The Correspondence of Mr. Justice Holmes and Sir Frederick Pollock, 1874-1932,* 2nd ed. (Cambridge, Mass.: Harvard University Press, 1961), vol. 1, 163.
69. Keller, *Affairs of State,* 370.

4

SAFEGUARDING
ENTREPRENEURIAL LIBERTY

Building upon earlier constitutional developments and fashioning innovative doctrines, the Fuller Court markedly intensified the constitutional protection of economic interests. The justices heard a steady stream of cases challenging the constitutionality of state and federal economic regulations and taxes. Never before had the Supreme Court exercised the power of judicial review so actively. Yet, somewhat surprisingly, given the Court's reputation as a bastion of laissez-faire thought, most regulations were found to pass muster.

RAILROAD REGULATION

One of the most persistent and difficult issues of the Fuller era was the extent to which the state or federal governments could control operations of privately-owned railroad companies. As the principal artery of interstate commerce and travel, railroads occupied a unique spot in American life during the Gilded Age.[1] Railroading was a capital-intensive enterprise that required a continuous flow of funds to establish new routes and make necessary improvements. Despite an enormous increase in the amount of track and volume of business, many railroads in the 1890s experienced financial problems resulting from keen competition between carriers as well as the depressed national economy. Many lines went bankrupt and were placed under federal court receivership. Shippers and farmers, on the other hand, perceived the railroads as wielding monopoly power and charging excessive rates. Responding to a clamor for public control, in the 1870s western and southern states enacted so-called Granger laws, under which commissions regulated the prices

---

1. Harold U. Faulkner, *Politics, Reform, and Expansion: 1890–1900* (New York: Harper and Row, 1959), 75–76

charged by railroads for the transportation of passengers and freight. In 1886, however, the Supreme Court ruled that under the commerce clause the states could not regulate rates for interstate transportation. This decision caused Congress to enact the Interstate Commerce Act the following year.

The first important affirmative use of federal regulatory authority, the act created a new agency, the Interstate Commerce Commission (ICC), to supervise railroad operations.[2] The ICC was authorized to conduct hearings, gather information, and issue orders against practices that violated the act. However, the ambiguous provisions of the act raised a number of interpretative problems for the Fuller Court. The measure declared that charges for interstate railroad transportation should be reasonable and just but did not define reasonableness or expressly give the ICC power to set rates. Section 4 made it unlawful for a carrier to discriminate between long hauls and short hauls in fixing rates "under substantially similar circumstances." The act also prohibited the pooling of traffic among carriers as well as the practice of granting rebates or preferred treatment to favored shippers.

Railroad leaders were ambivalent about the growing web of state and federal regulations.[3] They preferred federal supervision to inconsistent and sometimes oppressive state laws. Some carriers hoped that national controls might help to stabilize the highly competitive industry. But most railroad officials were hostile to government control of their rates. They feared that lawmakers would seek to benefit politically powerful shippers and farmers at the expense of the roads by imposing unreasonably low charges. Such an outcome would threaten the long-term economic health of the railroads by discouraging capital investment. Under these circumstances, the carriers looked to the Supreme Court as a bulwark against excessive regulation.

Although it was broadly sympathetic to the position of the railroads, the Court accepted the basic premise that they were subject to a degree of public control. Regulation of railroads was predicated on the notion that, as common carriers, the roads had assumed certain obligations to the public. In a line of decisions during the 1890s, however, the justices acted to curtail regulatory authority, leave key decision making in the hands of the lines, and preserve the operation of the free market.

---

2. Kermit L. Hall, *The Magic Mirror: Law in American History* (New York: Oxford University Press, 1989), 204–206.

3. Morton Keller, *Affairs of State: Public Life in Late Nineteenth Century America* (Cambridge, Mass.: Harvard University Press, 1977), 427–430.

The Fuller Court initially moved to intercede in the state regulation of intrastate railroad charges. The decision in *Chicago, Milwaukee & St. Paul Railway Company v. Minnesota* (1890) was a significant turning point in the Court's handling of rate regulations. At issue was a Minnesota commission order to reduce the charge for carrying milk on certain routes within the state. By a 6 to 3 vote the justices struck down the Minnesota rate law. Speaking for the Court, Justice Samuel Blatchford found a procedural infirmity because the statute did not provide for a hearing before the commission or for judicial review of rates set by the agency. Blatchford then moved beyond this procedural objection and asserted judicial authority to review the fairness of rates imposed by state law. He observed that "if the company is deprived of the power of charging reasonable rates for the use of its property, and such deprivation takes place in the absence of an investigation by judicial machinery, it is deprived of the lawful use of its property, and thus, in substance and effect, of the property itself, without due process of law and in violation of the Constitution of the United States."[4]

There were several noteworthy aspects to the *Chicago, Milwaukee* ruling. First, it signaled the Fuller Court's acceptance of the due process clause as a substantive restriction on state legislative authority. Second, it contradicted a fundamental principle of *Munn* that rate-setting was solely a legislative function. Once the justices came to understand that unlimited power to regulate might be used to destroy the value of railroad property, judicial supervision of rates followed logically. Otherwise regulated industries would have only those property rights that legislators chose to recognize. Third, the ruling expanded the range of property interests secured by the Constitution. The Court implicitly took the position that property ownership went beyond title and possession and encompassed the right to use property for economic value.

The Court's path with respect to rate regulation, however, was not unilinear. In *Budd v. New York* (1892) the justices upheld by a margin of 6 to 3 a New York law fixing the maximum charge for storing grain in the face of due process objections. The majority reasoned that this case could be distinguished from *Chicago, Milwaukee* because in *Budd* the charges were fixed directly by the legislature, not a commission. Affirming the *Munn*

---

4. *Chicago, Milwaukee & St. Paul Railway Company v. Minnesota*, 134 U.S. 418, 458 (1890). Richard C. Cortner, *The Iron Horse and the Constitution: The Railroads and the Transformation of the Fourteenth Amendment* (Westport, Conn.: Greenwood Press, 1993), 77–124. See James W. Ely, Jr., "The Railroad Question Revisited: Chicago, Milwaukee & St. Paul Railway v. Minnesota and Constitutional Limits on State Regulations," 12 *Great Plains Quarterly* 121 (1992).

doctrine, the Court declared that rates set by the legislature itself were not subject to judicial review. This prompted a forceful dissenting opinion by Justice David J. Brewer, who assailed the notion that a public interest in the use of private property constituted a valid basis to regulate prices. He maintained that government could prescribe prices only for a narrow category of businesses in which government conferred exclusive privileges or property was devoted to a public use. The distinction drawn in *Budd* between legislative and agency regulation was fundamentally flawed. Since lawmakers could exercise their authority to control transportation charges either by direct legislation or through a commission, it made little sense to reach a different result based on the regulatory device utilized. Rather, the Court should have focused on the economic impact of the regulation and the reasonableness of the rate. In any event, the outcome in *Budd* proved to be aberrational, and the Fuller Court moved swiftly into the thicket of rate regulation.

In *Reagan v. Farmers' Loan and Trust Co.* (1894) the Fuller Court served notice that it would inquire into the reasonableness of state rates imposed by either a legislature or a commission and would restrain any regulation that operated to divest a property owner of rights. To assess the reasonableness of rates prescribed by the Texas Commission, the Court undertook a review of the railroad's earnings, operating costs, and financial condition. Justice Brewer, who spoke for a unanimous bench, noted the importance of investment capital for the achievement of economic growth. "Would any investment ever be made of private capital in railroad enterprise," he asked, with such an insufficient return as was provided by the Texas rate? He also invoked "the spirit of common justice" to deny "that one class should by law be compelled to suffer loss that others may make gain."[5] From this perspective, judicial supervision of rates was both salutary and necessary.

Railroads were not the only business to claim the Supreme Court's protection against confiscatory rates. In *Covington and Lexington Turnpike Road Company v. Sandford* (1896) the justices unanimously held that legislative control over the tolls on a turnpike road was subject to the same constitutional limitations. The turnpike company alleged that a Kentucky statute would sharply reduce the toll allowed and thereby diminish the income of the company so that it could not meet ordinary expenses or pay any dividend. Such allegations were found to constitute a prima facie case of deprivation of property without due process.

---

5. *Reagan v. Farmers' Loan and Trust Co.*, 154 U.S. 362, 412, 410 (1894).

The culmination of this trend came in *Smyth v. Ames* (1898). In 1893 the Nebraska legislature, under Populist influence, established a maximum rate schedule for railroads operating in the state. The effect of the law was to compel an average 30 percent reduction in charges for intrastate freight. Writing for a unanimous Court, Justice John M. Harlan addressed the complex question of how courts should ascertain what compensation a railroad was entitled to receive. He first concluded that the reasonableness of a charge for intrastate transportation must be determined without reference to the return earned by the railroad on its interstate business. Otherwise, Harlan feared, low local rates would constitute a subsidy for state business at the expense of interstate shipping. He then spelled out a standard to guide judicial review of rates:

> We hold, however, that the basis of all calculations as to the reasonableness of rates to be charged by a corporation maintaining a highway under legislative sanction must be the fair value of the property being used by it for the convenience of the public. And in order to ascertain that value, the original cost of construction, the amount expended in permanent improvements, the amount and market value of its bonds and stock, the present as compared with the original cost of construction, the probable earning capacity of the property under particular rates prescribed by statute, and the sum required to meet operating expenses, are all matters for consideration, and are to be given such weight as may be just and right in each case. We do not say that there may not be other matters to be regarded in estimating the value of the property. What the company is entitled to ask is a fair return upon the value of that which it employs for the public convenience. On the other hand, what the public is entitled to demand is that no more be exacted from it for the use of a public highway than the services rendered by it are reasonably worth.[6]

Known as the fair value rule, the formula articulated by Harlan was full of ambiguity. He set forth a cluster of inconsistent factors with no indication as to the relative weight to be assigned to each item. Over time, however, courts defined fair value primarily in terms of current or replacement value of a company's assets rather than the actual or original cost.[7]

---

6. *Smyth v. Ames*, 169 U.S. 466, 546–547 (1898).
7. Stephen A. Siegel, "Understanding the Lochner Era: Lessons From the Controversy Over Railroad and Utility Rate Regulation," 70 *Virginia Law Review* 227–228 (1984).

The upshot of *Smyth v. Ames* was to place constitutional limits on the rate-making process of regulatory bodies. The Supreme Court became in effect the final arbiter as to the reasonableness of imposed rates. By promulgating the fair value rule, the Fuller Court sought both to protect investors and regulated industries against confiscatory rates and to safeguard the interests of consumers. Yet over time the fair value rule proved difficult to administer. In order to establish a rate base the federal courts had to make an intricate assessment of the present value of a company. This necessitated a substantial commitment of judicial resources to the review of rate-making. The Supreme Court passed upon appeals from a large number of state agency rate orders alleging a failure to adequately determine current market value. In practice, the Court during Fuller's tenure was reluctant to find challenged rates invalid. But *Smyth* shut the door on state-mandated reductions of existing rates and created a standard that would increasingly bind state regulatory authority in the years after Fuller's death. A rising level of prices in the early twentieth century meant a steady increase in the worth of assets. Under these circumstances, state agencies found it hard to impose meaningful limits on rates.[8] Progressives began to view the *Smyth* ruling as hampering regulatory bodies and unduly favoring the railroads and utilities.

By and large, scholars have not been kind to *Smyth*. Melvin I. Urofsky has declared that the decision "may be one of the worst mistakes the Court ever made, for it plunged the judiciary into the business of second-guessing both legislatures and administrative agencies on the complex issue of rate structures."[9] The *Smyth* ruling, however, should not be dismissed so completely. Despite the shortcomings of the fair value rule, the justices of the Fuller Court followed sound instincts. As suggested by the facts in *Smyth* itself, they were concerned that the regulatory process was often skewed by political manipulation that operated to the unfair disadvantage of railroads and utilities. Politicians seeking to curry favor would be tempted to use the rate-making process as a means of redistributing wealth. Such an outcome would at once infringe on the property rights of regulated industries and discourage capital investment. The fair value rule of *Smyth* was meant to serve a protective function and not leave railroads to the unrestrained rate-making of state agencies.[10] The

---

8. *Ibid.*, 233–234.

9. Melvin I. Urofsky, *A March of Liberty: A Constitutional History of the United States* (New York: Alfred A. Knopf, 1988), 526. For the liberal attack on *Smyth v. Ames* see Siegel, "Understanding the Lochner Era," 243–259.

10. Mary Cornelia Porter, "That Commerce Shall Be Free: A New Look at the Old Laissez-Faire Court," *1976 Supreme Court Review* 151–157.

hopes of the Court were only partially realized, but *Smyth* did provide a barrier against confiscatory rates.

The Fuller Court continued to scrutinize state rate regulations following *Smyth*. In *Lake Shore and Michigan Southern Railway Company v. Smith* (1899) the justices voted 6 to 3 to strike down a Michigan statute that required railroads to sell a thousand-mile ticket at a set price below the standard rate. The Court viewed the law as an improper interference with the right of the company to manage its business. Concluding that the legislation was not "for the safety, health or proper convenience of the public, but an arbitrary enactment in favor of" a certain group of passengers, the Court held that the act constituted a taking of property without due process.[11]

Notwithstanding its determination to review the reasonableness of imposed rates, the Fuller Court was by no means uniformly hostile to state regulation of railroads. In many cases it recognized broad state authority to control the rates for intrastate travel. The justices routinely rejected challenges to state regulation based upon claimed exemptions in corporate charters. Under the due process clause railroads could assert protection only against rates so low as to have a confiscatory effect. Charges fixed by a state regulatory process were presumed to be reasonable, and the burden of proof was placed on the carriers to show the contrary. Many state rate regulations were sustained. For example, the justices upheld the imposition of a joint through rate on connecting railroads in Minnesota. Likewise, they ruled that railroads were bound by state long-haul/short-haul antidiscrimination provisions governing traffic within the state even though such regulations might indirectly affect interstate commerce.[12]

In fact, the Fuller Court could be criticized for giving inadequate attention to the adverse impact of state rate regulations on the national railroad system.[13] Regulation of intrastate charges in effect compelled adjustments in interstate rates. The wonder is that the Fuller Court did not intervene more forcefully in the state rate-setting process in order to protect the economic health of the roads. This failure may be explained in terms of the Court's commitment to preserving an important role for the states in the federal union. But the Fuller Court's willingness to ac-

---

11. *Lake Shore and Michigan Southern Railway Company v. Smith*, 173 U.S. 684, 698–699 (1899).

12. *Minneapolis & St. Louis Railroad Company v. Minnesota*, 186 U.S. 257 (1902); *Louisville and Nashville Railroad Company v. Kentucky*, 183 U.S. 503 (1902).

13. Herbert Hovenkamp, *Enterprise and American Law, 1836–1937* (Cambridge, Mass.: Harvard University Press, 1991), 159–164.

cord the states regulatory authority over aspects of the national rail system hardly supports the older Progressive view of the Court as a prorailroad tribunal.

State regulation of railroads was by no means confined to the matter of shipping charges. The Fuller Court heard frequent due process challenges to a wide variety of regulations. Railroad operations often caused injury to adjacent landowners. Accordingly, many states enacted laws to enlarge the legal liability of the roads by holding them strictly liable, independent of any negligence, for such damages. In *St. Louis and San Francisco Railway Company v. Mathews* (1897) the issue was a Missouri statute that imposed absolute liability on railroads for any property damaged by fire communicated from locomotive engines. Noting that at English common law every person was strictly accountable for the spread of fire to the property of others, the Court unanimously decided that lawmakers could make railroads liable for fire damage caused by the use of dangerous instruments.

Yet there were limits as to what degree of regulation the justices would permit. At issue in *Louisville and Nashville Railroad Company v. Central Stock Yards Company* (1909) was a Kentucky law requiring that a railroad deliver its cars to a connecting carrier, but making no provision for adequate compensation. The purpose of this measure was to facilitate the movement of goods by mandating an interchange of railroad cars. By a 6 to 3 margin, the Court, in an opinion by Justice Oliver Wendell Holmes, found that such a duty amounted to a deprivation of property without due process. A year later, in *Missouri Pacific Railway Company v. Nebraska* (1910), the Court struck down a statute requiring railroads, at their own expense, to construct switch connections and a side track upon the application of any grain elevator operation. Again speaking for the Court, Justice Holmes proclaimed that "railroads after all are property protected by the Constitution, and there are constitutional limits to what can be required of their owners under either the police power or any other ostensible justification for taking such property away."[14] He concluded that the statute sought to confer a private benefit on the elevator operators and went beyond the limits of the police power.

National regulation of railroads also raised nettlesome questions of economic regulation, statutory construction, and federalism for the Fuller Court. The intent of Congress in enacting the Interstate Commerce Act of 1887 has long been the subject of historical debate. A compromise among divergent economic interests, the act was designed more

---

14. *Missouri Pacific Railway Company v. Nebraska*, 217 U.S. 196, 206 (1910).

to placate antirailroad agitation than to establish strict control over the roads. Congress created the Interstate Commerce Commission (ICC), a relatively weak regulatory body that had few express powers. The shadowy language of the act invited judicial interpretation. In a series of decisions the Fuller Court moved to curb what little authority the ICC attempted to exercise over railroads.

In keeping with its preference for private economic ordering, the Fuller Court took a narrow view of ICC power. In *ICC v. Cincinnati, New Orleans and Texas Pacific Railway Company* (1897) the commission decided that its authority to review the reasonableness of existing rates conferred by implication the power to prescribe rates. By an 8 to 1 margin the justices rejected this contention. "There is nothing in the act fixing rates," Justice Brewer pointed out, and such a power "is never to be implied."[15]

The railroads' practice of charging a higher price for short, usually intrastate, hauls than for long hauls gave rise to one of the most bitter and misunderstood rate controversies of the Gilded Age. In fact, much of this rate differential made good economic sense. Distance was not the determining factor in setting rates. The operating expenses of carrying local freight were usually higher than those for carrying long-distance freight. Moreover, most long-distance routes were highly competitive, and the resulting pressure forced long-haul rates downward. Local shippers, however, considered the differential between long hauls and short hauls a form of invidious rate discrimination. In section 4 of the Interstate Commerce Act, Congress prohibited railroads from charging more for transportation "under substantially similar circumstances and conditions for a shorter than a longer distance over the same line." Thus the act permitted railroads to retain the differential between long and short hauls when they were warranted by special circumstances.

Inevitably the long-haul–short-haul issue reached the Supreme Court. The Fuller Court's skeptical attitude toward the regulatory process is strikingly illustrated by the famous case of *ICC v. Alabama Midland Railway Company* (1897). At issue was an ICC order that the railroad cease charging a greater rate for shipments to and from Troy, Alabama, than for the longer distance to Montgomery, Alabama. The differential was prompted by the fact that Montgomery was served by several competing carriers. The justices held that the existence of competition was a factor to be considered when applying "the similar circumstances and conditions" clause. Hence the company could lawfully charge lower prices for

---

15. *ICC v. Cincinnati, New Orleans and Texas Pacific Railway Company*, 167 U.S. 479, 494 (1897).

shipments to Montgomery because the circumstances were not similar. In effect, the Court decided that the free market should continue to operate as a factor in setting prices. To underscore this point, the justices ruled that courts hearing appeals from the ICC were not bound by the factual findings of the commission and could consider additional evidence. Justice Harlan alone dissented, protesting that the decision "goes far to make that commission a useless body for all practical purposes."[16]

Indeed, between 1897 and 1906 the ICC prevailed in only one major case out of sixteen argued before Fuller and his colleagues. The agency virtually abandoned rate-making and directed its energy into gathering information and issuing reports about the financial condition of railroads. As a result, the ICC did not play a major role in fashioning transportation policy until passage of the Hepburn Act in 1906.

Many historians, influenced by the Progressive school, have accused the Fuller Court of emasculating the ICC and the policy of vigorous railroad regulation.[17] But this criticism is wide of the mark. The basic problems were not of the Court's making but were properly attributed to Congress, which failed to confer rate-making authority on the ICC. Faced with this clear omission in the statute, the justices correctly held that the agency could not claim such a far-reaching right by implication. In fact, during the late nineteenth century the ICC never developed a consistent position concerning rate-making. The same analysis pertains to the Court's interpretation of section 4. The Fuller Court's handling of the the long haul/short haul differential in *Alabama Midland* demonstrated a grasp of economic reality and the importance of competition in determining prices. Reaching a sensible result, the justices minimized the economic damages to railroads that would have resulted if the lines could not charge more on short-haul routes.[18] In any event, Congress was not troubled by the Court's railroad decisions and showed little inclination to strengthen the ICC during the 1890s. Congress's deep ambivalence over railroad regulations undermines any claim that the Fuller Court was blocking some clearly expressed congressional goal.

In the early twentieth century there were renewed calls for additional railroad regulation, and Congress gradually empowered the ICC to supervise interstate rates. The Hepburn Act of 1906 authorized the agency

---

16. *ICC v. Alabama Midland Railway Company*, 168 U.S. 144, 176 (1897).

17. Urofsky, *A March of Liberty*, 524–525; Faulkner, *Politics, Reform, and Expansion*, 78–79.

18. Albro Martin, *Railroads Triumphant: The Growth, Rejection, and Rebirth of a Vital American Force* (New York: Oxford University Press, 1992), 328; Herbert Hovenkamp, "Regulatory Conflict in the Gilded Age: Federalism and the Railroad Problem," 97 *Yale Law Journal* 1071–1072 (1988).

to declare an existing charge unreasonable and set a new one. Thus for the first time Congress conferred rate-making power on the commission. Late in Fuller's tenure, the Supreme Court also moved to bolster the ICC's authority. In *ICC v. Illinois Central Railroad Company* (1910), a case arising under the Hepburn Act, the justices redefined their position concerning judicial review of commission decisions. Adopting a narrow understanding of its role, the Court declared that it would not "under the guise of exerting judicial power, usurp merely administrative functions by setting aside a lawful administrative order upon our conception as to whether the administrative power has been wisely exercised."[19] If the ICC made orders within the scope of its authority, the Court would defer to the agency and not pass upon questions of rail policy. The Court adhered to this deferential approach in *ICC v. Chicago, Rock Island & Pacific Railway Company* (1910), in which the justices upheld an ICC order that reduced freight charges on certain shipments from the Atlantic seaboard to Missouri River destinations.

Clearly the Fuller Court was not disposed to resist the efforts of Congress to revitalize the ICC. The explanation for this apparent change of heart is not hard to find. Fuller and his colleagues never denied that Congress had substantial regulatory power over railroads. To be sure, they were prepared to interpret the vague terms of the original Interstate Commerce Act to leave economic decisions largely in the hands of the carriers. But it would be an entirely different matter for the Court to thwart the unequivocal intent of Congress to regulate railroad operations and rates. Despite their preference for the free market, Fuller and his associates were on the whole pragmatic rather than doctrinaire. They usually functioned within the parameters of dominant public opinion.

It should be emphasized, too, that the justices did not entirely retire from the field. The Supreme Court continued to review the reasonableness of rates imposed by the ICC and the states. Moreover, in several cases the justices continued to construe narrowly the provisions of railroad regulatory statutes. Fuller and his colleagues acted, for instance, to restrain the investigatory powers of the ICC. In *Harriman v. ICC* (1908) the Court ruled by a 5 to 3 margin that the Interstate Commerce Act authorized the commission to compel the testimony of witnesses only when it was investigating a specific breach of law, not for the purpose of recommending new legislation. Delivering the majority opinion, Justice Holmes decried "the enormous scope of the power asserted for the commission" and declared that "no such unlimited command over the liberty

---

19. *ICC v. Illinois Central Railroad Company*, 215 U.S. 452, 470 (1910).

of all citizens ever was given, so far as we know, in constitutional times, to any commission or court."[20] Lurking behind the *Harriman* decision was the Fuller Court's lasting distrust of administrative bodies.[21] Similarly, in *United States v. Delaware and Hudson Company* (1909) the justices placed a restricted construction on the commodities clause of the Hepburn Act, which was designed to divorce production of commodities from transportation. The commodities clause was aimed primarily at railroads that were thought to obtain an unfair advantage by shipping coal from their own mines. The Court interpreted the clause not to prevent railroads from transporting commodities belonging to a corporation in which they owned stock. The decision effectively allowed the roads to occupy the dual position of carrier and shipper.[22]

The Fuller Court's handling of the prolonged rate-setting controversy has commonly been pictured as a futile stand against the growth of the regulatory state. But the fears of Fuller and his colleagues about rate regulation proved to be well grounded. Government regulation of railroad charges steadily increased in the early decades of the twentieth century. Revisionist scholarship has identified heavy-handed rate regulations and cumbersome rate-setting procedures as major factors in the decline of America's railroads.[23] In 1980, following the near collapse of the national railroad system, Congress passed the Staggers Act, which substantially eliminated ICC control over rates. Thus Congress has belatedly arrived at the free-market position first pointed out by the Fuller Court in the 1890s.

SUBSTANTIVE DUE PROCESS

While wrestling with the problems of rate regulation, the Supreme Court under Fuller began to flesh out the doctrine of substantive due process in other areas of economic regulation. In essence, the Court as-

---

20. *Harriman v. ICC*, 211 U.S. 407, 417–418 (1908).

21. Holmes, for instance, had little confidence in the ICC and feared that the commission was constantly seeking to expand its delegated power. Liva Baker, *The Justice from Beacon Hill: The Life and Times of Oliver Wendell Holmes* (New York: HarperCollins, 1991), 428–429.

22. Clyde B. Aitchison, "The Evolution of the Interstate Commerce Act: 1887–1937," 5 *George Washington Law Review* 329 (1937). See also John E. Semonche, *Charting the Future: The Supreme Court Responds to a Changing Society, 1890–1920* (Westport, Conn.: Greenwood Press, 1978), 228–229.

23. Albro Martin, *Enterprise Denied: Origins of the Decline of American Railroads, 1897–1917* (New York: Columbia University Press, 1971), 358–360; John F. Stover, *The Life and Decline of the American Railroad* (New York: Oxford University Press, 1970), 247–248.

sessed state economic regulations against a reasonableness standard and invalidated measures seen as unduly restrictive of property rights or serving the interests of only one class. As the justices explained in *Lawton v. Steele* (1894), "The legislature may not, under the guise of protecting the public interest, arbitrarily interfere with private business, or impose unusual and unnecessary restrictions upon lawful occupations."[24] Under substantive due process, the mere fact that an enactment purported to protect the public was not conclusive upon the Court. Instead, the justices would scrutinize both the goal to be served by a governmental action and the means employed to achieve this end. They would independently weigh the evidence to ascertain whether a regulatory statute was a valid exercise of the police power that genuinely protected the health, safety, or morals of the public. In practice, the doctrine of substantive due process lodged in the hands of judges potentially wide discretionary authority over economic and social measures.

A crucial problem was to articulate a baseline from which the reasonableness of economic regulations could be measured. The justices drew upon common-law doctrines of property law, the private law of contracts, and the prevalent belief in entrepreneurial liberty to fashion the tenets of substantive due process.[25] The doctrine quickly became a mainstay of laissez-faire constitutionalism. Critics charged, with some merit, that it was difficult for the Court to draw a consistent line between permissible and impermissible legislation. But the Fuller Court was engaged in a legitimate inquiry into the nature and extent of due process protection. Although the attempt to formulate a test of reasonableness was far from perfect, the main thrust of the Fuller Court's due process jurisprudence was clear. Safeguarding liberty and property from state interference under the due process clause was widely seen as an appropriate judicial function. In Fuller's day most of the controversy surrounding substantive due process concerned particular applications of the doctrine rather than its existence.

LIBERTY OF CONTRACT

The Fuller Court also developed an important corollary of substantive due process, the liberty of contract principle. In *Allgeyer v. Louisiana* (1897) the justices unanimously struck down a state law that prohibited a person from obtaining insurance from a company that was not qualified to do business in Louisiana. Allgeyer, a resident of Louisiana, was pros-

---

24. *Lawton v. Steele*, 152 U.S. 133, 137 (1894).
25. Hovenkamp, *Enterprise and American Law*, 176–182.

ecuted for making a marine insurance contract with a New York company. Speaking for the Court, Justice Rufus W. Peckham defined liberty, as protected by the Fourteenth Amendment, in expansive terms:

> The liberty mentioned in that amendment means not only the right of the citizen to be free from the mere physical restraint of his person, as by incarceration, but the term is deemed to embrace the right of the citizen to be free in the enjoyment of all his faculties; to be free to use them in all lawful ways; to live and work where he will; to earn his livelihood by any lawful calling; to pursue any livelihood or avocation, and for that purpose to enter into all contracts which may be proper, necessary and essential to his carrying out to a successful conclusion the purposes above mentioned.[26]

It followed that a state could not prohibit its residents from making a valid contract outside its borders. Although the case was decided on a liberty of contract rationale, *Allgeyer* also had implications for commerce among the states. The outcome testified to the Fuller Court's protection of the national market against obstructionist state laws.

The concept of contract played a fundamental role in shaping American law during the nineteenth century.[27] Contracts were a vehicle by which private persons could make voluntary arrangements to govern their economic affairs. Individuals were deemed capable of looking out for their own best interests. Contractual freedom was at the heart of free-market exchanges and closely identified with laissez-faire economics. Accordingly, constitutional theorists such as Christopher G. Tiedeman called upon the courts to prevent legislative interference with the terms of a contract. It seemed reasonable therefore that the right to enter contracts deserved special protection by the judiciary.

The decision in *Allgeyer,* concerning the right to obtain marine insurance, did not create much of a stir. But *Allgeyer* became the leading case establishing the liberty of contract principle. The implications of this principle were potentially sweeping, especially with respect to employment relationships. Seeking to alleviate harsh industrial working conditions, state lawmakers limited contractual freedom by regulating the terms and conditions of labor. Employers regularly relied upon liberty of contract in challenges to state legislation regulating employment,

---

26. *Allgeyer v. Louisiana,* 165 U.S. 578, 589 (1897).

27. Lawrence M. Friedman, *A History of American Law,* 2nd ed. (New York: Simon and Schuster, 1985), 532–536. For the origins of the liberty of contract doctrine see Charles W. McCurdy, "The Roots of 'Liberty of Contract' Reconsidered: Major Premises in the Law of Employment, 1867–1937," *Yearbook 1984 Supreme Court Historical Society,* 20–33.

but the Fuller Court found no further occasion to apply the doctrine for several years.

Indeed, in a series of cases the Court rebuffed arguments that state labor laws abridged the right of employers and employees to make contracts. In *Holden v. Hardy* (1898) the justices upheld by a margin of 7 to 2 a Utah statute that limited employment in mines to eight hours a day. They stressed the unhealthy working conditions in underground mining and realistically noted that mine owners and their employees "do not stand upon an equality, and that their interests are, to a certain extent, conflicting."[28] Similarly, the court in *Knoxville Iron Company v. Harbison* (1901) sustained a Tennessee law that required that employers who paid their workers in script must, upon request, redeem the same in money. Convinced that the statute would promote good employment relations, the justices pointed out that the right to contract was not absolute. This pattern of decisions continued in *Atkin v. Kansas* (1903), which raised the question of whether a state could prescribe conditions for work of a public nature. Brushing aside a liberty of contract argument, the justices voted 6 to 3 to validate a statute limiting work on state or municipal projects to eight hours a day.

The reluctance of the Fuller Court to apply the liberty of contract doctrine was also evident in cases involving regulation of business. Thus in *W. W. Cargill Co. v. Minnesota* (1901) the justices unanimously concluded that states could require grain elevators and warehouses on railroad lines to obtain a license to do business. In *Nutting v. Massachusetts* (1902) the Court similarly ruled that a state could prohibit the sale of insurance within its jurisdiction by unlicensed brokers. The decision in *Nutting* was seemingly at odds with that in *Allgeyer,* but Fuller and his colleagues were prepared to allow the states greater latitude to control domestic insurance business. The justices were also sympathetic to state regulation of the commodity and stock markets. They sustained, by a margin of 7 to 2, a law prohibiting options to sell or buy grain at a future time in *Booth v. Illinois* (1902). Likewise, in *Otis v. Parker* (1903) the justices upheld a provision of the California Constitution that prohibited contracts for the sale of corporate stock on margin for future delivery. Although the provision admittedly limited contractual freedom, Justice Holmes, writing for the Court, urged that a state be allowed considerable latitude to regulate or prohibit commercial transactions. In addition, the Court rejected a liberty of contract challenge to a state mechanics' lien law in *Great Southern Fire Proof Hotel Company v. Jones* (1904). In marked contrast to the hesi-

---

28. *Holden v. Hardy,* 169 U.S. 366, 397 (1898).

tant Fuller Court, the state courts generally proved more willing to strike down legislation that violated the liberty of contract principle.

The Supreme Court under Fuller, however, continued to treat liberty of contract as the controlling constitutional norm and to require the states to justify legislation that restricted this right. The freedom to make individual contracts, including the right to sell one's own labor, could be curbed only to promote the health, safety, or morals of the community. Liberty of contract thus brought into possible conflict social legislation and individual economic freedom.

In the seminal case of *Lochner v. New York* (1905), the justices implemented the liberty of contract doctrine by invalidating a statute that limited work in bakeries to ten hours a day or sixty hours a week.[29] Speaking for a 5 to 4 majority, Justice Peckham pointed out that the "right to purchase or to sell labor is part of the liberty protected by the Fourteenth Amendment." He agreed that a state could enact legislation to protect the health of bakers, but he was not persuaded that the baking trade was unhealthy and could find no direct relationship between the number of working hours and the health of bakers. Peckham reasoned that "the real object and purpose" of the statute was to regulate labor relations rather than the purported end of safeguarding health. Because Peckham felt that bakers were fully capable of asserting their interests and were "in no sense wards of the state," he characterized statutes limiting hours of work "as mere meddlesome interferences with the rights of the individual." Therefore he concluded that the statute exceeded the permissible bounds of state police power. Peckham expressed broad disapproval of labor protective laws. "It is impossible for us to shut our eyes," he observed, "to the fact that many of the laws of this character, while passed under what is claimed to be the police power for the purpose of protecting the public health or welfare, are, in reality, passed from other motives."[30]

The two dissenting opinions also warrant comment. The justices had initially decided to sustain the statute, and Justice Harlan's dissent was first prepared for delivery as the opinion of the Court. But one jus-

---

29. See Howard Gillman, *The Constitution Besieged: The Rise and Demise of Lochner Era Police Powers Jurisprudence* (Durham, N.C.: Duke University Press, 1993), 126–136; Paul Kens, *Judicial Power and Reform Politics: The Anatomy of Lochner v. New York* (Lawrence: University Press of Kansas, 1990).

30. *Lochner v. New York,* 198 U.S. 45, 53, 64 (1905).

tice changed his position at a later conference.[31] Harlan accepted the legitimacy of the liberty of contract principle but contended that the Court misapplied it in this case. Emphasizing that contracts were subject to health and safety regulations, he pointed to evidence that prolonged work in bakeries endangered an employee's health. Thus Harlan maintained that the legislature acted reasonably for the common good.

Justice Holmes, in one of his most famous dissents, went a step further and rejected the notion of liberty of contract. In a brief but trenchant opinion, he first accused the majority of deciding the case on an economic theory rather than on legal grounds. Yet, as discussed in chapter 3, Holmes never convincingly demonstrated that the Court was influenced by Herbert Spencer and Social Darwinism. More significantly, Holmes articulated a philosophy of judicial restraint under which the Supreme Court should defer to "the right of a majority to embody their opinions in law." He lectured his colleagues that "a constitution is not intended to embody a particular economic theory. . . . It is made for people of fundamental differing views."[32] A harbinger of legal realism and New Deal jurisprudence, the celebrated Holmes dissent is not without problems. For all his powerful rhetoric, Holmes never addressed the scope of due process protection or explained why, on the facts of *Lochner*, the maximum hours statute was reasonable.[33] But the Holmes dissent became a rallying point for critics of the Supreme Court's defense of property rights. Holmes, much to his discomfort, was hailed by Progressives, who believed legislation was the path to social and economic reform.

The *Lochner* decision initially aroused little public interest. Reformers, however, gradually began to fear that the ruling was a serious setback to their hopes for legislative improvement of working and social conditions. In 1910 former president Theodore Roosevelt sharply attacked the federal courts for protecting property rights and maintained that "every man holds his property subject to the general right of the community to regulate its use to whatever degree the public welfare may require it."

---

31. Charles Henry Butler, *A Century at the Bar of the Supreme Court of the United States* (New York: G. P. Putnam's Sons, 1942), 170–172.

32. *Lochner v. New York*, 198 U.S., 75–76. For an analysis of the Holmes dissent in *Lochner* see G. Edward White, *Justice Oliver Wendell Holmes: Law and the Inner Self* (New York: Oxford University Press, 1993), 324–328.

33. Richard A. Posner, *Law and Literature: A Misunderstood Relation* (Cambridge, Mass.: Harvard University Press, 1988), 281–286.

Roosevelt singled out *Lochner* as a case that struck "against popular rights, against the Democratic principle of government by the people, under the forms of law."[34] Detached from its factual context, *Lochner* gradually acquired a life of its own. To liberals *Lochner* became a term of reproach, an emotionally charged symbol of everything they disliked about a property-conscious Supreme Court. Some historians have even described the history of the Supreme Court between 1900 and 1937 as the "*Lochner* era," a term that is somewhat misleading because it implies that the justices consistently applied the liberty of contract principle to invalidate social legislation.

Lochner has long been the subject of an intense scholarly debate. For decades liberal critics have successfully presented the case as a prime example of improper judicial activism and as a reflection of an antilabor bias by the Court. This negative view continues to hold sway in most accounts of *Lochner*.[35] More recently, a group of revisionist scholars has endeavored to rehabilitate *Lochner* and the underlying liberty of contract principle. Echoing Justice Peckham's majority opinion, they have argued that the ostensible purpose of the maximum working hours statute was only a facade for special-interest legislation. They picture the statute as an anticompetitive measure designed to drive small-scale immigrant bakers out of business.[36] This revisionist scholarship invites reconsideration of whether *Lochner* has been unfairly castigated.

In any event, *Lochner* was not typical of the Fuller Court's handling of liberty of contract claims. In practice, the justices allowed the states a large degree of authority to control employment and business activities. This was illustrated in the notable case of *Muller v. Oregon* (1908). The issue before the Court was whether a state could limit the number of working hours for women in factories and laundries to ten hours a day. Unanimously sustaining this measure, the Supreme Court stressed the

34. Theodore Roosevelt, "The New Nationalism", August 31, 1910, in *Social Justice and Popular Rule* (New York: Charles Scribner's Sons, 1926), 17. For Roosevelt's attack on the *Lochner* decision see William Henry Harbaugh, *The Life and Times of Theodore Roosevelt* (New York: Collier, 1963), 367.

35. Urofsky, *A March of Liberty*, 553–555; Russell W. Galloway, *Justice for All? The Rich and Poor in Supreme Court History, 1790–1990* (Durham, N.C.: Carolina Academic Press, 1991), 89; William M. Wiecek, *Liberty Under Law: The Supreme Court in American Life* (Baltimore: Johns Hopkins University Press, 1988), 123–125.

36. Bernard H. Siegan, *Economic Liberties and the Constitution* (Chicago: University of Chicago Press, 1980), 113–121. For a discussion of the revisionist efforts to defend *Lochner* see Mary Cornelia Porter, "Lochner and Company: Revisionism Revisited," in Ellen Frankel Paul and Howard Dickman, eds., *Liberty, Property and Government: Constitutional Interpretation Before the New Deal* (Albany: State University of New York Press, 1989), 11–38.

special health needs of women, their maternal function, and their dependent legal status as justifying different treatment. Liberty of contract applied only to persons who were deemed capable of managing their own economic affairs. Writing for the Court, Justice Brewer did not see women as equal competitors with men in the marketplace and thus accepted the necessity for protective legislation. The *Muller* case was a milestone because the Court relied upon social science information contained in the brief of Louis D. Brandeis as a factual basis for upholding the legislation. The Brandeis brief interjected a new element into constitutional decision making, one that would reach fruition after Fuller's death. Although it was a qualified victory for reformers, *Muller* accepted the basic premise upon which *Lochner* was predicated. But the decision demonstrates that the Fuller Court was prepared to recognize major exceptions to the liberty of contract when a state could demonstrate the reasonableness of its regulations.

The paternalistic assumptions behind the Progressive legislation to protect women and Justice Brewer's *Muller* opinion appear suspect to modern eyes. Laws grounded upon gender differences too often had the practical effect of placing women at a disadvantage in securing employment and pigeonholing them in particular occupations. Such paternalistic attitudes, however, accurately reflected the prevailing sentiment concerning a woman's role in society. This helps to explain why Justice Brewer so readily accepted the nascent social science evidence. The data supported an existing societal judgment regarding the desirability of limiting the amount of time women worked away from the house. Indeed, *Muller* was in accord with a line of state court decisions that sustained protective legislation for women as an appropriate exercise of the police power. In a sense, the Fuller Court merely ratified ascendant public belief concerning the unique position of women.[37]

The Fuller Court made clear its commitment to liberty of contract in a case rendered during the same term in which *Muller* was decided. In 1898 Congress enacted the Erdman Act to govern employment relations on railroads engaged in interstate commerce and to encourage arbitration of disputes. Among other provisions, the act outlawed so-called yellow dog contracts. Such contracts made it a condition of employment that employees not belong to any labor union. Widespread use of these agreements seriously hampered the union movement in the early twentieth century. In *Adair v. United States* (1908) the Court struck down the

---

37. Hall, *The Magic Mirror*, 239–240. See also Joan Hoff, *Law, Gender, and Injustice: A Legal History of U.S. Women* (New York: New York University Press, 1991), 196–203.

yellow dog contract provision by a 6 to 2 vote. Speaking for the Court, Justice Harlan said that the provision was "an invasion of the personal liberty, as well as the right of property" guaranteed by the due process clause of the Fifth Amendment. Citing *Lochner,* he reiterated "the general proposition that there is a liberty of contract which cannot be unreasonably interfered with by legislation." He pronounced the statute an arbitrary interference with the right of employers and employees to contract concerning terms of employment.[38]

Liberty of contract was invoked in *Adair* to invalidate legislation supportive of labor organizations. Since this was one of a handful of cases in which the Fuller Court applied the liberty of contract principle, it is hard to escape the conclusion that Fuller and his colleagues were uneasy with a growing labor movement. This judicial skepticism readily matched the reluctance of society at large to accept labor unions. It is revealing that Justice Harlan, who had previously been deferential to legislative judgement, wrote the majority opinion. As Loren P. Beth has observed, "Harlan was . . . a child of his times in many ways; for example, he shared to some degree the rest of the Court's marked antipathy to the rise of organized labor."[39] The *Adair* ruling provoked outrage among supporters of unions and contributed to the antilabor image of the Fuller Court.

Late in Fuller's tenure the justices went the opposite way, permitting the states to regulate the method of calculating wages owed to miners. In *McLean v. State of Arkansas* (1909) the Court, by a vote of 7 to 2, upheld a state law that required that wages be determined on the basis of what the mined coal weighed before being passed over a screen, a device used to sift the coal. The use of screens had been the subject of bitter disputes between operators and miners because miners believed that the screens often unfairly reduced the weight of the coal. Since mining companies commonly paid miners only for coal that passed over the screen, miners felt deprived of their just compensation. Rejecting a liberty of contract argument, the Court observed, "Laws tending to prevent fraud and to require honest weights and measures in the transaction of business have frequently been sustained in the courts, although in compelling certain modes of dealing they interfere with the liberty of contract."[40] The ma-

---

38. *Adair v. United States,* 208 U.S. 161, 172, 174 (1908). For an analysis of the *Adair* decision see Barry Cushman, "Doctrinal Synergies and Liberal Dilemmas: The Case of the Yellow-Dog Contract," *1992 Supreme Court Review* 238–243.

39. Loren P. Beth, *John Marshall Harlan: The Last Whig Justice* (Lexington: University Press of Kentucky, 1992), 202.

40. *McLean v. Arkansas,* 211 U.S. 539, 550 (1909).

jority reasoned that legislatures could take reasonable steps to insure that laborers receive their just wages.

The Fuller Court formulated the liberty of contract principle but employed the doctrine sparingly. The totality of cases that touched upon the liberty of contract does not sustain an interpretation of the Court as grimly determined to frustrate economic regulation. Although Justices Peckham and Brewer were consistent champions of liberty of contract, they could not persuade a majority of their colleagues in most cases. Consequently, a large number of regulatory measures passed judicial muster. In actuality, the justices endeavored to reconcile their commitment to entrepreneurial liberty and the free market with legislative efforts at economic reform.

At the same time, one must acknowledge the significance of the liberty of contract in shaping constitutional jurisprudence for the ensuing decades. The doctrine affirmed the Supreme Court's dedication to limited government and particularly to the belief that government did not have unfettered dominion over economic life. In this respect, it served as a potential check upon arbitrary governmental action, causing state legislatures to justify regulation more carefully. Moreover, the justices reserved for themselves the authority to decide when lawmakers exceeded the scope of the police power and trespassed upon property or contractual rights. Last, acceptance of liberty of contract as a constitutional principle set the stage for more aggressive use of the doctrine by succeeding justices.

THE TAKINGS CLAUSE

Drawing upon natural law theory and colonial experience,[41] the Fifth Amendment provides in part, "Nor shall private property be taken for public use without just compensation." The provision significantly limits the exercise of eminent domain power and implicitly rejects outright confiscation as an acceptable policy. In practice, however, the takings clause did not bulk large in constitutional thought before Fuller became chief justice. It was generally agreed, following the Supreme Court decision in *Barron v. Baltimore* (1833), that the Bill of Rights restricted only the federal government and was not applicable to the states.[42] Since the federal government undertook relatively few projects that necessitated

41. James W. Ely, Jr., " 'That due satisfaction may be made': The Fifth Amendment and the Origins of the Compensation Principle," 36 *American Journal of Legal History* 1 (1992).
42. Alfred H. Kelly, Winfred A. Harbison, and Herman Belz, *The American Constitution: Its Origins and Development,* 7th ed. (New York: Norton, 1991), vol. 1, 198.

taking private property, the Supreme Court had little opportunity to pass upon the scope of the takings clause. This changed markedly during Fuller's tenure as the justices heard a number of appeals in which property owners claimed the protection of the takings clause against government action. The Fuller Court was the first to wrestle in a sustained way with the takings issue, and it laid the groundwork for subsequent developments in this field. The justices never developed an overarching conception of takings jurisprudence; they proceeded on a case-by-case basis. In so doing, the Court tended to strengthen the position of property owners.

The relationship between the takings clause and substantive due process was elusive. Clearly the norm that government could not seize property without compensation shaped thinking about substantive due process rights, particularly in setting limits to the authority to regulate rates. The Fuller Court analyzed some cases under the due process framework that today would likely be treated as a takings problem. Fuller and his colleagues did not achieve doctrinal precision in their taking jurisprudence, a result which has evaded the grasp of later justices as well. Despite some confusion, however, the Court under Fuller did establish certain fundamental principles to govern application of the takings clause.

There are three critical components to takings jurisprudence. The initial inquiry is whether property has been "taken" by the government. A key issue in Fuller's time was whether injury to adjacent property owners resulting from public projects should be treated as a compensable taking. The Court heard a line of cases in which riparian owners suffered damage as a consequence of federal river and harbor improvements. At issue in *Gibson v. United States* (1897) was the construction of a dike on the Ohio River that drastically reduced the claimant's access to the river. Declaring that the title of riparian owners was subject to a navigational servitude in favor of the government, the Court, speaking through Fuller, unanimously ruled that the injury did not amount to a taking of property. Instead, it simply represented the incidental consequence of a proper exercise of governmental authority. Likewise, in *Scranton v. Wheeler* (1900) the Court, by a margin of 6 to 3, held that the takings clause was inapplicable when a riparian owner lost access to navigation because of the construction of a pier on submerged land in front of his property. Observing that "what is a taking of private property for public use, is not always easy to determine," the justices reasoned that the injury was not a taking of property but merely consequential damage that did not require compensation.[43] *Gibson* and *Scranton* established the rule that loss of access rights to a navigable river because of governmental action does not necessitate the payment of compensation.

On the other hand, when public works caused physical invasion of private property the Court was more likely to find that there had been a taking. Speaking for a 5 to 3 majority in *United States v. Lynah* (1903), Justice Brewer ruled that a river navigation project that caused permanent flooding of a rice plantation and rendered it useless constituted a taking. Yet in *Bedford v. United States* (1904) the justices unconvincingly distinguished *Lynah* and denied recovery for flooding damages resulting from erosion control by the federal government along the Mississippi River. In *Bedford* the Fuller Court appeared more anxious to facilitate government control over navigable rivers than to safeguard the property rights of individuals. The unsatisfactory upshot was continued confusion over the rights of an abutting owner to compensation for injury caused by navigation projects.

In an age before comprehensive zoning, the Fuller Court also dealt with early land use controls. Many of these statutes limited the profitable use of land or necessitated expenditures to change existing structures. As a general proposition the Fuller Court permitted localities to enact specific restrictions to safeguard public health or safety or to abate nuisance conditions. The justices decided in *Chicago, Burlington and Quincy Railway Company v. Illinois* (1906) that a state, as part of a drainage project, could compel a railroad to remove an existing bridge and erect a new bridge at its own expense. Brushing aside an argument that this requirement effectuated a taking of property, the Court concluded that the cost of rebuilding was merely an incidental injury resulting from exercise of the police power. Similarly, in *Tenement House Department of New York v. Moeschen* (1906) the Court sustained, in a per curiam opinion, a public health law requiring tenement owners to install modern sanitary facilities. The Court also unanimously upheld in *Welch v. Swasey* (1909) a limitation on the height of buildings in sections of Boston. The justices reasoned that the measure was a valid exercise of the police power to reduce the danger of fire in residential districts. A year later, in *Laurel Hill Cemetery v. San Francisco* (1910), the Court reaffirmed public control of land usage in broad terms. Declaring that "tradition and the habits of the community count for more than logic," Justice Holmes, speaking for the Court,

---

43. *Scranton v. Wheeler,* 179 U.S. 141, 153 (1900).

found that a municipal ordinance prohibiting burials within the city was constitutional.[44]

Yet there were limits to the Fuller Court's indulgence of land use regulations, particularly when local government disturbed the reasonable expectations of property owners. *Dobbins v. Los Angeles* (1904) involved a municipal ordinance fixing the geographic area in which a gasworks might be established. After a landowner obtained a permit and began to construct a works, the city adopted another ordinance that placed the land in a prohibited area. Treating the case under the rubric of due process, the justices unanimously held that the sudden change of limits amounted to "a taking of property without due process of law and an impairment of property rights protected by the Fourteenth Amendment."[45]

Another subject of contention in takings law is the requirement that private property be taken for "public use." Throughout most of the nineteenth century state courts encouraged an open-ended definition of public use by treating the exercise of eminent domain as a legislative responsibility. Legislators often delegated the power of eminent domain to business corporations, such as canal and railroad companies, for the purpose of serving the public. By the end of the century, however, many state courts began to define the concept of public use more narrowly and to insist upon some degree of actual usage by the public in order to take property by eminent domain. This was an attempt to curtail the wide-ranging exercise of eminent domain to benefit private entities.

The Fuller Court did not play a major role in shaping the public use doctrine. On the whole, the justices deferred to state determinations as to what should be deemed public use.[46] In *Missouri Pacific Railway Company v. Nebraska* (1896), however, they signaled that property could not be taken for private purposes. At issue was a Nebraska statute that authorized a state agency to compel a railroad to grant part of its land to private individuals for the purpose of establishing a grain elevator. Noting that there was no claimed public use, the Court decided that taking property for the private use of another was prohibited by the due process clause of the Fourteenth Amendment even though compensation was paid. In effect, the justices confined the taking of property by the states to public use.

---

44. *Laurel Hill Cemetery v. San Francisco*, 216 U.S. 358, 366 (1910).
45. *Dobbins v. Los Angeles*, 195 U.S. 223, 241 (1904).
46. For a discussion of the public use doctrine during Fuller's time see David A. Schultz, *Property, Power, and American Democracy* (New Brunswick: Transaction, 1992), 74–75.

Notwithstanding this step, Fuller and his colleagues were reluctant to treat the public use requirement as a significant restraint on the exercise of eminent domain power. In *Fallbrook Irrigation District v. Bradley* (1896) the justices heard a challenge to California's irrigation laws on grounds that the water to be procured was not for a public use but only aided certain landowners. Unanimously rejecting this argument, the Court adopted a broad definition of what makes up a public use. "It is not essential," Justice Peckham observed, "that the entire community or even any considerable portion thereof should directly enjoy or participate in an improvement in order to constitute a public use."[47] In like manner, the justices in *Hairston v. Danville and Western Railway Company* (1908) found condemnation of land for construction of a spur track to satisfy the public use requirement despite the fact that the track was used solely to reach a particular plant.

The Fuller Court also sustained the exercise of eminent domain by private individuals when it was deemed necessary for economic development. Many states in the Rocky Mountain region conferred the power of eminent domain upon private persons to obtain rights-of-way across the land of others for mining or irrigation.[48] This practice passed constitutional muster in *Clark v. Nash* (1905), which involved an action by an individual under Utah law to condemn a right-of-way through land of another for the purpose of irrigation. Recognizing the unique water problems of the arid and mountainous states, the Court ruled by a vote of 7 to 2 that "the use is a public one, although the taking of the right of way is for the purpose simply of obtaining the water for an individual." The Court was apparently persuaded that the private property was being taken to create some overall resource benefit for public advantage and not solely for the advantage of another individual. But such an analysis might be understood to legitimate any private takeover of property. Accordingly, Justice Peckham, writing for the Court, cautioned, "We do not desire to be understood by this decision as approving of the broad proposition that private property may be taken in all cases where the taking may promote the public interest."[49] The justices took the same position in *Strickley v. Highland Boy Mining Co.* (1906), sustaining the condemnation of a right-of-way by a mining company.

It is remarkable that the Fuller Court, which was not hesitant to employ substantive due process to review state laws, declined to put any

---

47. *Fallbrook Irrigation District v. Bradley,* 164 U.S. 112, 161 (1896).

48. Gordon Morris Bakken, *Rocky Mountain Constitution Making, 1850–1912* (Westport, Conn.: Greenwood Press, 1987), 29–34.

49. *Clark v. Nash,* 198 U.S. 361, 369–370 (1905).

teeth into the public use doctrine and attached great weight to the judgment of state courts. Despite some expressed qualifications, the Court for all practical purposes sanctioned the transfer of property from one private owner to another. This calls into question the reputation of the Fuller Court as a single-minded guardian of property rights. Perhaps the justices were persuaded that a generous view of eminent domain encouraged economic growth. In any event, the Court left lawmakers with virtually unrestrained discretion and thereby contributed to the process by which the public use clause was drained of any meaning.

The third critical element of takings jurisprudence is the requirement of just compensation when property is taken by the government. Fuller and his colleagues gave an expansive reading to the right of compensation and laid the basis for subsequent doctrinal developments. Insistence upon payment of compensation provided a check against excessive use of eminent domain authority. In the leading case of *Monongahela Navigation Company v. United States* (1893) the federal government appropriated a lock and dam as part of a river improvement project. The sole issue was the amount of compensation, with the government arguing that the owner was entitled only to the value of the tangible property and not to compensation for loss of the franchise to collect tolls. Justice Brewer, speaking for a unanimous Court, broadly asserted that "the fulness and sufficiency of the securities which surround the individual in the use and enjoyment of his property constitute one of the most certain tests of the character and value of the government." He explained that the right to compensation "prevents the public from loading upon one individual more than his just share of the burdens of government." Brewer then asserted that the determination of just compensation was a judicial function, not a legislative one: "It does not rest with the public, taking the property, through Congress or the legislature, its representative, to say what compensation shall be paid, or even what shall be the rule of compensation. The Constitution has declaimed that just compensation shall be paid, and the ascertainment of that is a judicial inquiry." He defined just compensation as "a full equivalent for the property taken" and maintained that the value of property was determined by its profitableness.[50] It followed, therefore, that just compensation mandated payment for the loss of tolls under the franchise as well as for the physical property taken. This ruling established the present value of the property to the owner as the proper determinant of compensation.

---

50. *Monongahela Navigation Company v. United States,* 148 U.S. 312, 324–328 (1893).

In an even more important holding, the Fuller Court ruled in *Chicago, Burlington and Quincy Railroad Company v. Chicago* (1897) that compensation for private property taken for public use was an essential element of due process as guaranteed by the Fourteenth Amendment. Writing for the Court, Justice Harlan declared that the mere form of the proceeding did not satisfy due process unless provision was made for compensation. Accordingly, the just compensation rule became in effect the first provision of the Bill of Rights to be applied to the states. By virtue of the *Chicago, Burlington* decision the due process clause operated as a takings clause binding on the states. This pioneering outcome is striking because the Fuller Court generally rejected arguments that the Fourteenth Amendment incorporated the Bill of Rights. It attests to the high regard in which Fuller and his associates held the ownership of private property and to their abhorrence of outright seizure. Surprisingly, after establishing that the just compensation guarantee was part of due process, the Court found that a nominal award made by the trial jury to the railroad represented just compensation under the circumstances.

Most of the takings cases heard by the Fuller Court concerned legislative action. But courts may reshape property law in ways that augment governmental authority and diminish previously recognized attributes of private ownership. This power raises the contested issue of whether court decisions that depart from prior law constitute an unconstitutional judicial taking of property. In *Chicago, Burlington* the Court pointedly observed that the Fourteenth Amendment, incorporating the just compensation protection, applied to all branches of state government including the judiciary. It did not, however, address the argument that courts could take property by changing the law.

Fuller and his colleagues grappled inconclusively with the concept of a judicial taking in *Muhlker v. New York and Harlem Railroad Company* (1905). The case arose out of prolonged litigation over the construction of elevated railroads in New York City.[51] New York state courts initially ruled that the abutting property owners had easements of light, air, and access in public streets and must be compensated for the loss of these interests. Thereafter, however, in a suit by an adjacent owner seeking compensation, the New York Court of Appeals reversed its earlier decision and held that the owners had no property interests that were infringed by the building of an elevated structure in place of a street-level railroad. In a

---

51. For the legal problems caused by the advent of elevated railroads in cities see Molly Selvin, *This Tender and Delicate Business: The Public Trust Doctrine in American Law and Economic Policy, 1789–1920* (New York: Garland, 1987), 299–339.

murky plurality opinion by Justice Joseph McKenna, the Supreme Court concluded that the previously recognized easements were property interests that could not be extinguished without compensation. Relying heavily on the contract clause, McKenna suggested that the state courts were not free to diminish property rights by abandoning precedent. He observed that the authority of state courts to declare property rules did not encompass the power "to take away rights which have been acquired by contract and have come under the protection of the Constitution of the United States."[52] The Court seemed anxious to protect the claimant's expectations when he acquired the abutting land. Justice McKenna's contract clause analysis was flawed because any contract was implied from the earlier court decisions, and the actual dispute pertained to property rights. Speaking for himself and three other members of the Court, including Fuller, Justice Holmes dissented. To Holmes the claimant's rights were "a construction of the courts," and he strenuously denied that property owners had a constitutional right to have general legal propositions remain unchanged. Thus the Fuller Court debated but failed to resolve the notion that judicial changes in existing law might constitute a taking of property.[53]

THE CONTRACT CLAUSE

Under the leadership of Chief Justice John Marshall the Supreme Court fashioned the contract clause into a significant limitation on state power to interfere with contractual arrangements and to regulate the economy. The contract clause continued to figure prominently in constitutional litigation throughout the nineteenth century. In 1896 Justice George Shiras cogently remarked, "No provision of the Constitution of the United States has received more frequent consideration by this Court than that which provides that no State shall pass any law impairing the obligation of contracts."[54] As this comment suggests, the Court decided numerous contract clause cases during Fuller's tenure. Indeed, it has been estimated that in Fuller's time nearly 25 percent of the cases challenging the constitutionality of state legislation involved the contract clause. In the hands of the Fuller Court the contract clause did not prove

---

52. *Muhlker v. New York and Harlem Railroad,* 197 U.S. 544, 570 (1905). The *Muhlker* decision is examined in Benjamin Fletcher Wright, *The Contract Clause of the Constitution* (Cambridge, Mass.: Harvard University Press, 1938), 240–241.
53. For a thoughtful treatment of judicial takings of property see Barton H. Thompson, Jr., "Judicial Takings," 76 *Virginia Law Review* 1449 (1990).
54. *Barnitz v. Beverly,* 163 U.S. 118, 121 (1896).

a reliable weapon to defend economic interests, but the clause retained a degree of vitality nonetheless. Although the justices sustained state action in the vast majority of cases, they relied upon the contract clause to strike down state laws in at least 28 cases, which amounted to approximately 21 percent of the contract clause cases heard.[55] Despite this activity, the contract clause declined in importance while Fuller was chief.

Most contract clause cases heard by the Fuller Court concerned public contracts. Still, the justices twice relied on the clause to invalidate state debtor-relief laws that infringed private contractual obligations. In *Barnitz v. Beverly* (1896) the Court unanimously voided a Kansas statute authorizing the redemption of foreclosed property where no such right previously existed as an impairment of a prior mortgage contract by subsequent legislation. Similarly, writing for a unanimous Court in *Bradley v. Lightcap* (1904), Fuller declared unconstitutional an Illinois measure that retroactively forfeited the legal title and right of possession of a foreclosing mortgagee for failure to obtain a deed within a set time. Although the Fuller Court did sustain some debt-relief legislation that was deemed to change only the available remedy and not to modify the substantive rights of the contract parties, it followed in the footsteps of previous courts by carefully scrutinizing statutes affecting debtor-creditor relationships.

The Fuller Court also invoked the contract clause to check attempts by states and municipalities to evade their financial obligations. At the behest of voters upset by high taxes, southern states and many western counties in the late nineteenth century sought ways to reduce their level of bonded indebtedness. They enacted a wide variety of legislation to scale down the amount of debt, reduce the rate of interest owed on bonds, and limit the remedies of bondholders. Not surprisingly, creditors instituted a host of lawsuits charging that such laws impaired bondholder contracts. Much of this litigation was resolved before Fuller became chief, and in any event the full story of the debt repudiation controversy is too complex for treatment here. In many cases the Supreme Court ruled that suits in federal court between bondholders and state governments were barred by the Eleventh Amendment.[56]

---

55. Wright, *The Contract Clause of the Constitution*, 95–96; J. Gordon Hylton, "David Brewer and the Rights of Property: A Conservative Justice Reconsidered," unpublished paper, Table 3. See also David P. Currie, *The Constitution in the Supreme Court: The Second Century, 1888–1986* (Chicago: University of Chicago Press, 1990), 7–13.

56. John V. Orth, *The Judicial Power of the United States: The Eleventh Amendment in American History* (New York: Oxford University Press, 1987), 58–120. For the Fuller Court's treatment of the Eleventh Amendment see chapter 7.

Nonetheless, Fuller and his associates sided with creditors in some bond repudiation cases. The extended contest over Virginia's bonds prompted a flood of lawsuits. Virginia lawmakers went to extraordinary lengths to undercut the tax-receivable coupons attached to state bonds. The case of *McGahey v. Virginia* (1890) involved a statute requiring production of the bond from which the tendered coupons were removed. The justices unanimously concluded that this duty was so onerous as to virtually destroy the value of the coupons and thus impaired the obligation of contract. In the companion case of *Cuthbert v. Virginia* (1890) the Court invalidated a prohibitory license tax on those offering the coupons for sale.

In other contract clause cases the Fuller Court protected the expectation of creditors against legislative schemes to diminish state financial responsibilities. For instance, a Texas statute authorized payment in state treasury warrants of interest on railroad bonds held by the state. In *Houston and Texas Central Railroad Company v. Texas* (1900) the Court held that a subsequent repeal of the statute, which in effect halted payments by warrant, impaired the state's contractual obligation. Nor would the Fuller Court allow states to restrict the power of taxation of local government when such authority was necessary to meet contractual engagements. In *Hubert v. New Orleans* (1909) the justices unanimously ruled that state legislation withdrawing municipal powers of taxation and leaving creditors without satisfaction impaired their contracts. They reasoned that creditors were entitled to rely on the existing tax laws as the means of making their obligations effectual.

Another group of cases involved contracts for tax exemption given to business enterprises to encourage economic growth. These decisions tended to turn upon the wording of particular grants, and generalization is difficult. The Fuller Court insisted that claims of tax immunity must be clearly demonstrated, and it generally resolved ambiguity in favor of the state's sovereign authority to levy taxes. Nonetheless, the Court applied the contract clause in several cases to uphold exemptions against subsequent attempts at taxation. The vexing problem of construing tax exemptions was illustrated by the Court's 5 to 4 vote in *Mobile and Ohio Railroad Company v. Tennessee* (1894), sustaining a tax immunity. At issue was a legislative grant that exempted a railroad from taxation for twenty-five years from completion of the road and further provided that "no tax shall ever be laid on said road or its fixtures which will reduce the dividends below eight per cent." No dividends had ever been paid. Finding that the language was plain, Justice Howell Jackson, writing for the majority, concluded that a state levy of taxes on the railroad was prohibited by the contract clause. He noted that the object of the grant provision "was to invite and encourage the investment of private capital in the enterprise of building the road."[57] Hence the majority reached a result consistent with one of the main themes of the Fuller Court's jurisprudence, the protection of investment capital. Yet Fuller himself, in dissent, argued that the language was unclear and did not constitute an indefinite exemption from taxation. He was joined in this position by Justice Brewer, who took the lead in attacking economic regulations on due process grounds. The division of the Court made clear that the justices did not always follow predictable voting patterns.

The Fuller Court also heard a large number of cases that involved attempts to alter the terms of franchises granted by municipalities to water, gas, or transportation companies. The justices rendered several decisions that protected exclusive franchises against competition by the city. In *Walla Walla City v. Walla Walla Water Company* (1898), for instance, the city gave the water company a franchise to provide water for twenty-five years and agreed not to "erect, maintain or become interested in any water works." Six years later the city took steps to establish a municipal water works. A unanimous Supreme Court ruled that the city's action represented an impairment of its agreement with the water company. Justice Henry Billings Brown's opinion displayed awareness that the contract clause safeguarded reliance interests. He focused on the fact that in "establishing a system of water works the company would necessarily incur a large expense" and would have a right to expect that the city would not enter into competition with it. Indicating judicial suspicion of urban government, Brown added that the company understandably obtained a contract provision to protect itself from "the sudden changes of public opinion to which all municipalities are more or less subject."[58] As with tax exemptions, however, the terms of a franchise grant were often determinative. In a line of cases in which the text of the franchise was more ambiguous, the Fuller Court rejected claims of an exclusive grant and allowed municipalities to provide utility services.

In addition, municipal efforts to change the rates charged by utility franchise holders swelled the Court's docket. The justices repeatedly rebuffed attempts by cities to compel a reduction in street railway charges. Thus in *City of Minneapolis v. Minneapolis Street Railway Company* (1910) they unanimously held that the city unconstitutionally impaired a charter provision guaranteeing a five-cent minimum rate by enacting a subsequent ordinance requiring the sale of six tickets for twenty-five cents.

---

57. *Mobile and Ohio Railroad Company v. Tennessee,* 153 U.S. 486, 501 (1894).
58. *Walla Walla City v. Walla Walla Water Company,* 172 U.S. 1, 17–18 (1898).

Justice William R. Day's opinion revealingly declared that "the right to charge passenger fares is of the very essence of the contract, essential to the operation and success of the enterprise."[59] Significantly, these street railway cases were decided while the Supreme Court was employing the due process clause to limit state authority to regulate railroad rates. This pattern showed the Fuller Court's fundamental skepticism about governmental control of charges and its belief in the need to encourage economic growth by protecting regulated industries.

Although most cases under the contract clause involved state legislation that arguably interfered with contractual arrangements, the Supreme Court in the nineteenth century occasionally indicated that judicial decisions that changed state law might constitute an impairment of obligations made in reliance on earlier propositions of law.[60] Fuller and his associates wrestled with the question of judicial impairment of contracts in several cases but failed to formulate a clear or consistent doctrine. In *Central Land Company v. Laidley* (1895) the justices flatly declared that for purposes of constitutional protection a contract "must have been impaired by some act of the legislative power of the State, and not by a decision of its judicial department only."[61] Yet the Fuller Court was often solicitous when the rights of municipal bondholders were undermined by the reversal of state court precedent. Where bonds were issued or contracts made upon the faith of state court decisions, the Court explained in *Wade v. Travis County* (1899) that "such contracts and bond have been held to be valid, upon the principle that the holders upon purchasing such bonds and the parties to such contracts were entitled to rely upon the prior decisions as settling the law of the State. To have held otherwise would enable the State to set a trap for its creditors by inducing them to subscribe to bonds and then withdrawing their own security."[62] The *Wade* ruling can perhaps best be understood as a manifestation of the Court's hostility toward municipal bond repudiation, but it left the way open for finding a judicial impairment of contracts.

As previously discussed in connection with the takings clause, a plurality of the Court in *Muhlker v. New York and Harlem Railroad Company* (1905) embraced the view that the contract clause prevented changes in state decisional law that undercut contractual obligations. Since Fuller's era, however, the Supreme Court has moved away from the notion that

---

59. *City of Minneapolis v. Minneapolis Street Railway Company,* 215 U.S. 417, 434 (1910).
60. Barton H. Thompson, Jr., "The History of the Judicial Impairment 'Doctrine' and Its Lessons for the Contract Clause," 44 *Stanford Law Review* 1405–1439 (1992).
61. *Central Land Company v. Laidley,* 159 U.S. 103, 109 (1895).
62. *Wade v. Travis County,* 174 U.S. 499, 509 (1899).

the contract clause constrained judicial changes in state law.[63] *Muhlker* strengthened the hand of the federal courts in another respect. It established the principle that, for purposes of applying the contract clause, the extent and existence of a contract is a federal question not controlled by state law.

Despite the Court's willingness to prohibit state interference with contractual relationships, the contract clause played only a secondary role in the protection of economic interests during Fuller's tenure. Several factors explain the diminishing importance of the once-powerful contract clause. The Fuller Court insisted that contracts and charters be strictly construed. Corporations claiming exemption from state regulation were required to demonstrate this privilege clearly by express language in their charter. As a result, the Court often found that few rights passed to the grantee under the contract. This tendency to give a crabbed reading to state grants was particularly evident in railroad rate cases. Even when the language of a charter seemingly granted a carrier the right to set its own rates, the justices managed to conclude that the charter was subject to state regulatory authority. Indeed, the Fuller Court never found a railroad rate invalid on the basis of the contract clause.

It is striking that the same justices who attached little weight to the contract clause as a means of curtailing state rate-making authority were receptive to substantive due process. The Fuller Court drove home its preference for due process in the landmark *Chicago, Milwaukee* decision discussed earlier. Brushing aside the railroad's contract clause argument, the justices proceeded to invalidate the challenged rate on due process grounds.[64] As Fuller and his associates broadened the scope of due process protection during the 1890s, counsel relied less frequently on the contract clause as a barrier to regulation. Increasingly the contract clause was invoked only in conjunction with due process claims.

In addition to employing the principle of strict construction of grants, the Fuller Court restricted the substantive protection available under the contract clause. One of the most important demonstrations of this was its decision in *Illinois Central Railroad v. Illinois* (1892). This case involved an 1869 state statute granting the railroad a large area of submerged land along the Chicago waterfront. The legislature later repealed this law and sought to reclaim the land. Rejecting the argument that Illinois was impairing its land grant, the Court ruled, by a 4 to 3 margin, that a state

---

63. Wright, *The Contract Clause,* 240–242; Richard A. Epstein, "Toward a Revitalization of the Contract Clause," 51 *University of Chicago Law Review* 747–750 (1984).

64. Ely, "The Railroad Question Revisited," 125–126.

could not irrevocably alienate land under navigable waters.[65] Justice Field, writing for the Court, maintained that such lands were held in trust for the public and could be conveyed only to the limited extent that their disposition was consistent with the public interest in navigation and commerce. Because the original grant of submerged land was necessarily revocable, there was no infringement of a contractual obligation when the grant was rescinded.

Justice Field's reasoning in *Illinois Central* is problematic. He admitted that there were no precedents for finding a legislative grant of submerged lands to be invalid. Nonetheless, he was prepared to make a novel application of the traditional public trust doctrine and to erode the contract clause. The dissenters forcefully pointed out that a state had the same power to convey submerged lands as to convey any other public land, and therefore Illinois could not impair its grant to the railroad. Moreover, the *Illinois Central* decision is difficult to square with Justice Field's historical reputation as a champion of property rights. One scholar has explained Field's position as a manifestation of his hostility to special privileges conferred by government.[66] But the upshot of *Illinois Central* was a weakened contract clause and an encouragement for states to rely on an expanded public trust doctrine to assert ownership of waterfront property.

Closely related to the public trust doctrine was the police power exception to the contract clause. Starting before Fuller's appointment, the Supreme Court had ruled in a series of cases that a state legislature could not bargain away its police power over public health, safety, and morals. This concept of an inalienable police power opened the door for state legislatures to modify or revoke public contracts to which a state was a party.[67] In *Manigault v. Springs* (1905), the Fuller Court further restricted the scope of the contract clause by extending this police power exception to private contracts. This case involved an agreement between private parties to leave a navigable creek unobstructed. Subsequently a state statute authorized one of the parties to construct a dam across the creek. Upholding the statute against an attack based on the contract clause, the Court unanimously declared that the police power "was paramount to

---

65. Fuller recused himself because he had represented the city as counsel in the lower court. Justice Blatchford did not participate because he was a stockholder in the Illinois Central Railroad.
66. Currie, *The Constitution in the Supreme Court*, 10–12; Charles W. McCurdy, "Justice Field and the Jurisprudence of Government-Business Relations: Some Parameters of Laissez-Faire Constitutionalism, 1863–1897," 61 *Journal of American History* 993–994 (1975).
67. Wright, *The Contract Clause*, 196–210.

any rights under contracts between individuals" and added that "parties by entering into contracts may not estop the legislature from enacting laws intended for the public good."[68] Yet if contractual arrangements could be abridged whenever a state deemed it necessary, the contract clause obviously afforded little protection to the contracting parties.

Although the contract clause remained one of the most litigated provisions of the Constitution, it did not bulk large in the Fuller Court's defense of the rights of property owners. The justices ceased to read the provision creatively and began to constrict its meaning. As a result, the clause was gradually eclipsed by the emergence of substantive due process as the primary safeguard of economic liberty.

TAXATION

The power of taxation has direct implications for the security of property ownership. As a general proposition, Fuller and his associates sustained both federal and state taxes and made no systematic attempt to shield wealth from taxation. But this record is overshadowed by the fierce controversy over the federal income tax enacted in 1894.

The Constitution vested Congress with broad authority to levy taxes but at the same time placed certain restrictions on the taxing power. Among these was the requirement that "no Capitation or other direct Tax shall be laid except in proportion to the number of inhabitants." Throughout the nineteenth century Americans were notoriously adverse to a heavy tax burden. To meet its revenue needs the federal government relied primarily on excise taxes and customs duties. In 1862 Congress enacted an unprecedented income tax to help finance the Civil War. But the income tax became increasingly unpopular after the war, and eastern business groups charged that they paid a disproportionate share of it. Congress allowed the income tax to expire in 1872. Thereafter, in *Springer v. United States* (1881), the Supreme Court upheld the constitutionality of the tax against the contention that it was a direct tax that had to be apportioned among the states as prescribed in the Constitution.

In the 1890s there was agitation to revive the income tax. Western and southern congressmen took the lead in pressing for a levy on incomes. The Populists called for a graduated income tax in the presidential election of 1892. Proponents of the income tax sought to accomplish dual objectives. They hoped that an alternative source of revenue would make reductions of the high tariff possible. Further, there was an egalitarian

---

68. *Manigault v. Springs*, 199 U.S. 473, 480 (1905).

motive behind the push for an income tax. It was widely perceived that property was increasingly concentrated in a few hands, and supporters saw the income tax as a means of redistributing wealth. After bitter debate, Congress, under Democratic Party control, enacted the first peacetime income tax in 1894 as part of the Wilson-Gorman tariff. The measure placed a tax, at a flat rate of 2 percent, on individual income and corporate profit over $4,000 a year.

Public debate over the income tax bared political, sectional, and class divisions. Republicans in Congress uniformly opposed the income tax. It was calculated that the tax would fall upon a handful of individuals living in the industrial northeastern states and California. Opponents charged that western and southern enthusiasm for the income tax was dictated by the fact that few persons in those regions would have to pay it. They pictured the tax as a spiteful attack on eastern capital and as the opening wedge for socialism. The income tax was vulnerable too because it constituted class legislation as that concept was understood in the nineteenth century. By burdening only one segment of society, the income tax breached the widely shared constitutional maxim enjoining equality of rights and duties.[69]

Opponents of the income tax wasted no time in bringing a lawsuit to challenge the constitutionality of the measure. The central legal issue in *Pollock v. Farmers' Loan & Trust Company* (1895) was whether the income tax was a direct tax that had to be apportioned among the states according to population. Since personal income did not bear any correlation to population, such a proportional levy was a practical and political impossibility. In *Pollock* Fuller wrote his two most famous and most criticized decisions, striking down the income tax. Commentators have vied with each other to denounce Fuller's handiwork in often harsh terms. The standard critique proceeds as follows: The Fuller Court in *Pollock* disregarded established precedent and frustrated popular support for an income tax with a class-oriented decision that protected the interests of the

69. Morton J. Horwitz, *The Transformation of American Law, 1870–1960: The Crisis of Legal Orthodoxy* (New York: Oxford University Press, 1992), 25–26; Arnold M. Paul, *Conservative Crisis and the Rule of Law: Attitudes of Bar and Bench, 1887–1895* (Ithaca, N.Y.: Cornell University Press, 1960), 160–163; Keller, *Affairs of State,* 308; Elmer Ellis, "Public Opinion and the Income Tax, 1860–1900," 27 *Mississippi Valley Historical Review* 225, 226–239 (1940).

wealthy by narrowly construing the powers of Congress.[70] There is room to doubt, however, that this conventional interpretation adequately explains the outcome.

A full account of the *Pollock* litigation is beyond the scope of this work. The case was argued twice before the Supreme Court. In April 1895 Fuller, writing for a 6 to 2 majority, held that a tax on income from land was the equivalent of a tax on land and therefore constituted a direct tax that must be apportioned. To reach this conclusion Fuller distinguished the earlier *Springer* decision upholding the Civil War income tax. He pointed out that *Springer* involved professional income, not income from real estate, a fact that reduced its force as a precedent. Drawing upon a historical analysis, Fuller concluded that the framers expected direct taxes to be used only in extraordinary circumstances. He further intimated that a peacetime tax stood on a different footing from a war tax. According to Fuller, the apportionment requirement was "manifestly designed to operate to restrain the exercise of the power of direct taxation to extraordinary emergencies, and to prevent an attack upon accumulated property by mere force of numbers." If this "rule of protection" was subverted, he warned, "one of the great landmarks defining the boundary between the Nation and the States of which it is composed, would have disappeared, and with it one of the bulwarks of private rights and private property."[71] In sum, Fuller employed the direct tax clause to protect the role of the states and the owners of property by limiting the federal taxing authority. Although it is not immune from criticism, Fuller's opinion certainly offers at least a debatable reading of the constitutional text. Indeed, a prominent constitutional scholar of that day, Christopher G. Tiedeman, maintained that an income tax was within the concept of a direct tax as understood by the framers and that Fuller's opinions were "unanswerable from that standpoint."[72]

The justices were unable to resolve the income tax issue fully in the April decision. In addition to invalidating the tax on income from land, the Court also unanimously held that the tax upon the income from mu-

---

70. For example, Urofsky, *A March of Liberty*, 535–538; Wiecek, *Liberty Under Law*, 122–123; Friedman, *A History of American Law*, 566–567; Currie, *The Constitution in the Supreme Court*, 24–26; Paul, *Conservative Crisis and the Rule of Law*, 198–220; Edwin S. Corwin, *Court over Constitution* (Princeton: Princeton University Press, 1938), 177–209.

71. *Pollock v. Farmers' Loan & Trust Company*, 157 U.S. 429, 583 (1895).

72. Christopher G. Tiedeman, "The Income Tax Decision As an Object Lesson in Constitutional Construction," 6 *Annals of the American Academy of Political and Social Science* 274 (1895). Interestingly, Tiedeman disputed framer intent as a basis for constitutional adjudication and argued that "the real reason" for the decision in *Pollock* was the justices' "profound disbelief in the economic merits of the income tax law." *Ibid.*, 81.

nicipal bonds was unconstitutional because the federal government lacked power to tax state bonds. This aspect of the decision rested largely on the concept of intergovernmental immunity. But with Justice Jackson absent for reasons of health, the Court was equally divided concerning the validity of the tax on incomes from personal property. Since this result left unsettled the validity of the tax on most income, the matter was reargued in May before the full bench.

One incident provides a glimpse of the inner workings of the Fuller Court concerning the income tax. Slightly more than a week after *Pollock* was reargued, Field wrote to Fuller suggesting "that it might be well, considering my condition, that the decision of the Income Tax case be announced as soon as practicable." Field explained that the previous evening he had been given an injection of carbolic acid in his knee joint in an attempt to alleviate chronic pain. Instead, the treatment produced such intense suffering that Field feared for his life. He added, "And what gave me additional pain was the thought that if I did not survive, our action in reference to the Income Tax cases would be entirely defeated." This evidence underscores Field's determination to strike down the entire levy on incomes.[73]

Three days later Fuller delivered his second *Pollock* opinion, invalidating the entire income tax. Speaking this time for a 5 to 4 majority,[74] Fuller reasoned that taxes on income from personal property should be treated in the same manner as income from land. He disclaimed any judicial policy making and carefully pointed out that the Court was not concerned "with the question whether an income tax be or not be desirable." Indeed, he observed that a constitutional amendment expressly to

---

73. Field to Fuller, May 17, 1895, Fuller Papers, LC.

74. Since Justice Jackson was a supporter of the income tax, his participation should have produced a majority in favor of the income tax on personal property. It was therefore assumed for years that one justice must have changed his mind and voted to strike down the levy. Belief that the income tax had been invalidated by a justice who switched sides heightened the drama surrounding *Pollock*. The vacillating justice thesis has spawned much inconclusive historical speculation over the identity of the justice who supposedly changed his position. This approach overlooks the possibility that there was no switch and that five justices from the outset felt the tax was unconstitutional. For the debate over the vacillating justice theory see Willard L. King, *Melville Weston Fuller: Chief Justice of the United States, 1888–1910* (New York: Macmillan, 1950, reprint Chicago: University of Chicago Press, 1967), 218–220; Semonche, *Charting the Future*, 70–71; George Shiras III, *Justice George Shiras, Jr., of Pittsburgh* (Pittsburgh: University of Pittsburgh Press, 1953), 168–183; Paul, *Conservative Crisis and the Rule of Law*, 214–218; Robert Stanley, *Dimensions of Law in the Service of Order; 1861–1913* (New York: Oxford University Press, 1993), 302–303n.43

confer income tax authority would allow time "for the sober second thought of every part of the country to be asserted."[75] Fuller also pointed out that states were free to levy income taxes.

Since historians have largely echoed the views of the dissenters in *Pollock*, it is important to consider their arguments in support of the income tax. Pointing to *Springer*, Justice Edward Douglas White stressed the binding force of stare decisis and accused the majority of judicially amending the Constitution to deny Congress an essential power of taxation. "The fundamental conception of a judicial body," he stated, "is that of one hedged about by precedents which are binding on the court without regard to the personality of its members." White warned of the unjust result produced by the majority opinion that "takes invested wealth and reads it into the Constitution as a favored and protected class of property."[76] Justice Harlan went beyond White and made affirmative arguments for the constitutionality of the income tax. He described taxation on income as a "just and equitable" means of sharing the tax burden. He concluded that the practical effect of the decision was "to give certain kinds of property a position of favoritism and advantage inconsistent with the fundamental principles of our social organization."[77]

The income tax controversy aroused heated emotions across the country, and the decisions were rendered amid a crisis atmosphere. The justices did not escape these divisive feelings. As noted in chapter 3, much has been made of Justice Field's concurring opinion: "The present assault upon capital is but the beginning. It will be but the stepping-stone to others, larger and more sweeping, till our political contests will become a war of the poor against the rich."[78] Justice Harlan privately complained that Field "has acted often like a mad man" during the Court's income tax deliberations. But the angry dissenters were even more impassioned. Visibly agitated, Justice Harlan caused a furor with the delivery of his extemporaneous dissent. He made an almost personal attack on the majority justices and pounded his fist to add emphasis. For this Harlan was soundly criticized by the press for giving an intemperate po-

---

75. *Pollock v. Farmers' Loan & Trust Company,* 158 U.S. 601, 634–635 (1895).

76. *Pollock,* 157 U.S., 652; 158 U.S., 712. For an assessment of Justice White's attitude toward the taxing power and his belief in stare decisis see Robert B. Highsaw, *Edward Douglass White: Defender of the Conservative Faith* (Baton Rouge: Louisiana State University Press, 1981), 119–130.

77. *Pollock,* 158 U.S., 676, 685. Harlan's thinking about the income tax is explored in Beth, *John Marshall Harlan,* 240–248.

78. *Pollock,* 157 U.S., 607.

litical tirade.[79] Justice Brown, who had joined in the first *Pollock* decision, now saw the matter in conspiratorial tones. He decried the outcome as "nothing less than a surrender of the taxing power to the moneyed class" and expressed hope that "it may not prove the first step toward the submergence of the liberties of the people in a sordid despotism of wealth."[80]

Most commentators have taken Fuller to task for overturning well-settled precedent in order to shield property from taxation. Such an assessment is puzzling. The line of previous decisions giving the direct tax clause a limited meaning was hardly decisive on the question of an income tax. As Fuller correctly noted, most of the statements defining direct taxes as just capitation and land taxes were simply dicta in cases addressing unrelated issues. Only *Springer* represented a formidable precedent in favor of the income tax, and this case Fuller attempted to distinguish. More important, modern jurisprudence has hardly been characterized by adherence to stare decisis. The New Deal Court and the Warren Court overruled precedent on a massive scale, to the acclaim of many scholars. It seems fanciful and less than principled, considering this record, to assail Fuller for not following precedent and for examining the direct tax clause anew.

Allegations of class bias are likewise misleading. No doubt the political and economic views of the justices influenced their voting, but this was true for the dissenters as well as the majority. Harlan, for instance, had long favored imposition of an income tax, a fact which explains his vigorous dissent. An accurate appraisal of the Fuller Court's performance in *Pollock* must take into account the pronounced sectional dimensions of the income tax struggle. The justices who voted to invalidate the tax — Fuller, Field, Gray, Brewer, and Shiras — came from states with high per capita wealth. Three of the dissenters — Harlan, Jackson, and White — were from southern states with low per capita wealth. In short, the division of the justices tended to match voting in Congress on the income tax law.[81] The sectional aspect of the dispute was not lost on contemporary

---

79. Beth, *John Marshall Harlan,* 244–248; David Farrelly, "Justice Harlan's Dissent in the Pollock Case," 24 *Southern California Law Review* 175 (1951).

80. *Pollock,* 158 U.S., 695. Brown subsequently explained his dissent in terms of opposition "to judicial legislation where the law has been settled by a series of adjudications." Charles A. Kent, *Memoir of Henry Billings Brown* (New York: Duffield, 1915), 95. Justice Brown's change of position concerning taxation of income from land is treated in Robert J. Glennon, Jr., "Justice Henry Billings Brown: Values in Tension," 44 *University of Colorado Law Review* 553, 570–573 (1973).

81. King, *Fuller,* 214–215;

observers. The *Nation* asserted, "Remembering . . . that it was to the Southern members mainly that we owed the insertion of the income tax in the tariff-reform bill, it is not surprising that of the four judges who stood by the tax three should be Southerners."[82] Moreover, there is a marked states' rights dimension to *Pollock*. Fuller was motivated in part to preserve the existing balance in state and federal relations. He instinctively realized that an income tax would greatly expand federal revenue and power as well as portend further moves to reallocate wealth in a more egalitarian fashion.

Last, there is evidence that the *Pollock* decision was in step with public opinion in the late nineteenth century. To be sure, the Court's action ignited a firestorm. Populists and many Democrats denounced the ruling, and newspapers in the West and South largely followed suit. On the other hand, eastern political figures and newspapers applauded the outcome and stoutly defended the justices. As one noted historian has observed, the Pollock decision "may not have been too far from the actual desires of the public."[83] Public sentiment was more directly tested in the presidential election of 1896. The Democratic Party platform blasted *Pollock*, and William Jennings Bryan urged that the decision be reversed by a reconstituted Court or a constitutional amendment. The victory of Republican William McKinley, however, doomed the income tax for nearly twenty years. The political process seemingly ratified the *Pollock* decision.[84] By 1904 even the Democrats dropped their call for an income tax. Not until public opinion changed markedly during the Progressive era would the Sixteenth Amendment effectively overrule *Pollock*.

Efforts to arraign the Fuller Court as a partisan of the wealthy are contradicted by a look at its handling of other taxation cases. By the late nineteenth century many states enacted some type of inheritance tax. Typically these laws provided for lower tax rates on legacies to family members than on legacies to strangers.[85] The Fuller Court had no difficulty in upholding such a progressive inheritance tax in *Magoun v. Illinois*

---

82. *Nation*, May 30, 1895, 417.

83. Loren P. Beth, *The Development of the American Constitution, 1877–1917* (New York: Harper & Row, 1971), 42; Ellis, "Public Opinion and the Income Tax, 1860–1900," 239–242.

84. Alan Furman Westin, "The Supreme Court, the Populist Movement and the Campaign of 1896," 15 *Journal of Politics* 30–41 (1953); Paul, *Conservative Crisis and the Rule of Law*, 221–226.

85. Friedman, *A History of American Law*, 570–571; Morton Keller, *Regulating a New Economy: Public Policy and Economic Change in America, 1900–1933* (Cambridge, Mass.: Harvard University Press, 1990), 211–212; Stanley, *Dimensions of Law in the Service of Order*, 168–172.

Trust and Savings Bank (1898). Pointing out that states had long levied taxes on property passing at death, the justices reasoned that an inheritance tax is not a levy on property but on the privilege to transmit property. Since property ownership encompasses the right of disposition, the distinction drawn by the Court is suspect. Nonetheless, the justices relied on the same rationale in *Knowlton v. Moore* (1900) to sustain a federal progressive inheritance tax passed to help finance the Spanish-American War. Although the burden of inheritance taxes would inevitably fall most heavily on large personal fortunes, Fuller and his colleagues were disinclined to challenge death duties legitimated by long-settled practice. Their action opened the door for steeper taxation on estates in the twentieth century.

Other federal taxes also passed constitutional muster. In *Nicol v. Ames* (1899) the Supreme Court unanimously ruled that Congress could impose stamp taxes on sales at stock exchanges and boards of trade. Justice Peckham, speaking for the Court, declared in broad terms that the "power to tax is the one great power upon which the whole national fabric is based."[86] He maintained that the stamp tax was not a tax on business but a duty on the facilities used in transacting business. Likewise, in *Thomas v. United States* (1904) Fuller upheld the federal stamp tax on a contract to sell stock against claims that the levy constituted a direct tax.

In addition, Fuller and his colleagues permitted a wide exercise of state taxing authority. They repeatedly upheld state franchise taxes on corporations that conducted business in many states for the privilege of doing business within the taxing jurisdiction.[87] In *Adams Express Company v. Ohio State Auditor* (1897), moreover, Justice Brewer accepted that "no finespun theories about situs should interfere to enable these large corporations" to escape taxation on the value of their intangible property.[88]

At the same time, the Court was prepared to block improper use of state taxing power. Special assessments imposed on landowners who presumably received a special benefit from a particular public improvement proved troublesome. The usual assessment in the late nineteenth century was to take land for streets or to pay for the paving of an existing street. Taxation of special benefit was thus closely related to the use of eminent domain power. In several cases the Fuller Court endeavored to fashion restraints on the use of special assessments to finance projects. At issue in *Norwood v. Baker* (1898) was a street opening. A single abutting land-

86. *Nicol v. Ames,* 173 U.S. 509, 515 (1899).
87. For example, *Home Insurance Company v. New York,* 134 U.S. 594 (1890); *Maine v. Grand Trunk Railway Company,* 142 U.S. 217 (1891).
88. *Adams Express Company v. Kentucky,* 166 U.S. 171, 225 (1897).

owner was assessed for the land taken for the street as well as the cost of the condemnation proceeding. By a margin of 6 to 3 the Court invalidated the assessment as an uncompensated taking of property. "In our judgment," Justice Harlan asserted, "the exaction from the owner of private property of the cost of a public improvement in substantial excess of the special benefits accruing to him is, *to the extent of such excess,* a taking, under the guise of taxation, of private property for public use without compensation."[89] The premise of *Norwood* was that a marked disparity between the imputed benefit to the landowner and the amount of the assessment constituted a backdoor means of taking private property without paying compensation.

The justices retreated, however, from the full implications of *Norwood* in later cases. They did not require a close fit between the benefit and the assessment, and they tended to defer to legislative calculations of benefit. Still, the Fuller Court continued to review special assessments and intervened to halt abusive assessment practices in individual cases. In *Martin v. District of Columbia* (1907) the justices invalidated a special assessment for widening an alley. Finding that the assessment charges greatly exceeded the benefit conferred, Justice Holmes construed the governing statute to limit the apportionment of costs to the amount of the benefit.

EQUAL PROTECTION

The Fuller Court also resolved a number of cases in which economic regulations were challenged under the equal protection clause of the Fourteenth Amendment.[90] This provision, however, was of limited significance during Fuller's period. In *Minneapolis and St. Louis Railway Company v. Emmons* (1893), for instance, the justices unanimously rejected an equal protection argument against a state statute that required railroads to fence their roads and imposed liability for damages resulting from failure to fence. They reasoned that this measure was an exercise of the police power to protect the safety of the public as well as that of railroad passengers and employees. Likewise, in *Atchison, Topeka and Santa Fe Railroad Company v. Matthews* (1899) the Court, by a vote of 5 to 4, sustained

---

89. *Norwood v. Baker,* 172 U.S. 269, 279 (1898). For the history of special assessments see Richard A. Epstein, *Takings: Private Property and the Power of Eminent Domain* (Cambridge, Mass.: Harvard University Press, 1985), 286–289; Stephen Diamond, "The Death and Transfiguration of Benefit Taxation: Special Assessments in Nineteenth-Century America," 12 *Journal of Legal Studies* 227–232 (1983).

90. See generally Richard S. Kay, "The Equal Protection Clause in the Supreme Court, 1873–1903," 29 *Buffalo Law Review* 709–716 (1980).

a Kansas law that permitted the recovery of attorneys' fees in actions for damages by fire resulting from railroad operations. Although the statute applied only to railroads, the majority found that railroad fires constituted a peculiar hazard and that the lawmakers did not violate equal protection by imposing a special burden on the carriers.

On occasion, however, Fuller and his colleagues employed the equal protection clause to safeguard economic interests from discriminatory treatment. At issue in *Gulf, Colorado and Santa Fe Railway Company v. Ellis* (1897) was a Texas statute allowing a person with a bona fide small claim against a railroad to recover attorneys' fees. By a vote of 6 to 3 the Court struck down the statute as an unconstitutional discrimination against railroad companies. Forcefully declaring that courts must enforce "those constitutional provisions intended to secure that equality of rights which is the foundation of free government," Justice Brewer concluded that the statute arbitrarily singled out railroads for a penalty not imposed on other corporations or individuals. He emphasized that courts must inquire into the reasonableness of attempted classifications so that the equal protection clause would not become "a mere rope of sand, in no manner restraining state action."[91] In another case, *Cotting v. Kansas City Stock Yard Company* (1901), the justices invalidated on equal protection grounds a state law that regulated only stockyards in Kansas City and did not apply to other companies engaged in such business elsewhere in the state.

BULWARK OF PROPERTY RIGHTS

As this record demonstrates, the Supreme Court under Fuller took a hard look at state and federal regulations that impinged on the rights of property owners. Relying in part on an enlarged understanding of the due process, takings, and direct taxation clauses, the justices freely used judicial review to invalidate legislation. The Court's concern for economic liberty was also manifest in its handling of law governing interstate commerce, a subject treated in the following chapter.

---

91. *Gulf, Colorado and Santa Fe Railway Company v. Ellis*, 165 U.S. 150, 160, 154 (1897).

Melville W. Fuller in 1891, three years after he became Chief Justice of the United States. (Office of the Curator, Supreme Court of the United States.)

The Supreme Court met in the old Senate chamber during Fuller's tenure. (Office of the Curator, Supreme Court of the United States.)

Justice Stephen J. Field, who pioneered the doctrine of substantial due process, was an intellectual force on the Fuller Court. (Prints and Photographs Division, Library of Congress.)

Justice David J. Brewer was an outspoken defender of the rights of property owners. (Prints and Photographs Division, Library of Congress.)

Justice John Marshall Harlan often dissented in important cases, but he remained close friends with Fuller. (Prints and Photographs Division, Library of Congress.)

A PARTY OF PATCHES.
Grand Balloon Ascension—Cincinnati, May 20th, 1891.

The Populists were frequent critics of the Supreme Court under Fuller. This 1891 cartoon satirizes Populist demands for government intervention in the economy. (*Judge*, June 6, 1891; Heard Library, Vanderbilt University.)

KING DEBS.

The Pullman strike in 1894 aroused a bitter controversy and led to the famous case of *In re Debs* (1895). This cartoon pictures the labor leader Debs as constituting an obstacle to interstate commerce. (Prints and Photographs Division, Library of Congress.)

CROWNED "KING OF BLUNDERERS."

"It was the most foolish thing the Democratic party ever did—and it has done a great many foolish things—to enact this income-tax. The Supreme Court of the United States is entitled to the thanks of the country for its decision."—D. B. HILL.

The income tax of 1894, the subject of intense debate, was invalidated by the Supreme Court in two opinions by Fuller. In this cartoon Fuller is crowning President Grover Cleveland with a dunce cap for having signed the legislation. (*Judge*, June 8, 1895; Heard Library, Vanderbilt University.)

HARPER'S WEEKLY

A JOURNAL OF CIVILIZATION

Vol. XLI.—No. 2102.
Copyright, 1897, by Harper & Brothers.
All Rights Reserved.

NEW YORK, SATURDAY, MARCH 13, 1897.

TEN CENTS A COPY.
FOUR DOLLARS A YEAR.

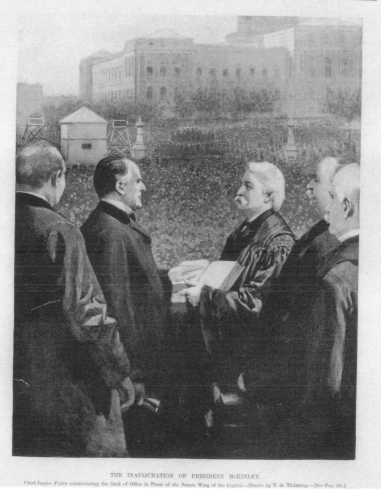

THE INAUGURATION OF PRESIDENT McKINLEY.
Chief-Justice Fuller administering the Oath of Office in Front of the Senate Wing of the Capitol.—Drawn by T. de Thulstrup.—[See Page 259.]

Fuller administering the oath of office to President William McKinley in March 1897. (Office of the Curator, Supreme Court of the United States.)

The Fuller court in 1905, the year in which *Lochner v. New York* was decided. (Office of the Curator, Supreme Court of the United States.)

5

DEFENDING THE NATIONAL MARKET

Fuller's tenure marked a watershed in the development of affirmative congressional power under the commerce clause. Prior to his chief justiceship, the Supreme Court was called upon primarily to decide whether state laws usurped congressional authority with respect to interstate commerce. By the late nineteenth century, however, Congress began actively to exercise its authority over commerce. The Interstate Commerce Act of 1887 was subject to extensive judicial construction, but there was no dispute about congressional power to regulate railroads engaged in interstate transportation. In contrast, the second important exercise of commerce power by Congress, the Sherman Anti-Trust Act of 1890, raised questions about the extent of congressional authority to regulate commerce. Congress also started to assert a federal police power through control of interstate commerce. Moreover, increased attempts by the states to regulate and tax business activity threatened to obstruct commerce across state lines. Accordingly, the Fuller Court wrestled with the commerce clause in light of the new industrial order.

The judicial response to federal regulation reflected unresolved societal tensions between the needs of a national industrial market and the persistence of localism and states' rights sentiments. Considerations of federalism and federal jurisdiction were thus closely linked to substantive issues over the scope of the commerce power. In effect Fuller and his colleagues allocated power between the federal government and the states by defining the concept of commerce. They endeavored to find an appropriate balance between federal and state spheres. Since the justices were committed both to preserving a role for the states in economic life and to protecting commerce against state interference, their efforts were often unsure and contradictory. Consequently there was a measure of doctrinal confusion in the Fuller Court's delineation of the commerce power. The Court gingerly expanded federal authority, but large areas of economic activity remained outside the power of Congress. Consistent with the original constitutional design of a limited federal government, the justices insisted that the commerce clause was not a comprehensive grant of power.

THE SHERMAN ANTI-TRUST ACT

One of the most conspicuous features of rapid industrial growth was the emergence of large-scale corporate enterprise that conducted multistate business operations. In order to stabilize volatile markets, many businesses employed a variety of devices, such as mergers, trust arrangements, and holding companies, to control the marketing of goods and to fix prices. Such business consolidations were perceived as diminishing economic competition and thus aroused long-standing antimonopoly sentiments among the public. Many people feared that concentrated economic power in private hands posed a threat to political liberty, productive efficiency, and economic opportunity. There was a widespread demand for some type of regulation to restrain these huge corporations and preserve competition.

Congress responded to this pressure by near unanimous enactment of the Sherman Anti-Trust Act in 1890. In some respects the legislation was rather traditional in outlook. The act built upon the common-law concept that conspiracies in restraint of trade were against public policy. Further, it did not create an administrative agency to enforce its provisions but relied upon judicial interpretation and enforcement through both government and private litigation. The measure was premised on the notion that the prohibition of wrongful practices would permit competition to determine prices and regulate economic activity. It was a symbolic affirmation of the ideal of free markets.[1] Beyond this, however, there was little agreement among proponents of the Sherman Act as to what the law was expected to accomplish. As one scholar has noted, the act "hardly reflected any coherent economic theory at all."[2]

The Sherman Act was a compromise written in ambiguous language that provided no guidance as to practical application. It outlawed "every contract, combination in the form of trust or otherwise, or conspiracy, in restraint of trade or commerce among the several states or with foreign nations." The statute also made it a crime "to monopolize or attempt to

---

1. Kermit L. Hall, *The Magic Mirror: Law in American History* (New York: Oxford University Press, 1989), 206–207.
2. Lawrence M. Friedman, *A History of American Law,* 2nd ed. (New York: Simon and Schuster, 1985), 465.

monopolize, or combine or conspire . . . to monopolize any part of the trade or commerce among the several states." With these vague words Congress virtually invited the Supreme Court to give meaning to the act and to share in formulating public policy toward corporate consolidation. The Sherman Anti-Trust Act proved a fruitful source of litigation during Fuller's tenure. The justices addressed the related issues of the scope of the commerce power and the ambiguity inherent in the Sherman Act.

In *United States v. E. C. Knight Company* (1895), the first case under the Sherman Act to reach the Supreme Court, the justices accepted the constitutionality of the measure but restricted congressional power to prevent manufacturing monopolies. The case involved an action against the American Sugar Refining Company, which controlled more than 90 percent of the sugar refining in the country. The government maintained that the contracts that secured this monopoly constituted combinations in restraint of trade and enabled the company to charge higher prices. The Court rejected this argument in an opinion that circumscribed federal antitrust enforcement. Speaking for a majority of eight justices, Fuller adhered to the traditional view that manufacturing was local in nature and subject only to state control. "Commerce succeeds to manufacture," he explained, "and is not part of it."[3] Because the refining of sugar was manufacturing rather than commerce, such activity could not be governed by Congress. Fuller further differentiated between "direct" and "indirect" effects on interstate commerce and asserted that combinations to control manufacturing or agriculture constituted only an indirect restraint on trade. He conceded that contracts to sell goods among the states were part of interstate trade and could be regulated by Congress, but he drew a sharp line between manufacturing and sales in interstate markets.

Alarmed about the power of "gigantic monopolies" that recognized "none of the restraints of moral obligations controlling the action of individuals," Justice John M. Harlan dissented alone.[4] He forcefully argued that the challenged merger was devised to control both the refining and the selling of sugar throughout the country. Charging that the majority opinion defeated the main object for which the Sherman Act was passed, Harlan concluded that only federal regulation could protect freedom of commerce from monopolistic business combinations.

---

3. *United States v. E. C. Knight Company,* 156 U.S. 1, 12 (1895).
4. *Ibid.,* 19, 44.

The *E. C. Knight* decision narrowed the reach of the Sherman Act and hampered federal antitrust enforcement. To modern eyes there is an air of economic unreality about Fuller's opinion. The distinction between production and commerce appeared to ignore the basic interdependence of economic activity. This has led some observers to contend that the Fuller Court was seeking to thwart robust implementation of the Sherman Act in order to defend the interests of big business from federal controls.[5]

But the most compelling explanation of *E. C. Knight* points in another direction. A primary consideration to Fuller was the preservation of the existing balance between federal and state authority over the economy. He asserted that respect for reserved power of the states was "essential to the preservation of the autonomy of the States as required by our dual form of government." Fuller went on to declare, "Slight reflection will show that if the national power extends to all contracts and combinations in manufacture, agriculture, mining, and other productive industries, whose ultimate result may affect external commerce, comparatively little of business operations and affairs would be left for state control."[6] Thus, while denying federal jurisdiction, Fuller proclaimed that the states retained power to move against manufacturing monopolies. This was a realistic analysis in the setting of the 1890s, not a friendly gesture to big business. In fact, the states played an important role in the ongoing efforts to check corporate aggregations throughout Fuller's tenure.[7] Over time, experience would call into question the adequacy of state antitrust enforcement. To Fuller, however, a deep commitment to federalism and limited government transcended economic considerations. In his view the prospect of unlimited federal commerce authority was more dangerous to the constitutional system than the threats posed by business consolidations, "however grave and urgent they may appear to be."[8]

---

5. John P. Roche, "Entrepreneurial Liberty and the Commerce Power: Expansion, Contraction and Casuistry in the Age of Enterprise," 30 *University of Chicago Law Review* 696–703 (1963); Russell W. Galloway, *Justice For All? The Rich and Poor in Supreme Court History 1790–1990* (Durham, N.C.: Carolina Academic Press, 1991) 83–85.

6. *United States v. E. C. Knight Company,* 156 U.S. 1, 13, 16 (1895).

7. Charles W. McCurdy, "The *Knight* Sugar Decision of 1895 and the Modernization of American Corporation Law, 1869–1903," 53 *Business History Review* 304, 328–336 (1979); James May, "Antitrust in the Formative Era: Political and Economic Theory in Constitutional and Antitrust Analysis, 1880–1918," 50 *Ohio State Law Journal* 331–383 (1989).

8. *United States v. E. C. Knight Company,* 156 U.S., 13. Hall, *The Magic Mirror,* 237; Melvin I. Urofsky, *A March of Liberty: A Constitutional History of the United States* (New York: Alfred A. Knopf, 1988), 531. For a defense of the *E. C. Knight* decision see Richard A. Epstein, "The Proper Scope of the Commerce Power," 73 *Virginia Law Review* 1432–1442 (1987).

The Fuller Court also restricted the scope of federal power over commerce in *Hopkins v. United States* (1898). The government brought suit to dissolve the Kansas City Live Stock Exchange, a voluntary association of commission merchants buying and selling livestock consigned to them in the city stockyards. It was alleged that the rules of the Exchange restrained interstate commerce by fixing the amount of commissions and by prohibiting members from buying livestock from nonmembers. Speaking for the Court, Justice Rufus Peckham declared that the business of the commission merchants was local in nature and consisted of furnishing services and facilities. The effects of the stockyard agreement were deemed to have only an indirect impact on interstate commerce and therefore did not come within the Sherman Act.

Yet Fuller and his associates were not reluctant to enforce the Sherman Act when the authority of Congress was plainly established. The Court struck down railroad pooling arrangements to determine rates in *United States v. Trans-Missouri Freight Association* (1897) despite tacit approval of this practice by the Interstate Commerce Commission. By a 5 to 4 margin, the justices seemingly adopted a literal interpretation of the Sherman Act as applicable to all combinations in restraint of trade. Warning that powerful combinations drove out of business "small dealers and worthy men," Justice Peckham, speaking for the majority, ruled that the scope of the act was not confined to contracts and combinations that produced an unreasonable restraint of trade. He declined to "read into the act by way of judicial legislation an exemption that is not placed there by the law-making branch of the Government."[9] In dissent, Justice White articulated what became known as the rule of reason. The act should be construed, he suggested, in terms of the traditional common-law distinction between reasonable and unreasonable restraints of trade. Hence White maintained that the Sherman Act prohibited only unreasonable restraints and that the pooling arrangement at issue was a reasonable attempt to prevent secret undercutting of rates.[10] White's dissenting opinion highlighted a critical question of statutory construction that was not resolved during Fuller's time. Subsequent developments, however, vindicated White's approach. In 1911 the Supreme Court adopted the rule of reason for applying the Sherman Act, a step that gave the justices broad discretion to pass upon which restraints were reasonable.[11]

---

9. *United States v. Trans-Missouri Freight Association,* 166 U.S. 290, 323, 340 (1897).

10. For an analysis of Justice White's role in formulating the rule of reason see Robert B. Highsaw, *Edward Douglass White: Defender of the Conservative Faith* (Baton Rouge: Louisiana State University Press, 1981), 92–93.

11. Urofsky, *A March of Liberty,* 534–535.

In *Addyston Pipe and Steel Company v. United States* (1899) the justices again demonstrated their willingness to uphold antitrust restrictions. At issue in this case was a suit to enjoin an express agreement by cast-iron pipe manufacturers to divide territorial markets among themselves and control prices. The Court unanimously held that Congress had the power to prohibit private contracts that directly affected interstate commerce. Distinguishing *E. C. Knight,* the Court stressed that this combination had a direct bearing on interstate transportation and sales and was not related solely to manufacturing.

After 1900 President Theodore Roosevelt sought to reinvigorate enforcement of the Sherman Act. He instituted several well-publicized antitrust suits and prevailed in two important cases. In *Northern Securities Company v. United States* (1904) the government sued to break up the Northern Securities Company, a railroad holding company organized to eliminate competition between three interstate railroads and thereby to control freight and passenger transportation in the Northwest. By a vote of 5 to 4 the Supreme Court declared that, under the Sherman Act, the company was an illegal combination. Justice Harlan, writing for only four justices, gave full expression to his antimonopoly leanings. He sternly lectured that "it is the history of monopolies . . . that predictions of ruin are habitually made by them when it is attempted, by legislation, to restrain their operations and to protect the public against their exactions." Harlan rejected the contention that a holding company was not engaged in commerce and thus was beyond the reach of the Sherman Act. He reiterated the Court's literalistic position in the *Trans-Missouri Freight Association* case. "The act is not limited," Harlan observed, "to restraints of interstate and international trade and commerce that are unreasonable in their nature, but embraces all direct restraints imposed by any combination, conspiracy, or monopoly upon such trade or commerce."[12] Justice David J. Brewer concurred on grounds that the holding company represented an unreasonable restraint of trade.

Both Justices White and Oliver Wendell Holmes wrote dissenting opinions, and they were joined by Fuller and Peckham. White maintained that the ownership of stock in railroads by a holding company did not constitute commerce and was therefore not subject to control by Congress. Stock ownership was a matter for state law.[13] In the first of his famous dissents, Holmes emphasized that Congress could not regulate economic

---

12. *Northern Securities Company v. United States,* 193 U.S. 197, 351, 331 (1904). Justice Harlan's antitrust views are treated in Loren P. Beth, *John Marshall Harlan: The Last Whig Justice* (Lexington: University Press of Kentucky, 1992), 194–199.
13. Highsaw, *Edward Douglass White,* 102–103.

activity without some direct impact on interstate commerce. He further argued that the Northern Securities Company did not amount to a combination in restraint of trade within the meaning of the Sherman Act. Holmes concluded by decrying "an interpretation of the law which in my opinion would make eternal the *bellum omnium contra omnes* and disintegrate society so far as it could into individual atoms. If that were its intent I should regard calling such a law a regulation of commerce as a mere pretense. It would be an attempt to reconstruct society."[14] As in *E. C. Knight,* the dissenters sought to place some limits on congressional power under the commerce clause.

The Holmes dissent was a dramatic moment for the Fuller Court. President Roosevelt, who appointed Holmes to the high court, anticipated that the justice would vigorously support his antitrust crusade. With his dissent in *Northern Securities* Holmes bitterly disappointed Roosevelt. Fuller reported the scene to his wife: "When his voice, refined and clear, rose in the Court Room you could have heard a pin drop and his sentences were as incisive as the edge of a knife."[15]

Despite its symbolic importance, the decision in *Northern Securities* was not a harbinger of the future. As indicated above, the Supreme Court soon moved away from a literal understanding of the Sherman Act in favor of the rule of reason.[16] Moreover, even the specific holding was overtaken by events. In 1970 the competing railroads once controlled by the Northern Securities Company were merged, suggesting that, at the end, economic forces triumphed.[17]

The second major antitrust success of the Roosevelt administration was *Swift and Company v. United States* (1905), in which the government sought to halt collusive practices with respect to buying cattle and selling meat. Writing for a unanimous Court, Justice Holmes asserted that "commerce among the States is not a technical legal conception, but a

---

14. *Northern Securities Company v. United States,* 193 U.S. 197, 411 (1904). For a consideration of Holmes's dissenting opinion see Liva Baker, *The Justice from Beacon Hill: The Life and Times of Oliver Wendell Holmes* (New York: HarperCollins, 1991), 398–405; Alfred S. Neely, "'A humbug based on economic ignorance and incompetence'—Antitrust in the Eyes of Justice Holmes," 1993 *Utah Law Review* 23–31. Epstein, "The Proper Scope of the Commerce Power," 1438–1439.

15. Fuller to Mrs. Fuller, March 15, 1904, as quoted in Willard L. King, *Melville Weston Fuller: Chief Justice of the United States, 1888–1910* (New York: Macmillan, 1950, reprint Chicago: University of Chicago Press, 1967), 296.

16. Morton Keller, *Regulating a New Economy: Public Policy and Economic Change in America, 1900–1933* (Cambridge, Mass.: Harvard University Press, 1990), 29–34.

17. Albro Martin, *Railroads Triumphant: The Grown, Rejection and Rebirth of a Vital American Force* (New York: Oxford University Press, 1992), 329.

practical one, drawn from the course of business." He then ruled that the operation of stockyards, although local in nature, was an integral part of "a current of commerce among the states" because the meat products were shipped to other states.[18] Hence the Sherman Act could be constitutionally applied against meat packers. The *Swift* case was the source of the stream of commerce doctrine, which was later employed to expand application of the commerce power to local enterprises. At the same time, nothing in *Swift* challenged the line between production and interstate commerce set forth in *E. C. Knight.*[19]

Although they were divided with respect to the definition of commerce and the proper construction of the Sherman Act, Fuller and his colleagues were not hostile to federal antitrust enforcement. In actuality they strongly supported application of the Sherman Act in a variety of situations. But the Fuller Court insisted that the commerce power did not extend to manufacturing or production. Behind this view of the commerce clause was the genuine conviction of Fuller and most of his associates that comprehensive congressional authority over economic life was fundamentally inconsistent with the constitutional system of enumerated powers. The line between manufacturing and commerce, drawn by Fuller in *E. C. Knight,* was recognized by the Supreme Court until the New Deal era and the constitutional revolution of 1937.

THE LABOR MOVEMENT

Severe economic distress animated an increasingly militant labor movement after 1893. Although formation of unions was not illegal, strikes and boycotts had a direct impact on the conduct of interstate business. Gradually the federal courts were drawn into labor disputes. In the 1890s federal judges began to issue injunctions to halt strikes, picketing, or other union activities that were seen as interfering with an employer's property interests. Moreover, federal courts sometimes relied upon the Sherman Anti-Trust Act to enjoin strikes or boycotts as unlawful restraints of trade. Injunctions were a mighty judicial weapon because fail-

---

18. *Swift and Company v. United States,* 196 U.S. 375, 398, 399 (1905).
19. David Gordon, "Swift & Co. v. United States: The Beef Trust and the Stream of Commerce Doctrine," 28 *American Journal of Legal History* 244 (1984); Barry Cushman, "A Stream of Legal Consciousness: The Current of Commerce Doctrine From *Swift* to *Jones & Laughlin,*" 61 *Fordham Law Review* 108–116 (1992).

ure to obey a court order was punishable as a contempt of court without a jury trial.[20]

Conflict over the use of labor injunctions came to a head in the famous case of *In re Debs* (1895). The case originated in the Pullman strike of 1894. In response to an imposed wage reduction of 20 percent, employees of the Pullman Palace Car Company went on strike. The American Railway Union, under the leadership of Eugene V. Debs, engaged in a secondary boycott by refusing to handle trains with Pullman cars. To make the work stoppage effective, strikers forcibly obstructed railroad transportation and the passage of mail through Chicago. This action paralyzed much of the national rail transportation network. President Grover Cleveland's administration then obtained a sweeping injunction from the federal circuit court in Chicago. Relying on the Sherman Act to sustain its jurisdiction, the court ordered union officials and all persons conspiring with them to cease stopping any trains operating in interstate commerce or carrying the mail. When mob violence continued, President Cleveland sent federal troops to Chicago and effectively crushed the strike. Debs and other union leaders were found guilty of contempt of court for disregarding the injunction and were sentenced to jail. They applied to the Supreme Court for a writ of habeas corpus.[21]

Writing for a unanimous Court, Justice Brewer denied the writ and powerfully asserted federal authority "to brush away all obstructions to the freedom of interstate commerce or the transportation of the mails."[22] In the absence of any relevant statute, Brewer invoked the public nuisance doctrine. Declaring that the government could summon military force to compel obedience to law, Brewer commended the government for resort to the judicial process. He broadly sustained the equity jurisdiction of federal courts to prevent unlawful interference with commerce. Unlike the circuit court, Brewer did not rest upon the Sherman Act. Instead, he upheld injunctive relief on the basis of both the government's property interest in the mails and the sovereign power to protect the general welfare. Brewer also stressed that a court of equity

---

20. Hall, *The Magic Mirror,* 244–245; Christopher L. Tomlins, *The State and the Unions: Labor Relations, Law, and the Organized Labor Movement in America, 1880–1960* (Cambridge: Cambridge University Press, 1985), 49–51.

21. Alfred H. Kelly, Winfred A. Harbison, and Herman Belz, *The American Constitution: Its Origins and Development,* 7th ed. (New York: Norton, 1991), vol. 2, 397–400; Ray Ginger, *Altgeld's America: The Lincoln Ideal Versus Changing Realities* (New York: Funk & Wagnalls, 1958), 157–163; Loren P. Beth, *The Development of the American Constitution, 1877–1917* (New York: Harper & Row, 1971), 160.

22. *In re Debs,* 158 U.S. 564, 582 (1895).

could punish by contempt actions that might violate criminal law. In so doing, he placed the Supreme Court's imprimatur on the growing use of labor injunctions. More significantly, in *Debs* the Fuller Court had a major impact on remedial jurisprudence by opening the door for more extensive use of injunctive power by the government.

Most Americans disapproved of the Pullman strike, and consequently the *Debs* decision was widely applauded. Labor unions and their political allies, however, furiously assailed the Supreme Court. The 1896 platform of the Democratic Party decried "government by injunction as a new and highly dangerous form of oppression by which Federal Judges, in contempt of the law of the States and rights of citizens, become at once Legislators, Judges and executioners."[23] Coming at the same term of Court as the *E. C. Knight* and *Pollock* decisions, the outcome in *Debs* aroused allegations that the justices were biased in favor of the propertied classes.[24] Critics charged that Fuller and his associates construed federal power broadly when it served to protect economic rights and narrowly when legislation threatened property rights. These perceptions have been readily echoed by historians.[25]

There are problems in explaining *Debs* solely in terms of class prejudice. To be sure, Fuller and his colleagues shared the prevalent antipathy to organized labor. Judges are commonly influenced by the dominant social and economic thought of the age, and the Fuller Court was no exception. But other factors were also at work. The central legal issue in *Debs* was quite distinct from that raised in *E. C. Knight* and *Pollock*. These latter cases turned upon the scope of the federal government's commerce and taxation power. In contrast, *Debs* concerned the exercise of judicial authority with respect to railroad transportation, an economic activity manifestly within the concept of interstate commerce. The Fuller Court made clear in many decisions its determination to protect interstate commerce from interference. It is hardly surprising, therefore, that the justices acted firmly in *Debs* to safeguard the movement of goods and mail in the face of a crisis.

---

23. Democratic Platform of 1896, in Donald Bruce Johnson and Kirk H. Porter, comps., *National Platforms 1840–1972* (Urbana: University of Illinois Press, 1973), 99.

24. Charles Warren, *The Supreme Court in United States History*, rev. ed. (Boston: Little, Brown, 1926), vol. 2, 700–704; Arnold M. Paul, *Conservative Crisis and the Rule of Law: Attitudes of Bar and Bench, 1887–1895* (Ithaca, N.Y.: Cornell University Press, 1960), 223; Alan Furman Westin, "The Supreme Court, The Populist Movement and the Campaign of 1896," 15 *Journal of Politics* 3, 22–30 (1953).

25. John E. Semonche, *Charting the Future: The Supreme Court Responds to a Changing Society, 1890–1920* (Westport, Conn.: Greenwood Press, 1978), 74; Allan Nevins, *Grover Cleveland: A Study in Courage* (New York: Dodd, Mead, 1933), 666–673.

In addition to fashioning labor injunctions, the federal courts in the 1890s began to apply the Sherman Anti-Trust Act to union activities. Although union leaders maintained that Congress did not intend unions to be covered by the act, the evidence indicates that Congress expected it to reach all combinations, business or labor, that restrained trade. In *Loewe v. Lawlor* (1908) the Fuller Court, in the words of Herbert Hovenkamp, "adopted the consensus view and applied the Sherman Act to a labor union."[26] As part of its campaign to organize the employees of a small Connecticut hat factory, the hatters' union began a nationwide drive to urge merchants and the public not to purchase Loewe's hats. Loewe brought suit for a conspiracy in restraint of trade under the Sherman Act and requested treble damages. Speaking for a unanimous Court, Fuller declared that "the Act prohibits any combination whatever to secure action which essentially obstructs the free flow of commerce between the States, or restricts, in that regard, the liberty of a trader to engage in business."[27] Hence a secondary boycott aimed at compelling third parties not to engage in trade might constitute a direct restraint of interstate commerce. Having established jurisdiction under the Sherman Act, Fuller remanded the case for a trial on the merits.[28] The *Loewe* decision invited greater judicial scrutiny of the coercive power of unions as possible violations of the antitrust laws.

After Fuller's death Congress sought to curtail application of the antitrust laws to unions. The Clayton Anti-Trust Act of 1914 provided that "the labor of a human being is not a commodity or article of commerce." Section 20 of the act further stated that no injunctions should be granted by federal courts in labor disputes "unless necessary to prevent irreparable injury to property, or to a property right." However, these vague provisions did not serve to overturn the principle established in *Loewe*. Distinguishing between strikes and boycotts, the Supreme Court ruled in 1921 that the Clayton Act labor exemption did not protect secondary boycotts from judicial control.[29]

---

26. Herbert Hovenkamp, *Enterprise and American Law, 1836–1937* (Cambridge, Mass.: Harvard University Press, 1991), 229.

27. *Loewe v. Lawlor*, 208 U.S. 274, 293 (1908). Justice Holmes's participation in *Loewe* is explored in Neely, " 'A humbug based on economic ignorance and incompetence'— Antitrust in the Eyes of Justice Holmes," 39–43.

28. After trial Loewe was awarded a large monetary recovery. This judgment was unanimously upheld by the Supreme Court in *Lawlor v. Loewe*, 235 U.S. 522 (1915).

29. *Duplex Printing Press Company v. Deering*, 254 U.S. 443 (1921); Hovenkamp, *Enterprise and American Law*, 236–238; Keller, *Regulating a New Economy*, 131–132. For the relationship between the *Loewe* ruling and the labor provisions of the Clayton Act see Daniel R. Ernst, "The Labor Exemption, 1908–1914," 74 *Iowa Law Review* 1151 (1989).

Notwithstanding *Debs* and other cases in which broad federal power over interstate transportation was recognized, the Fuller Court drew the line at legislation that seemed to alter drastically the boundaries of congressional authority. At issue in the *Employers' Liability Cases* (1908) was the validity of the Employers' Liability Act, enacted by Congress in 1906. The act imposed liability on common carriers for the injury or death of any employee resulting from negligence and effectively abrogated the common-law fellow servant rule. It also modified the doctrine of contributory negligence, providing that employee negligence would only diminish the amount of the recovery. The Court had previously accepted without difficulty federal legislation requiring safety devices on railroads, but the Employers' Liability Act was a novel attempt to regulate labor relations more directly.

A badly splintered Court decided by a vote of 5 to 4 that the act imposed liability without restriction as to whether the injury occurred in interstate business, and thus it embraced "subjects wholly outside of the power of Congress to regulate commerce." Justice White, who announced the judgment, conceded that Congress could regulate the employment conditions of persons actually engaged in interstate commerce. But he rejected the contention that a firm engaged in interstate commerce submitted its entire business to the regulatory authority of Congress. Such a position, White asserted, "would extend the power of Congress to every conceivable subject, however inherently local, would obliterate all the limitations of power imposed by the Constitution, and would destroy the authority of the States."[30] Justice Peckham, joined by Fuller and Brewer, went a step further, questioning whether Congress had power to legislate upon employment relations. The dissenting justices agreed that Congress could not regulate intrastate commerce but argued that the statute should be construed to restrict its application to employees engaged in interstate commerce at the time of the injury. In 1908 Congress passed a second Employers' Liability Act, which applied only to workers in interstate commerce.

TOWARD A FEDERAL POLICE POWER

The Fuller Court's understanding of the commerce clause was closely linked to the type of goods being shipped in interstate commerce. Despite the Court's attempt to preserve a meaningful role for the states in

---

30. *Employers' Liability Cases*, 207 U.S. 463, 498, 502 (1908). See Semonche, *Charting the Future*, 212–214.

governing economic life, a majority of the justices sustained unprecedented use of federal commerce authority to safeguard the public from morally questionable products. This tie between commerce and supervision of public morals was exemplified by *Champion v. Ames* (1903), in which the justices, by a margin of 5 to 4, construed the commerce power broadly to facilitate the suppression of a morally suspect device. In 1895 Congress enacted a statute making it a criminal offense to transport lottery tickets from state to state. The obvious purpose of the statute was to suppress lotteries. The case raised troublesome issues and had to be argued three times. Justice Harlan, speaking for the majority, held that lottery tickets were subjects of commerce and that congressional power over commerce included the power to exclude items from commerce. Harlan's opinion was infused by his manifest dislike of lotteries. He spoke of congressional concern that "commerce shall not be polluted by the carrying of lottery tickets" and of "the mischiefs of the lottery business."[31] Harlan left open the question of whether Congress could ban useful or valuable commodities from commerce.

Fuller, in dissent, pointed out that Congress was in effect seeking to exercise a police power to promote public morals. Traditionally the police power had belonged to the states. According to Fuller, the majority opinion was inconsistent with the intention of the framers of the Constitution and threatened to upset the constitutional balance between the national and state governments. "To hold that Congress has general police power," Fuller asserted, "would be to hold that it may accomplish objects not entrusted to the General Government, and to defeat the operation of the Tenth Amendment."[32]

As Fuller correctly perceived, the practical result of *Champion* was to sanction a federal police power through the device of professing to regulate interstate commerce. The outcome was in sharp contrast to the doctrine of delegated powers and indicates that even the conservative Fuller Court found it hard to cabin the exercise of congressional commerce power. Congress, influenced by the Progressive movement, moved swiftly to enact social reform legislation grounded on the commerce power. For instance, the Pure Food and Drug Act of 1906 excluded adulterated and misbranded foods from interstate commerce. In 1910 Congress passed the Mann Act, outlawing the transportation of women from

---

31. *Champion v. Ames*, 188 U.S. 321, 356, 357 (1903). For a treatment of this case see Beth, *John Harlan Marshall*, 203; Semonche, *Charting The Future*, 155–158.
32. *Champion v. Ames*, 188 U.S. 365.

state to state for immoral purposes. The Supreme Court relied upon the doctrine established in *Champion* to uphold both statutes after Fuller's death.[33]

The Fuller Court also approved the use of taxation to regulate or prohibit economic activity that could not be reached directly by Congress under the commerce clause. In *McCray v. United States* (1904) the Court, divided 6 to 3, upheld the imposition of a prohibitory tax on yellow oleomargarine. The government sued McCray, a margarine dealer, for a statutory penalty because he purchased colored oleomargarine without the required revenue stamps. Although the evident intent of this tax was not to raise revenue but to assist the dairy industry by prohibiting oleomargarine, the majority declined to consider the motivation of Congress in passing the levy. Justice White, who delivered the opinion for the Court, declared that "the taxing power conferred by the Constitution knows no limit except those expressly stated in that instrument."[34] Because the taxing power was not restricted to interstate commerce, the *McCray* decision seemingly opened the door for Congress to regulate indirectly all aspects of the economy.[35] This generous understanding of taxing power was at odds with *E. C. Knight*, and not surprisingly, Fuller dissented.

The *Champion* and *McCray* decisions made clear that the Fuller Court was no monolith dedicated to defining congressional power over commerce in narrow terms. These cases indicate that the justices sometimes worked at cross-purposes in fashioning commerce-clause jurisprudence, heeding the political and economic currents toward centralization while simultaneously trying to maintain the dual form of government implicit in the federal system. Moreover, the upshot of the decisions in *Champion* and *McCray* demonstrated Fuller's inability to mold a consistent majority behind his commitment to federalism.

DORMANT COMMERCE POWER

Since Congress made only sparing use of its affirmative commerce power, the Fuller Court focused on the negative or dormant aspect of the commerce clause in light of the national market and emerging industrial order. Long before Fuller became chief justice, the Supreme Court established the principle that the commerce clause, by its own force, re-

---

33. Warren, *Supreme Court in United States History,* 736–737.
34. *McCray v. United States,* 195 U.S. 27, 59 (1904).
35. David P. Currie, *The Constitution in the Supreme Court: The Second Century, 1888–1986* (Chicago: University of Chicago Press, 1990), 30.

stricted the power of the states to obstruct interstate commerce.[36] The failure of Congress to impose any regulations was taken to signify that commerce between the states should be free. Under this view, the commerce clause was intended to secure a national market for goods.[37] Yet the states remained the primary locus of regulatory authority in the late nineteenth century. State laws to protect the public health, safety, or morals often had an incidental impact on the movement of goods and persons across state lines. A recurring inquiry, therefore, was the extent to which a state regulation entrenched congressional authority over commerce.

Fuller and his colleagues heard a steady stream of cases in which state laws were attacked as violative of the dormant commerce clause. "It is curious to note the fact," Justice Brewer observed in 1895, "that in a large proportion of the cases in respect to interstate commerce brought to this court the question presented was of the validity of state legislation in its bearings upon interstate commerce."[38] The Fuller Court considered on a case by case basis whether a challenged regulation unreasonably burdened interstate commerce. In essence, the justices weighed the interests of the state in imposing economic regulation against the barrier created to commerce among the states and the needs of a national market. Since cases were dependent upon particular factual circumstances, the Fuller Court found it difficult to achieve uniform results in dormant commerce decisions or to draw precise lines between permissible state regulations and invasions of federal authority. Still, the Court tended to strike down state laws that directly attempted to regulate interstate commerce or discriminated against the interstate movement of goods. Despite some uncertainty in application, Fuller and his associates wielded the dormant commerce clause forcefully to eliminate state-imposed obstacles to commerce across state lines. Hence the commerce clause provided another vehicle by which the Court could invalidate state economic legislation.[39]

---

36. James W. Ely, Jr., *The Guardian of Every Other Right: A Constitutional History of Property Rights* (New York: Oxford University Press, 1992), 71–75.

37. J. Willard Hurst, *Law and the Conditions of Freedom in the Nineteenth-Century United States* (Madison: University of Wisconsin Press, 1956), 44–51.

38. *In re Debs,* 158 U.S. 564, 581 (1895).

39. The Fuller Court's handling of the dormant commerce power is explicated in Currie, *The Constitution in the Supreme Court,* 31–40. One study concluded that the Fuller Court relied on the commerce clause to strike down state laws in 56 cases, which constituted 31 percent of the cases raising commerce clause challenges. J. Gordon Hylton, "David Brewer and the Rights of Property: A Conservative Justice Reconsidered," unpublished paper, Table 4.

The Fuller Court viewed with a critical eye local regulations that denied equality in the marketplace to products from other states. Relying on the commerce clause, the justices began to restrict the authority of the states to inspect goods shipped in interstate commerce. In several cases the Court took the position that a state could not, under the guise of inspection laws, impede the import of food products from other jurisdictions. The problem posed by state inspection laws was illustrated in *Minnesota v. Barber* (1890). At issue was a statute requiring the inspection of cattle twenty-four hours before slaughter. Ostensibly a health measure to insure purity, the effect of the law was to exclude out-of-state meat from markets in Minnesota. Reasoning that the inspection requirement constituted discrimination in favor of home products, Fuller and his associates unanimously struck down the statute as an unreasonable burden on commerce. Similarly, in *Voight v. Wright* (1891) the Court declared unconstitutional a Virginia law mandating an inspection of flour from other states when no such inspection was required of flour manufactured in Virginia. The justices also looked askance at other types of regulations that caused an exclusion of products from state markets. For example, in *Brimmer v. Rebman* (1891) the Court voided a Virginia law prohibiting the sale of meat from animals slaughtered more than one hundred miles from the place of sale unless such meat was previously inspected by Virginia officials. The seller was also required to pay heavy charges for the inspection. The justices unanimously concluded that this legislation, as a practical matter, excluded from Virginia meat from animals slaughtered in other states.

At the same time, Fuller and his colleagues were not hostile to state inspection laws for which the justification was compelling. In *Reid v. Colorado* (1902) the issue was a state statute prohibited the transportation of cattle or horses into Colorado unless the owner procured a document from Colorado state officials certifying that the livestock were free from contagious diseases. The Court recognized that the movement of animals from state to state was part of interstate commerce but unanimously concluded that the statute did not unnecessarily burden commerce. Pointing out that shippers could comply with the law without unreasonable cost or delay, the Court sustained the measure as a valid police power regulation to protect domestic animals.

State efforts to forbid the shipment of certain products from other states posed nettlesome problems for the Fuller Court. Such bans rested upon the state police power to guard its residents from harmful or deceptive products. During Fuller's era, state laws were directed against the interstate shipment of alcoholic beverages, oleomargarine, and cigarettes. As a result, Fuller and his associates were frequently called upon to reconcile exercise of police power with the need to protect freedom of commerce.

Laws prohibiting the sale of alcoholic beverages were a source of heated controversy. Before Fuller became chief justice, the Supreme Court upheld a state law that prohibited the manufacture and sale of intoxicating liquors within the state. But the sale of imported liquor raised different issues. The notable case of *Leisy v. Hardin* (1890) involved the application of an Iowa prohibition measure to beer imported from another state and still in the original packages. Writing for a majority of six, Fuller declared that alcoholic beverages were articles of commerce within the protection of the commerce clause. Relying on a dictum by Chief Justice John Marshall in *Brown v. Maryland* (1827), dealing with state taxing authority, Fuller formulated the original package doctrine under which no state could prevent an importer from selling commodities that were recognized articles of commerce in their original packages. The decision underscored Fuller's belief that the commerce clause secured freedom of trade among the states unless Congress indicated otherwise. As a practical matter, however, the *Leisy* ruling seriously impaired state prohibition laws by compelling states to receive liquor from other jurisdictions.

Toward the end of the *Leisy* opinion Fuller observed that Congress could "remove the restriction upon the State in dealing with imported articles of trade within its limits, which have not been mingled with the common mass of property therein, if in its judgment the end secured justifies and requires such action."[40] Influenced by the burgeoning prohibitionist sentiment, Congress responded promptly to Fuller's invitation. The Wilson Act of 1890 attempted to restore control of liquor to the states by providing that imported alcoholic beverages were subject "upon arrival" to state laws to the same extent as if they had been produced in the state. Writing for a unanimous Court in *In re Rahrer* (1891), Fuller sustained the statute. He again emphasized the importance of freedom of commerce among the states. "The power over interstate commerce," Fuller stated, "is too vital to the integrity of the nation to be qualified by any refinement of reasoning."[41] Nonetheless, Fuller maintained that Congress could divest imported liquor of its interstate character immediately upon the product's arrival within a state.

But the Fuller Court's commitment to free trade with respect to alcoholic beverages soon resurfaced. At issue in *Scott v. Donald* (1897) was South Carolina's controversial dispensary law that created a state mo-

---

40. *Leisy v. Hardin,* 135 U.S. 100, 123–124 (1890).
41. *In re Rahrer,* 140 U.S. 545, 562 (1891).

nopoly for the sale of liquor and prohibited private importation or sale of alcoholic beverages. All traffic in liquor was to be handled by a state agency, which was required to give preference to domestic manufacturers. By a vote of 7 to 1 the justices invalidated the seizure of wine and liquor imported into the state by private parties. They reasoned that, since South Carolina recognized the sale of alcoholic beverages as lawful, the state could not discriminate against importing such articles from other states. The dispensary law was voided as both a hindrance to interstate commerce and "an unjust preference to the products of the enacting State." Nor could the legislation be justified under the Wilson Act because that measure did not give the states authority to discriminate against the products of other jurisdictions. Dissenting alone, Justice Brown protested that the Wilson Act was undermined if a state could not prevent its residents from importing liquor. A year later, in *Vance v. W. A. Vandercook Company* (1898), the Court sustained South Carolina's amended state monopoly scheme but affirmed the right of residents to order liquor from outside the state for their own use. The scope of the Wilson Act was more significantly limited in *Rhodes v. Iowa* (1898). In that case the Fuller Court determined, by a margin of 6 to 3, that the statutory phrase "upon arrival" did not mean physical arrival but rather receipt by the consignee. This outcome undercut enforcement of state prohibition laws. Federal authority over liquor shipments remained paramount until Congress, after Fuller's death, passed the Webb-Kenyon Act in 1913. This law broadly forbade the shipment in interstate trade of liquor to be used in violation of state law.

States also turned their attention to denying the public access to oleomargarine. Acting at the behest of the dairy lobby, which wished to eliminate competition from margarine, many states during the 1880s either prohibited or severely regulated sales of the substance. This prohibitory legislation was avowedly based upon a state's authority to suppress the distribution of harmful or deceptive products.[42] In a line of cases the Fuller Court tended to protect the sale of margarine in the channels of commerce.

The dairy lobby won the first round before the Court. In *Plumley v. Massachusetts* (1894) the justices, divided 6 to 3, held that a law prohibiting the sale of yellow oleomargarine could be applied to forbid the sale of such product shipped from other states. Brushing aside the argument

---

42. An able treatment of the oleomargarine issue can be found in Geoffrey P. Miller, "Public Choice at the Dawn of the Special Interest State: The Story of Butter and Margarine," 77 *California Law Review* 83 (1989).

that the statute conflicted with congressional power over interstate commerce, Justice Harlan, speaking for the Court, declared that a state could exclude yellow margarine as a deceptive product that might mislead the public into purchasing margarine instead of butter. The *Plumley* decision was out of step with the general direction of the Fuller Court's dormant commerce cases, and the chief wrote for the dissenters. "I deny," he emphatically remarked, "that a state may exclude from commerce legitimate subjects of commercial dealings because of the possibility that their appearance may deceive purchasers in regard to their qualities."[43] Later margarine cases revealed movement by the Court toward Fuller's position. At issue in *Schollenberger v. Pennsylvania* (1898) was a statute totally prohibiting the sale of margarine in the state. By a vote of 7 to 2 the justices ruled that a state could not interfere with the right of an importer, under the commerce clause, to transport and sell a lawful article of commerce in original packages. Similarly, in *Collins v. New Hampshire* (1898) the Court struck down a statute banning the sale of margarine unless it was colored pink. In response to these developments, Congress sought to strengthen state control over margarine by enacting the Oleomargarine Act of 1902. Like the Wilson Act, this measure provided that "upon the arrival" of margarine in a state the substance was subject to the state police power.

The Fuller Court also followed the original package doctrine with respect to the interstate shipment of cigarettes. Animated by health concerns as well as the goal of protecting the valuable cigar trade, states began in the 1890s to ban the sale and use of cigarettes. Commercial dealers argued that such restrictions infringed upon interstate commerce.[44] The justices in *Austin v. Tennessee* (1900) recognized tobacco products as legitimate articles of commerce and declined to take judicial notice that cigarettes were injurious to health. But they split 5 to 4 over the nature of the original package in this situation. The majority decided that a ten-cigarette parcel was not the original package for purposes of protection under the commerce clause against state interference. Rather, the original package doctrine contemplated large shipping containers. Tennessee could therefore halt the distribution of imported cigarettes in small boxes. In a strongly worded dissent Justice Brewer accused the majority of defining the size of the original packages in such a manner as to deny the right of importation. "It is better," he insisted, "that in certain

---

43. *Plumley v. Massachusetts,* 155 U.S. 461, 481 (1894).
44. Rivka Widerman, "Tobacco Is A Dirty Weed. Have We Ever Liked It? A Look At Nineteenth Century Anti-Cigarette Legislation," 38 *Loyola Law Review* 398–403 (1992).

instances one state should be subjected to temporary annoyance rather than that the whole framework of commercial unity created by the Constitution should be destroyed by relegating to each State the determination of what particular articles it will permit to be imported into its borders."[45]

The original package doctrine was not without difficulties. It begged the questions of what constituted shipment in original packages and at what point federal protection of imported goods came to an end. Nonetheless, despite a somewhat confusing course of decisions, the Fuller Court fashioned the original package doctrine into an important weapon for safeguarding interstate transportation of commodities. Fuller himself consistently championed free trade among the states and was usually able to win a majority of justices to his view.[46]

State quarantine laws posed another potential obstacle to interstate commerce. In marked contrast to the original package cases, Fuller and his colleagues regularly sustained quarantine laws as within the state police power to protect public health. For example, in *Compagnie Francaise de Navigation a Vapeur v. Louisiana State Board of Health* (1902) the justices stressed that a state could enforce quarantine laws although their operation affected interstate or foreign commerce. Consequently, the state could forbid the entry of healthy persons into infected areas in order to reduce the danger of contagion. In *Smith v. St. Louis and Southwestern Railway Company* (1901) the Court, by a margin of 6 to 3, saw no infirmity in Texas quarantine regulations prohibiting the importation of cattle from Louisiana. Notwithstanding long commercial rivalry between the states, Justice McKenna, writing for the majority, took the position that a state could embargo the interstate shipment of livestock because of a threat that contagious disease was likely to break out in the state of origin. Arguably in both of these cases the quarantine imposed went beyond the necessities of the situation and represented drastic interference with interstate commerce. Yet this pair of cases well illustrates the Fuller Court's willingness to defer to state control of public health even at the expense of trade across state lines.

The justices accorded the states considerable latitude in other areas as well. They unanimously rejected a commerce clause attack on a state statute imposing a licensure requirement on itinerant peddlers. Pointing to a lengthy history of laws regulating peddlers, the Court concluded in

---

45. *Austin v. Tennessee,* 179 U.S. 343, 387 (1900). Widerman, "Tobacco Is A Dirty Weed," 404–407. The Court adhered to the *Austin* decision in *Cook v. Marshall County,* 196 U.S. 261 (1905).

46. See King, *Fuller,* 238–241.

Emert v. Missouri (1895) that a state could impose a penalty for peddling goods without a license, provided that there was no discrimination against goods or persons from other states.

State regulation of railroad operations was a fruitful source of commerce clause challenges for Fuller and his colleagues. The carriers often claimed that a state regulation constituted an unconstitutional burden on interstate commerce. Carefully reviewing different factual circumstances, the justices evaluated these cases on an individual basis. The results were decidedly mixed, and consistent patterns are difficult to discern. There was a large volume of railroad litigation, and only a few representative cases are examined here.

Notwithstanding its professed dedication to unrestricted commerce, the Court sustained a number of regulations affecting interstate rail transportation. Safety provisions invariably passed judicial muster despite an incidental impact on commerce. In *New York, New Haven and Hartford Railroad Company v. New York* (1897) the Court unanimously upheld a state law that prevented heating passenger cars by stoves in the cars. This measure was deemed to be within the police power to promote the safety of passengers. Likewise, the justices determined in *Erb v. Morasch* (1900) that a city could restrict the speed of all trains within the city limits. The same attitude was reflected at the end of Fuller's tenure in *Southern Railway Company v. King* (1910), in which the justices ruled that Georgia could require carriers to slow their trains at grade crossings even if this caused delays to interstate travel.

Attempts by the states to compel the stoppage of interstate trains at designated points or times generated recurring litigation. At issue in *Hennington v. Georgia* (1896) was a state law forbidding the operation of freight trains on Sunday. The justices divided 6 to 2 in an opinion sustaining the statute. Justice Harlan's majority opinion characterized the law as a police power regulation designed to promote public health and morals. Fuller, for the dissenters, compellingly asserted that the statute "in requiring the suspension of interstate commerce for one day in the week amounts to a regulation of that commerce, and is invalid because the power of Congress is that regard is exclusive."[47] The Court also deferred to state authority in *Lake Shore & Michigan Southern Railway Company v. Ohio* (1899). By a 5 to 4 vote the justices found that a law compelling railroads to stop three passenger trains daily at villages of more than three thousand inhabitants did not infringe on national power over commerce.

---

47. *Hennington v. Georgia*, 163 U.S. 299, 318 (1896).

Yet the Fuller Court struck down other state statutes that mandated train stops. In *Illinois Central Railroad Company v. Illinois* (1896) the justices unanimously voided a law requiring an interstate mail train to stop at every county seat, even if this entailed a detour out of its course. Since the effect of this measure was to delay interstate transportation, Fuller and his colleagues had no difficulty in pronouncing it an unconstitutional hindrance of commerce. *Mississippi Railroad Commission v. Illinois Central Railroad Company* (1906) provided another example of the Court's willingness to protect interstate travel. In this case the justices, speaking through Peckham, held that the orders of a state commission that directed the stopping of trains at certain local stations, when adequate facilities were already provided, was an unlawful obstacle to commerce. Peckham's analysis was clearly shaped by the working of the free market. "Competition between great trunk lines is fierce and at times bitter," he explained, and consequently even a small obstacle "ought not, in fairness, to be placed in the way of an interstate road, which may thus be unable to meet the competition of its rivals."[48] In another decision, *Herndon v. Chicago, Rock Island and Pacific Railway Company* (1910), the Court invalidated a Missouri law ordering interstate trains to stop at junction points with other railroad lines.

Fuller and his associates also assumed a critical posture toward other types of state railroad regulation. In *Louisville & Nashville Railroad Company v. Eubank* (1902) the Court declared by a vote of 7 to 2 that application of Kentucky's long-haul–short-haul provision to interstate carriers had the direct effect of regulating interstate rates and amounted to an interference with commerce. Three years later, in *Central of Georgia Railway Company v. Murphey* (1905), the justices unanimously ruled that a state could not impose on an initial carrier the duty of tracing lost freight where the loss occurred on another carrier. Such liability, the Court reasoned, although convenient for shippers, directly burdened interstate commerce.

NATURAL RESOURCES

In a series of cases the Fuller Court broadly affirmed the authority of the states to control natural resources within their boundaries despite a potential conflict between this authority and the principle of free movement of goods across state lines. This was made clear in *Geer v. Connecticut* (1896), which involved the power of the state to prevent the

---

48. *Mississippi Railroad Commission v. Illinois Central Railroad Company*, 203 U.S. 335, 346 (1906).

transportation of killed game outside the jurisdiction. Rejecting an argument that a ban on the transportation of killed game interfered with interstate commerce, the justices held that since a state could regulate the taking and ownership of game, it could forbid the removal of game. Justices Field and Harlan dissented on grounds that the Connecticut law impeded the freedom of interstate commerce. Late in Fuller's tenure the Court extended the *Geer* analysis to the control of water. A New Jersey statute made it unlawful to transport water from any river or lake of the state into other jurisdictions. Brushing aside the challenge of a riparian owner, Justice Holmes, writing for the Court in *Hudson County Water Company v. McCarter* (1908), stressed that "the constitutional power of the State to insist that its natural advantages shall remain unimpaired by its citizens is not dependent upon any nice estimate of the extent of present use or speculation as to future needs."[49] It followed that the private rights of riparian owners were subject to the state police power to maintain a water supply for its citizens.

The willingness of Fuller and his colleagues to uphold state legislation blocking the transportation of natural resources across state lines was consistent with their respect for state autonomy. But this approach has not stood the test of time. The *Geer* case was overruled in *Hughes v. Oklahoma* (1979), with the Supreme Court holding that asserted state ownership of natural resources did not prevent application of the dormant commerce clause to a statute forbidding the export of minnows. In *Sporhase v. Nebraska* (1982) the justices held that water was an article of interstate commerce subject to commerce clause scrutiny. A broader understanding of federal commerce power doomed the Fuller Court's inclination to permit in state preferences in the use of natural resources.

---

49. *Hudson County Water Company v. McCarter,* 209 U.S. 349, 356–357 (1908).

6

CIVIL LIBERTIES, EQUAL RIGHTS, AND CRIMINAL JUSTICE

Although the Fuller Court was willing to give heightened protection to the rights of property owners and the operation of the national market, the justices were generally unconcerned with guarding other asserted rights from government regulation. Hence the Supreme Court during Fuller's tenure displayed little sympathy for the claims of racial minorities, women, criminal defendants, dissidents, or individuals who breached accepted codes of moral behavior. Several factors account for this aloof judicial attitude. One root cause was the Fuller Court's profound commitment to federalism. With the important exception of the just compensation requirement, the justices steadfastly maintained that the guarantees of the Bill of Rights did not extend to the states. Despite adoption of the Fourteenth Amendment, the Court continued to view the states as the primary protectors of individual rights. Moreover, the Fuller Court's treatment of minorities and criminal defendants reflected the larger societal currents of the era. The justices shared the dominant public understanding with respect to personal status, race relations, and crime control. Consequently, they were disinclined to interfere with local autonomy in these areas.

As a result, the Fuller Court's record on civil liberties issues seems dismal in terms of modern constitutional liberalism. It has often been censured for inadequately safeguarding noneconomic liberties.[1] While this criticism is justified to some extent, it can be overdrawn. Any assessment of the performance by Fuller and his colleagues must take into account the political constraints that limited the range of effective judicial behavior. Further, one must bear in mind that the justices upheld many restrictions on private economic activity. It was hardly remarkable, therefore,

---

1. John P. Roche, "Civil Liberty in the Age of Enterprise," 31 *University of Chicago Law Review* 103 (1963).

that the Court would similarly recognize broad governmental authority to control other types of individual conduct. Finally, in a few cases the Supreme Court under Fuller gave a generous reading to provisions of the Bill of Rights and cautiously pointed toward a more expansive judicial role in protecting individuals.

PUBLIC MORALS AND HEALTH

The time-honored American inclination to regulate public morals found new expression in the late nineteenth century. The social disruptions of the era fueled the passage of state legislation to control individual behavior by imposition of a social code. Justified as an exercise of the police power to protect the interests of society, such regulations often clashed with minority values and claimed individual liberties.[2] Yet Americans of the late nineteenth century placed little premium on the supposed right of individuals to live according to their personal notions of morality. Instead, as Michael Les Benedict has cogently observed, they believed that society "had a legitimate interest in promoting morality, suppressing immoral behavior, and fostering those institutions that inculcated moral virtue."[3]

Reflecting this sentiment, Fuller and his colleagues consistently repulsed attacks against morals and health laws and allowed the states wide discretion to control individual behavior. For instance, in *Petit v. Minnesota* (1900) the justices unanimously upheld a state law prohibiting most work on Sundays as an appropriate exercise of the police power. Accepting the contention that the statute was designed to insure workers a day of rest, Fuller, speaking for the Court, ruled that the legislature could direct the closing of barbershops on Sunday. The Court also permitted the states to control prostitution. This was established in *L'Hote v. New Orleans* (1900), in which Justice David J. Brewer declared that New Orleans could establish a red-light district. Brushing aside objections from property owners within the district who feared that the ordinance destroyed the pecuniary value of their property, Brewer noted that "one of the difficult social problems of the day is what shall be done in respect to those vocations which minister to and feed upon human weaknesses, ap-

2. Morton Keller, *Affairs of State: Public Life in Late Nineteenth Century America* (Cambridge, Mass.: Harvard University Press, 1977), 59–94.
3. Michael Les Benedict, "Victorian Moralism and Civil Liberty in the Nineteenth–Century United States," in Donald G. Nieman, ed., *The Constitution, Law, and American Life: Critical Aspects of the Nineteenth-Century Experience* (Athens: University of Georgia Press, 1992), 104.

petites and passions."[4] This approach to prostitution, he concluded, was a valid exercise of the police power even if it indirectly caused the value of land to depreciate.

Fuller and his colleagues rarely heard cases involving the free exercise of religion guaranteed by the First Amendment. In the famous case of *Davis v. Beason* (1890), however, legislative supervision of public morals collided with the Mormon practice of polygamy. Polygamy deeply offended the moral sensibilities of most Americans.[5] An Idaho territorial statute denied the suffrage to any person who was a polygamist or a member of any association that encouraged polygamy. Writing for a unanimous Court, Justice Stephen J. Field unsparingly denounced bigamy and polygamy. "They tend," he stated, "to destroy the purity of the marriage relation, to disturb the peace of families, to degrade woman and to debase man. Few crimes are more pernicious to the best interests of society and receive more general or more deserved punishment".[6] The crux of Field's opinion was the established constitutional doctrine that distinguished between religious belief and action. While one was free to adopt any religious doctrine, the free exercise clause did not bar punishment for practices inimical to the good order and morals of society. Since polygamy was a criminal offence, it followed that the suffrage restriction was valid.

The Fuller Court gave only passing attention to the meaning of the establishment clause of the First Amendment. In *Davis* the justices declared that the clause prohibits "legislation for the support of any religious tenets, or the modes of worship of any sect."[7] This comment intimates that lawmakers could not grant special exemptions or favors to religious organizations. But two years later, in *Church of the Holy Trinity v. United States* (1892), the Court invoked a different understanding of church-state relations. At issue was a congressional statute that outlawed the importation of aliens to perform contract labor. Inadvertently the defendant church violated the literal terms of this act when it contracted for the services of an English minister. The Court, speaking through Justice Brewer, sensibly construed the statute as inapplicable to religious societies. To buttress this decision Brewer stated that "no purpose of action against religion can be imputed to any legislation" and asserted that the

---

4. *L'Hote v. New Orleans*, 177 U.S. 587, 596 (1900).

5. On the controversy over polygamy see Robert T. Handy, *Undermined Establishment: Church-State Relations in America, 1880–1920* (Princeton, N.J.: Princeton University Press, 1991), 30–36.

6. *Davis v. Beason*, 133 U.S. 333, 341 (1890).

7. *Ibid.*, 342.

United States was "a Christian nation."[8] Although the case turned upon a question of statutory interpretation, the Court's language suggests a close identification between church and state. In any event, the Fuller Court never had an opportunity to address the establishment clause squarely and thus never amplified the holding in *Holy Trinity*. The decision remains exceptional, but it did foreshadow later controversy over the separation of church and state.

Public health regulations, too, could come into conflict with claims of individual rights. The case of *Jacobson v. Massachusetts* (1905) involved a state compulsory vaccination statute intended to eliminate smallpox. Rejecting the argument that compulsory vaccination deprived individuals of liberty, the Court, by a vote of 7 to 2, held that liberty "does not import an absolute right in each person to be, at all times and in all circumstances, wholly freed from restraint."[9] The justices emphasized that a community could adopt health regulations to protect itself against an epidemic of disease. Thus the views of individuals were subordinate to community welfare as determined by the legislature.

FREE SPEECH

In an attempt to stabilize the social order, both federal and state governments in the late nineteenth century enacted laws that curtailed the freedom of public discussion. Invoking the police power, lawmakers took the position that society's interest in self-protection was entitled to greater weight than the expressive rights of individuals. It was widely believed that obscenity, defamation, and dissident political speech lay outside the guarantees of the First Amendment. Indeed, few Americans saw free speech as inviolate under all circumstances.[10] At the same time, there was no federal sedition statute and little sustained attempt to restrain the exercise of free speech.

Fuller and his colleagues heard only a handful of cases dealing with free speech and did little to define the parameters of the First Amendment.[11] In step with dominant public opinion, they demonstrated no inclination to accept a libertarian position and sustained the regulatory authority of government. For instance, the Fuller Court permitted Con-

---

8. *Church of the Holy Trinity v. United States,* 143 U.S. 457, 465, 471 (1892).

9. *Jacobson v. Massachusetts,* 197 U.S. 11, 26 (1905).

10. See Alexis J. Anderson, "The Formative Period of First Amendment Theory, 1870–1915," 24 *American Journal of Legal History* 56 (1980).

11. Mark A. Graber, *Transforming Free Speech: The Ambiguous Legacy of Civil Libertarianism* (Berkeley: University of California Press, 1991), 24.

gress to use its power over the mails to control indirectly the dissemination of materials. In *In re Rapier* (1892) the Court, in an opinion by Fuller, unanimously agreed that Congress could exclude from the mails matter deemed injurious to public morals. Thus Congress could ban any articles pertaining to lotteries despite the fact that it was granted no express power to regulate morals. Fuller denied that the freedom of communication was abridged by such congressional action. This ruling opened the door for an expansion of federal authority through control of the mails to reach subjects over which Congress possessed no direct power. Similarly, the Court upheld a conviction for sending obscene materials through the mail. In *Rosen v. United States* (1896) the justices ruled that a defendant's right under the Sixth Amendment to be informed of the accusation against him was not impaired by omission of the indecent matter from the indictment. Apparently reasoning that the nature of obscenity was self-evident, the Court concluded that everyone who used the mail "must take notice of what, in this enlightened age, is meant by decency, purity, and chastity in social life, and what must be deemed obscene, lewd, and lascivious."[12]

The Fuller Court's most important case involving free speech was *Patterson v. Colorado* (1907). A newspaper editor published articles that criticized as partisan the conduct of the Supreme Court of Colorado. The Colorado court found the editor to be in contempt, notwithstanding his argument that he was performing a public duty. By a vote of 7 to 2 the Fuller Court sustained the contempt conviction. Justice Oliver Wendell Holmes, speaking for the majority, declined to decide whether the Fourteenth Amendment encompassed a protection of speech and press similar to the protection provided by the First Amendment. He went on to declare that the First Amendment simply prevented prior restraint upon publication, not "the subsequent punishment of such as may be deemed contrary to the public welfare."[13] Expressing fear that articles impugning the motives of judges might obstruct the administration of justice, Holmes said that state courts could determine what constituted contempt. Justice Harlan, dissenting, asserted that the right of free speech was an essential part of liberty protected against state infringement by the Fourteenth Amendment. Justice Brewer dissented separately on grounds that the defendant's claim of a

---

12. *Rosen v. United States,* 161 U.S. 29, 42 (1896).
13. *Patterson v. Colorado,* 205 U.S. 454, 462 (1907). For Holmes's record on free speech matters before World War I see Liva Baker, *The Justice from Beacon Hill: The Life and Times of Oliver Wendell Holmes* (New York: HarperCollins, 1991), 520–521 and G. Edward White, *Justice Oliver Wendell Hholmes: Law and the Inner Self* (New York; Oxford University Press, 1993), 348–352.

federally protected right should have been heard. With the *Patterson* decision the Fuller Court placed its stamp of approval on the restrictive common-law understanding of free speech. The justices also allowed the states tremendous authority over freedom of expression issues. A more generous interpretation of the First Amendment would slowly emerge only after Fuller's tenure.

RACIAL SEGREGATION

Nothing has clouded the historical image of the Fuller Court more than charges that the justices were insensitive to the plight of racial minorities. Scholars have vied with each other to condemn the Court's treatment of the segregation issue.[14] Yet much of their criticism fails to consider the political and social realities that severely restricted the Court in dealing with race relations. Racist assumptions permeated both popular attitudes and scientific thought in late-nineteenth-century America.[15] Reconstruction was widely seen as a political mistake and a constitutional error. Sectional reconciliation between the North and South was highly valued, and elite opinion makers were anxious not to disturb regional harmony. The political branches of the federal government, the president and Congress, displayed no enthusiasm for an assault on legally imposed racial separation in the South.[16] Moreover, before Fuller's tenure the Supreme Court had already drained the Fourteenth Amendment of much of its potential as a safeguard for the rights of blacks. Fuller and his colleagues were hardly writing on a fresh slate. Indeed, as John Braeman has observed, the "Fuller Court's acquiescence in the relegation of the Negro to second-class citizenship represented accommodation to the facts of life in turn-of-the-century America."[17]

There is little doubt that Fuller shared the prevalent racial outlook. Recall that the chief justice entered Illinois politics as a supporter of Stephen A. Douglas and had opposed the Emancipation Proclamation. In addition, he was supportive of state authority. Aside from protection

14. Robert J. Steamer, *Chief Justice: Leadership and the Supreme Court* (Columbia, S.C.: University of South Carolina Press, 1986), 145; William M. Wiecek, *Liberty Under Law: The Supreme Court in American Life* (Baltimore: Johns Hopkins University Press, 1988), 101–105;
15. Charles A. Lofgren, *The Plessy Case: A Legal-Historical Interpretation* (New York: Oxford University Press, 1987), 93–115; Lawrence M. Friedman, *A History of American Law,* 2nd ed. (New York: Simon and Schuster, 1985), 504–508.
16. Melvin I. Urofsky, *A March of Liberty: A Constitutional History of the United States* (New York: Alfred A. Knopf, 1988), 483.
17. John Braeman, *Before the Civil Rights Revolution: The Old Court and Individual Rights* (Westport, Conn.: Greenwood Press, 1988), 121.

of property rights and interstate trade, Fuller usually championed a major role for the states in determining public policy. He was not emotionally or intellectually inclined to assail racial segregation, a move that would have reopened sectional wounds and posed acute difficulties of enforcing judicial orders.

Railroad segregation developed gradually in the late nineteenth century and generated a series of cases for the Fuller Court. Although practices varied, many railroads in the South voluntarily segregated black passengers or provided them inferior services. By 1890, however, states began to mandate separate accommodations for black passengers. Many railroads disliked these separate-car laws because of the additional expense entailed, but they were hesitant to oppose community sentiment openly. At issue in *Louisville, New Orleans and Texas Railway Company v. Mississippi* (1890) was a state statute requiring separate cars for rail transportation within Mississippi. Treating as conclusive a state court determination that the law applied only to intrastate travel, the Supreme Court concluded by a margin of 7 to 2 that the regulation did not infringe on federal commerce power. Justice Brewer, writing for the Court, found that the requirement that railroads add a separate car at the state line did not unduly burden interstate commerce. He compared the separate-car law to laws compelling trains to stop at specific points. He expressly reserved judgment as to whether interstate passengers could be forced to use the separate accommodations.

In the famous case of *Plessy v. Ferguson* (1896) the Fuller Court rebuffed a challenge to railroad segregation based on the Thirteenth Amendment and the equal protection clause of the Fourteenth Amendment.[18] Homer A. Plessy, in an arranged test case, sought to invalidate Louisiana's separate-car law, which imposed criminal penalties on passengers who went into a coach other than the one to which they were assigned on account of race. The Supreme Court sustained the Louisiana law by a vote of 7 to 1.[19] Justice Henry Billings Brown, who wrote the majority opinion, gave little attention to the Thirteenth Amendment argument. He simply maintained that a distinction based on race "has no tendency to . . . reestablish a state of involuntary servitude." Brown acknowledged that the purpose of the Fourteenth Amendment "was to en-

---

18. The best account of the *Plessy* litigation is Lofgren, *The Plessy Case: A Legal-Historical Interpretation*.

19. Justice Brewer did not participate in the decision. For an analysis of his attitude toward civil rights and his abstention in *Plessy* see J. Gordon Hylton, "The Judge Who Abstained in *Plessy v. Ferguson*: Justice David Brewer and the Problem of Race," 61 *Mississippi Law Journal* 315 (1991).

force the absolute equality of the two races before the law." But he emphasized that laws requiring racial separation were widely regarded as within the state police power. To support this conclusion Brown specifically noted the practice of separate schooling and laws forbidding racial intermarriage. Articulating a reasonableness test, Brown asserted that the Louisiana legislature was free "to act with reference to the established usages, customs and traditions of the people" in order to promote public peace. He then sharply questioned the premise that legislation could overcome deeply rooted racial distinctions:

> We consider the underlying fallacy of the plaintiff's argument to consist in the assumption that the enforced separation of the two races stamps the colored race with a badge of inferiority. If this be so, it is not by reason of anything found in the act, but solely because the colored race chooses to put that construction upon it. . . . The argument also assumes that social prejudices may be overcome by legislation, and that equal rights cannot be secured to the negro except by an enforced commingling of the two races. We cannot accept this proposition. . . . Legislation is powerless to eradicate racial instincts or to abolish distinctions based upon physical differences, and the attempt to do so can only result in accentuating the difficulties of the present situation. If the civil and political rights of both races be equal, one cannot be inferior to the other civilly or politically. If one race be inferior to the other socially, the Constitution of the United States cannot put them upon the same plane.[20]

The upshot of *Plessy* was judicial affirmation that separate but equal facilities passed constitutional muster.

In an impassioned dissent, Justice Harlan assailed the Louisiana statute and forcefully contended that the Reconstruction Amendments banned racial discrimination. Endorsing the ideal of equal rights, Harlan maintained that the Thirteenth and Fourteenth Amendments "removed the race line from our governmental systems." Declaring the majority opinion to be as "pernicious" as the *Dred Scott* case, he broadly observed,

> Our Constitution is color-blind, and neither knows nor tolerates classes among citizens. In respect of civil rights, all citizens are equal before the law. The humblest is the peer of the most powerful. The law regards man as man, and takes no account of his sur-

---

20. *Plessy v. Ferguson,* 163 U.S. 537, 543, 544, 550, 551 (1896). Justice Brown's opinion in *Plessy* is criticized in Robert J. Glennon, Jr., "Justice Henry Billings Brown: Values in Tension," 44 *University of Colorado Law Review* 595–597 (1973).

roundings or of his color when his civil rights as guaranteed by the supreme law of the land are involved.[21]

Though it was eloquent, Harlan's dissent was out of harmony with the racial sentiments of the age, and it fell on deaf ears.

Although the case was a source of later controversy, *Plessy* attracted little notice at the time. Because the decision embodied popular attitudes, it was not a source of protest. Nor did *Plessy* institute the racial caste system in the South. Laws that mandated separate schooling and travel facilities antedated *Plessy*. Yet the decision marked an important turning point in race relations. It legitimated segregation laws and opened the door to more intrusive state control of racial minorities. Moreover, *Plessy* signaled the Fuller Court's abandonment of any efforts to achieve racial equality.[22]

Lacking support from the political branches of the federal government, there was little the Court could do to stem the segregationist tide. But the justices can rightly be faulted for not even enforcing the separate but equal standard. In practice, the public facilities available to whites and blacks grew increasingly unequal. The Fuller Court seemingly ratified this result in *Cumming v. Richmond County Board of Education* (1899). A Georgia county subsidized the student tuition at private high schools for white students but voted to convert the single black high school into a primary school. This move deprived the black high school students of any educational opportunity. Charging that the board's action denied equal protection of the law, the black plaintiffs sought to enjoin the board from supporting the white schools. They evidently hoped that the board would respond to an injunction by reopening the black high school. In an opinion by Justice Harlan, however, the Court unanimously denied the requested relief. Notwithstanding his *Plessy* dissent, Harlan appeared to regard school segregation as an established fact. He uncharacteristically accepted at face value the school board's protestation that it acted for economic reasons and not to discriminate against blacks. Indeed, Harlan stressed that public education was a matter of state jurisdiction and that the federal courts should not intervene without clear

---

21. *Plessy v. Ferguson*, 163 U.S., 555, 559. For a discussion of Harlan's dissent see Loren P. Beth, *John Marshall Harlan: The Last Whig Justice* (Lexington: University Press of Kentucky, 1992), 233–234. Harlan's call for a color-blind Constitution never found ready acceptance and in the late twentieth century has been increasing supplanted by race-conscious policies. Andrew Kull, *The Color-Blind Constitution* (Cambridge, Mass.: Harvard University Press, 1992).

22. Braeman, *Before the Civil Rights Revolution*, 72–73; Keller, *Affairs of State*, 453–454.

evidence of a constitutional violation.[23] As a consequence of *Cumming*, public agencies could give a disproportionate share of benefits to whites so long as they could offer some rationale other than race.

The segregationist tide also engulfed private institutions. The Fuller Court proved unwilling to protect the right of a private school to conduct its business on a basis of racial equality. Berea College in Kentucky provided educational opportunities for both white and black students. In 1904 the Kentucky legislature enacted a law forbidding any person or corporation to operate a school in which students of both races were instructed together. Citing *Lochner*, Berea College argued that the legislation constituted an arbitrary interference with the right to pursue a lawful occupation. Writing for the Court in *Berea College v. Kentucky* (1908), Justice Brewer, usually a defender of the rights of property owners, sidestepped the broad constitutional issues. Instead he concentrated on the authority of a state over the corporations it chartered. Brewer upheld the statute as an exercise of reserved power to amend corporate charters. The outcome is particularly glaring because, in other contexts, Fuller and his colleagues were quite prepared to strike down state laws infringing the rights of corporate enterprise. Indeed, Justice Harlan, in dissent, invoked the doctrine of substantive due process and pronounced the measure "an arbitrary invasion of the rights of liberty and property guaranteed by the Fourteenth Amendment against hostile state action."[24]

Likewise, Fuller and his associates did not resist the growing movement in the South to disenfranchise blacks. Southern legislatures employed many devices, including the literacy and understanding tests and the poll tax, to restrict black political participation. Yet any exclusionary device that superficially appeared even-handed was upheld by the Supreme Court despite evidence of discriminatory administration. In *Williams v. Mississippi* (1898), for instance, the Court unanimously approved Mississippi's literacy test on grounds that the requirement applied to both white and black voters. Looking only at the text of the statute, the justices declined to examine the actual working of the literacy test. Another challenge to the disfranchisement policy was presented in *Giles v. Harris* (1903). An Alabama black complained that he was denied registration because of his race and requested a federal court to order his registration. Speaking for a 6 to 3 majority, Justice Holmes declined to grant relief for technical reasons. Significantly, he

---

23. J. Morgan Kousser, "Separate but *not* Equal: The Supreme Court's First Decision on Racial Discrimination in Schools," 46 *Journal of Southern History* 17 (1980). For a different view of Harlan's opinion in *Cumming* see Kull, *The Color-Blind Constitution*, 126–130.

24. *Berea College v. Kentucky,* 211 U.S. 45, 67 (1908).

added that the Court had little practical power to deal with racial disfranchisement. If whites were determined to keep blacks from voting, Holmes pointed out, putting the plaintiff's "name on a piece of paper will not defeat them." Relief from a political wrong by the people or a state, he stated, "must be given by them or by the legislative and political department of the government of the United States."[25] Although they were seemingly oblivious to the deteriorating legal and social position of blacks in the South, Fuller and his colleagues were clearly mindful of the political realities that governed race relations.

The Court's indifference to the plight of black citizens continued through Fuller's tenure. As separate-car laws spread, many railroads, for the sake of convenience, adopted their own regulations to segregate both interstate and local travelers. In *Chiles v. Chesapeake and Ohio Railway Company* (1910) the justices validated a carrier's policy of segregating interstate passengers. They reasoned that the failure of Congress to legislate in this area amounted to a declaration that railroads could separate white and black passengers in interstate commerce.[26]

NATIVE AMERICANS

During the late nineteenth century the exceptional legal status of Native Americans confounded policymakers. Congress sought to compel eventual assimilation of Indians into society at large by passing the Dawes Severalty Act in 1887 to break up reservations and allot land to individual Indians. But the view persisted that Indians constituted a separate cultural group that could not be easily integrated.[27] Caught between these cross-currents, the Supreme Court under Fuller did not play a major role in determining Indian affairs. The justices continued to treat Indian tribes as distinct and dependent political communities whose members were neither aliens nor citizens. They also reiterated the long-standing principle that Indian tribes had merely the right to occupy their lands and that title to those lands was vested in the United States.

Fuller and his colleagues treated congressional decisions concerning Native Americans with considerable deference. A leading case was *Lone Wolf v. Hitchcock* (1903). At issue was the validity of congressional legislation disposing of several million acres of "surplus" tribal lands. The

---

25. *Giles v. Harris*, 189 U.S. 475, 488 (1903).

26. Catherine A. Barnes, *Journey from Jim Crow: The Desegregation of Southern Transit* (New York: Columbia University Press, 1983), 12.

27. Kermit L. Hall, *The Magic Mirror: Law in American History* (New York: Oxford University Press, 1989), 147–148; Keller, *Affairs of State*, 457–461.

plaintiff, a Chief of the Kiowa tribe, contended that this transfer was in violation of treaty requirements as well as the due process clause of the Fifth Amendment. Rejecting this argument, Justice White forcefully asserted for a unanimous Court, "Plenary authority over the tribal relations of the Indians has been exercised by Congress from the beginning, and the power has always been deemed a political one, not subject to be controlled by the judicial department of the government."[28] Likening Indians to foreign nations, White held that Congress possessed authority to abrogate the provisions of treaties and to exercise unfettered control over tribal lands. The Court, he added, would presume that Congress acted in good faith in dealing with Indians.

Under *Lone Wolf* there was apparently no judicial limit on congressional power to allot Indian lands. This decision opened the way for the government to take Indian lands without tribal consent and transfer such property to non-Indian owners. Unlike other rulings of the Fuller Court concerning racial minorities, *Lone Wolf* remains influential, and Congress continues to enjoy almost absolute authority to legislate in the field of Indian matters.[29]

Although the Fuller Court was disinclined to question congressional choices, it was prepared to scrutinize the administration of federal Indian policy. Cases calling for an interpretation of treaties with Indian tribes were frequently before the Court. In *Jones v. Meehan* (1899) the justices held that property rights of individual Indians specifically conferred by treaty could not be subsequently divested by Congress. Justice Horace Gray, writing for the Court, echoed the ethnocentric outlook of the era. He noted that Indians "are a weak and dependent people, who have no written language and are wholly unfamiliar with all the forms of legal expression." Because the Indians were at a disadvantage in negotiations with the government, Justice Gray declared that "the treaty must therefore be construed, not according to the technical meaning of its words to learned lawyers, but in the sense in which they would naturally be understood by the Indians."[30] This ruling helped to establish the principle that ambiguous treaty provisions should be resolved liberally in favor of the Indians. Again applying this canon, the Fuller Court in *Win-*

---

28. *Lone Wolf v. Hitchcock,* 187 U.S. 553, 565 (1903).

29. Petra T. Shattuck and Jill Norgren, *Partial Justice: Federal Indian Law in a Liberal Constitutional System* (New York: Berg, 1991), 118–127; Nell Jessup Newton, "Federal Power Over Indians: Its Sources, Scope, and Limitations," 132 *University of Pennsylvania Law Review* 195, 219–222 (1984).

30. *Jones v. Meehan,* 175 U.S. 1, 11 (1899).

ters v. United States (1908) interpreted a reservation treaty to preserve Indian water rights against non-Indian claimants.

WOMEN

Few cases involving the legal status of women reached the Supreme Court during Fuller's tenure. With women, as with blacks, the justices applied a restrictive meaning to the provisions of the Fourteenth Amendment, and they permitted the states to exercise wide latitude over gender relations. This tendency was illustrated by *In re Lockwood* (1894). Belva Lockwood, a prominent feminist, asked the Court to order her admission to practice law in Virginia.[31] Virginia law provided that "any person" practicing elsewhere could be licensed, but the Virginia courts rejected her application. A unanimous Supreme Court, speaking through Fuller, adhered to its previous position that the privileges and immunities of citizenship guaranteed by the Fourteenth Amendment did not encompass the right to practice law. Hence Virginia courts had the final word on whether admission to the bar was confined to males.

In reaching this result the Fuller Court simply gave credence to widely shared societal norms concerning the appropriate role for women.[32] The states had long treated women differently from men. As in the *Muller* case, discussed earlier, the Court proceeded on the assumption that there were innate differences between men and women and that lawmakers could properly take these into account in determining the legal status of women. At the same time, it should be noted that Fuller and his colleagues did not impose any barriers to the advancement of women. Legislators were free to expand opportunities for professional or political participation by women.

IMMIGRANTS AND ALIENS

Chinese immigrants were another minority group that did not fare well before the Fuller Court. In a line of cases the justices broadly affirmed the authority of Congress over immigration policy and the status of aliens. Lured by the prospect of employment in mining and railroad construction, many Chinese laborers arrived on the West Coast in the

---

31. Peter Wallenstein, " 'These New and Strange Beings': Women in the Legal Profession in Virginia, 1890–1990," 101 *Virginia Magazine of History and Biography* 196–201 (1993).

32. For the status of women in late-nineteenth-century polity see Braeman, *Before the Civil Rights Revolution,* 50–52; Joan Hoff, *Law, Gender, and Injustice: A Legal History of U.S. Women* (New York: New York University Press, 1991), 183–184.

mid-nineteenth century. But in time fear of competition for jobs and concern about the assimilation of immigrants from China fueled virulent anti-Chinese sentiment in the western states. Responding to the resulting pressure, in 1882 Congress suspended the immigration of Chinese laborers for ten years. Supplementary legislation in 1888 went a step further to prevent Chinese laborers who left the United States from returning, even if they had certificates of identity entitling them to reenter the country. The 1888 act directly contravened treaty provisions between the United States and China.

In the *Chinese Exclusion Case* (1889) a detained Chinese laborer sought a writ of habeas corpus. He assailed the 1888 act as a violation of existing treaties and statutory provisions and asserted that he had a vested right to return. Rejecting this argument, the justices unanimously decided that Congress had the power to abrogate treaty stipulations by enacting inconsistent legislation. Justice Field, who wrote for the Court, explained that the restrictions on Chinese immigration "have been caused by a well-founded apprehension—from the experience of years—that a limitation to the immigration of certain classes from China was essential to the peace of the community on the Pacific Coast, and possibly to the preservation of our civilization there."[33] Field also asserted that the power to exclude foreigners was inherent in national sovereignty. He suggested that returning Chinese laborers could seek redress from the political arms of the government.

Congress further tightened the prohibition on Chinese migrants with an 1892 act requiring that Chinese laborers living in the United States register and obtain a certificate of residence from federal treasury officials. Administrators were given broad discretion to determine whether an applicant was eligible for a certificate. Chinese laborers who failed to secure such a certificate were subject to summary deportation by a federal judge.[34] By a 6 to 3 vote the Court in *Fong Yue Ting v. United States* (1893) insisted that aliens resided in the country under the absolute authority of Congress to expel them whenever it deemed their removal necessary. Fuller, Brewer, and Field, writing separate opinions, vigor-

---

33. *Chinese Exclusion Cases,* 130 U.S. 581, 594 (1889). For a critical assessment of this case see Louis Henkin, "The Constitution and United States Sovereignty: A Century of *Chinese Exclusion* and Its Progeny," 100 *Harvard Law Review* 853 (1987).

34. Shin-Shan Henry Tsai, *The Chinese Experience in America* (Bloomington: Indiana University Press, 1986), 74–75. On the implementation of Chinese immigration laws see generally Lucy Salyer, "Captives of Law: Judicial Enforcement of the Chinese Exclusion Laws, 1891–1905," 76 *Journal of American History* 91 (1989).

ously dissented.[35] They argued that resident aliens were protected by the Constitution against deportation without due process of law. Demonstrating that his concern for liberty was not confined to the rights of property owners, Fuller eloquently declared,

> No euphuism can disguise the character of the act in this regard. It directs the performance of a judicial function in a particular way, and inflicts punishment without a judicial trial. It is, in effect, a legislative sentence of banishment, and, as such, absolutely void. Moreover, it contains within it the germs of the assertion of an unlimited and arbitrary power, in general, incompatible with the immutable principles of justice, inconsistent with the nature of our government, and in conflict with the written Constitution by which that government was created and those principles secured.[36]

Fong Yue Ting again signaled the Court's unwillingness to interfere with Congressional policy toward Chinese immigration.

The citizenship of children born to Chinese aliens living in the United States also became a contentious issue. Congress had previously declared that Chinese immigrants were ineligible to become citizens by naturalization. The application of the citizenship clause of the Fourteenth Amendment to the children of Chinese parents who were excluded from naturalization came under discussion in *United States v. Wong Kim Ark* (1898). A majority of six justices determined that all persons born in the United States of parents of Chinese descent became citizens at birth. It followed that no act of Congress could abridge citizenship acquired as a birthright under the Fourteenth Amendment. The *Wong Kim Ark* decision made clear that there were limits to the Supreme Court's deference to the will of Congress concerning the status of Chinese aliens.

In a lengthy dissenting opinion Fuller argued that citizenship was not acquired simply by birth within the geographic limits of the country. He contended that the children of aliens who owed allegiance to their native countries were not "subject to the jurisdiction" of the United States within the meaning of the Fourteenth Amendment. The justices debated this matter for nearly two years, and Fuller worked hard for his position.

---

35. Justice Brewer was an outspoken defender of Chinese aliens in the United States. For an analysis of his dissent in *Fong Yue Ting* see Hylton, "The Judge Who Abstained in *Plessy v. Ferguson*," 340–341.

36. *Fong Yue Ting v. United States*, 149 U.S. 698, 763 (1893). For a discussion of *Fong Yue Ting* see John E. Semonche, *Charting the Future: The Supreme Court Responds to a Changing Society, 1890–1920* (Westport, Conn.: Greenwood Press, 1978), 43–45.

According to Willard L. King, Fuller's inability to persuade his colleagues in *Wong Kim Ark* "was perhaps his worst defeat on the Court".[37]

The Fuller Court recognized the plenary authority of Congress to control immigration in other situations as well. In 1903 Congress imposed a political test by barring from entry "anarchists, or persons who believe in or advocate the overthrow by force or violence of the Government of the United States or of all governments or of all forms of law." In *United States ex rel Turner v. Williams* (1904) the justices unanimously denied a First Amendment challenge to this ban. Emphasizing congressional authority to exclude undesirable aliens, Fuller, speaking for the Court, brushed aside objections that the law curtailed freedom of speech. He observed that "those who are excluded cannot assert the rights in general obtaining in a land to which they do not belong as citizens or otherwise."[38] Fuller likened the ban on alien anarchists to an exercise of the power of societal self-preservation.

CRIMINAL JUSTICE

The administration of criminal justice did not occupy a prominent place in the jurisprudence of the Fuller Court. The most salient reason for this was the Court's dedication to federalism. The justices steadfastly refused to extend the procedural guarantees of the Bill of Rights to the states, and they allowed the states tremendous autonomy over criminal process.[39] Consequently, the state courts remained the principal agencies of criminal justice and the primary protectors of the rights of the accused.[40] These states' rights doctrines rested on foundations established before Fuller became chief, and the Court under his leadership continued in a path blazed by its predecessors. In federal prosecutions, on the other hand, Fuller and his colleagues frequently placed a broad con-

---

37. Willard L. King, *Melville Weston Fuller: Chief Justice of the United States, 1888–1910* (New York: Macmillan, 1950, reprint Chicago: University of Chicago Press, 1967), 235. On the *Wong Kim Ark* litigation see Semonche, *Charting the Future,* 111–114.

38. *United States ex rel Turner v. Williams,* 194 U.S. 279, 292 (1904).

39. In treating the Fuller Court and criminal justice I have drawn extensively from Braeman, *Before the Civil Rights Revolution,* 87–115; Richard C. Cortner, *The Supreme Court and the Second Bill of Rights: The Fourteenth Amendment and the Nationalization of Civil Liberties* (Madison: University of Wisconsin Press, 1981), 12–50; and David J. Bodenhamer, *Fair Trial: Rights of the Accused in American History* (New York: Oxford University Press, 1992), 67–91.

40. See generally William F. Duker, "The Fuller Court and State Criminal Process: Threshold of Modern Limitations on Government," 1980 *Brigham Young University Law Review* 275.

struction on provisions in the Bill of Rights. By the late nineteenth century there were in effect two distinct systems of criminal justice operating in the United States. It is therefore instructive to treat separately the Fuller Court's review of state and federal criminal proceedings.

Criminal defendants frequently argued that the privileges and immunities clause or the due process clause of the Fourteenth Amendment embraced at least some of the guarantees of the Bill of Rights. Throughout Fuller's tenure, however, the majority of the justices resisted nationalization of the Bill of Rights and respected state sovereignty over the criminal justice system. As a result, the states were at liberty to modify traditional criminal procedures, experiment with different methods of prosecution, and institute new modes of punishment. This deferential attitude was reflected in a line of cases, culminating in *O'Neil v. Vermont* (1892), in which the Fuller Court made clear that the inhibition on cruel and unusual punishments in the Eighth Amendment did not apply to the states.

Attempts by the states to reform cumbersome criminal proceedings gave rise to complaints that procedural innovations violated the Bill of Rights. For instance, in *Maxwell v. Dow* (1900) a criminal defendant attacked his conviction because it was based upon a proceeding by information rather than indictment by a grand jury and because he was tried by a jury of eight members rather than the common-law jury of twelve. Dismissing these objections, the Court upheld the conviction by a vote of 8 to 1. Justice Rufus W. Peckham, who spoke for the Court, adhered to the established view that the privileges and immunities clause did not necessarily include all the rights protected by the Bill of Rights against the federal government. Accordingly, neither a conviction based on an information nor a trial before a jury of only eight members abridged the defendant's privileges and immunities. Justice Peckham also took the position that trial by jury was not a requisite element of due process of law. Rather, the states could decide for themselves the form of procedure in criminal trials. Evincing his confidence in state administration of criminal justice, Peckham stated that "there can be no just fear that the liberties of the citizen will not be carefully protected by the States respectively. It is a case of self-protection, and the people can be trusted to look out and care for themselves."[41]

Similarly, the Supreme Court ruled in *West v. Louisiana* (1904) that the Sixth Amendment right to confront witnesses did not apply to proceedings in state courts. The justices pointed out that the states could control criminal cases subject only to the general constitutional prohibition

---

41. *Maxwell v. Dow*, 176 U.S. 581, 605 (1900).

against depriving a defendant of liberty without due process of law. The Court found that the due process requirement did not entail the right of an accused in state court to confront the witnesses against him.

The strong deference accorded state criminal process extended to the punishment of crime. Writing for a unanimous Court in *In re Kemmler* (1890), Fuller upheld New York's switch from hanging to electrocution as the mode of execution. Rejecting a due process argument almost out of hand, the chief justice observed, "Punishments are cruel when they involve torture or a lingering death; but the punishment of death is not cruel, within the meaning of that word as used in the Constitution. It implies there is something inhuman and barbarous, something more than the mere extinguishment of life."[42] Since the state legislature determined that electrocution was not a cruel punishment, Fuller could find no deprivation of due process of law. Moreover, in *McElvaine v. Brush* (1891) the justices sustained a law mandating that persons awaiting execution be held in solitary confinement until death was inflicted. The Fuller Court in *Moore v. Missouri* (1895) also validated habitual offender laws under which states imposed a more severe punishment on persons previously convicted of an offense.

Fuller and his colleagues put a stamp of approval on state immunity statutes that compelled witnesses to give possibly incriminating testimony under a grant of immunity from prosecution. In *Jack v. Kansas* (1905) the Court voted 7 to 2 to uphold a contempt conviction for failure to answer questions propounded as part of a state antitrust investigation. Brushing aside as a remote possibility the defendant's objection that an answer might incriminate him as a violator of federal law, the majority saw no deprivation of liberty without due process.

To be sure, the Fuller Court insisted that state authority over criminal procedure was not final. The justices reiterated the position, initially set forth in *Hurtado v. California* (1884), that under the due process clause no state could interfere with "those fundamental principles of liberty and justice which lie at the base of all our civil and political institutions."[43] This formula left open the question of which of the rights enumerated in the Bill of Rights were deemed fundamental principles. But experience demonstrated that Fuller and his associates were reluctant to conclude that any of the provisions of the Bill of Rights were binding on state criminal process.

---

42. *In re Kemmler*, 136 U.S. 436, 447 (1890). See also David Fellman, "Cruel and Unusual Punishments," 19 *Journal of Politics* 35–36 (1957).
43. *Hurtado v. California*, 110 U.S. 516, 535 (1884)

Only Justice Harlan consistently took the position that the purpose of the due process clause of the Fourteenth Amendment was to impose on the states the restrictions in the Bill of Rights. Dissenting in case after case, Harlan called for nationalization of the rights of the accused. He tellingly highlighted a seeming inconsistency in the Court's interpretation of the due process clause. Harlan asked how the majority could reconcile the holding in *Chicago, Burlington and Quincy Railroad Company v. Chicago* (1897) that just compensation for property taken was guaranteed by due process with the line of decisions that due process did not include the procedural protections in the Bill of Rights. He charged that "it would seem that the protection of private property is of more consequence that the protection of the life and liberty of the citizen."[44] In short, it appeared that the Fuller Court treated only economic liberty as constituting fundamental principles of justice.

Late in Fuller's tenure, however, the Supreme Court gingerly intimated that some provisions of the Bill of Rights might be effective against the states. At issue in *Twining v. New Jersey* (1908) was a state trial judge's negative comment on a defendant's failure to testify. The Supreme Court, by an 8 to 1 margin, ruled that the privilege of immunity against self-incrimination was not an essential principle of liberty encompassed in the concept of due process. In reaching this conclusion, the justices rejected a historical understanding of the due process clause. Such an approach, Justice William H. Moody worried, would fasten ancient common-law procedures "upon the American jurisprudence like a straight-jacket." Yet Moody ambiguously suggested that "it is possible that some of the personal rights safeguarded against National action may also be safeguarded against state action, because a denial of them would be a denial of due process of law."[45] The Court, he observed, would determine what rights were included in the notion of due process in the course of its future decisions. The implications of *Twining* would not be realized until long after Fuller's death, but the case raised the possibility that the due process clause could be read to encompass some of the terms of the Bill of Rights.

Contrary to their hands-off attitude toward state criminal process, the justices accorded defendants in federal prosecutions the full protection of the Bill of Rights. Before Fuller's tenure the Supreme Court had little opportunity to interpret the scope of the Bill of Rights. When in 1889 and 1891 Congress enlarged the right of criminal defendants in federal cases to appeal to the Supreme Court, the justices began for the first time

---

44. *Maxwell v. Dow*, 176 U.S. 581, 614 (1900).
45. *Twining v. New Jersey*, 211 U.S. 78, 101, 99 (1908).

to address criminal procedure guarantees. Alert to safeguarding individual liberties against the federal government, Fuller and his colleagues generally adopted a generous understanding of the rights afforded criminal defendants. The Court may have been influenced in this direction by the fact that some of the leading cases under review grew out of investigations into business practices.

This tendency can be seen in *Counselman v. Hitchcock* (1892), in which the Supreme Court broadened the Fifth Amendment privilege against self-incrimination. The case arose when a witness called to testify in a grand jury investigation into alleged violations of the Interstate Commerce Act declined to answer questions and invoked the Fifth Amendment. Justice Samuel Blatchford delivered a unanimous opinion holding that the purpose of the self-incrimination provision was "to insure that a person should not be compelled, when acting as a witness in any investigation, to give testimony which might show that he himself had committed a crime." Blatchford emphasized that the Fifth Amendment privilege applied not only to criminal trials but to inquiries in any official proceeding. Nor was the Court impressed by the government's reliance on a federal immunity statute. Finding that the statute afforded no protection from the use of compelled testimony to locate other evidence of a crime, Blatchford declared that a valid immunity statute must offer "absolute immunity against future prosecution for the offence to which the question relates."[46]

Although the decision in the case was an important victory for civil liberty, the practical effect of *Counselman* was to hamper federal investigations of illegal business activity. A year later Congress enacted a new and more comprehensive immunity statute covering Interstate Commerce Commission inquiries. In *Brown v. Walker* (1896) the Supreme Court voted 5 to 4 to sustain contempt convictions for failure to answer questions under the new law. The majority brushed aside the objection that the witness was imperfectly protected because he might by virtue of his disclosure be subject to prosecution in state courts. Maintaining that Congress could not by statute divest a person of his constitutional right not to be a witness against himself, the dissenters expressed doubt that the immunity act was a sufficient substitute for the Fifth Amendment guarantee.

The Fuller Court again contended with the privilege against self-incrimination in *Hale v. Henkel* (1906). Voting 7 to 2, the justices ruled that the Fifth Amendment provision was restricted to natural persons and did not extend to corporations. It followed that a federal grand jury could compel a corporate official to produce business documents relating to

---

46. *Counselman v. Hitchcock*, 142 U.S. 547, 562, 586 (1892).

possible antitrust violations and that the official could not set up the criminality of the corporations as a defense to a subpoena.

Moreover, in *Hale* the Court proceeded to establish a second important principle of law. Drawing a distinction between the Fourth and Fifth Amendments, the justices ruled that corporations were entitled to protection under the Fourth Amendment against unreasonable searches and seizures. In so doing they stressed the vital place of corporate enterprise in American life: "Corporations are a necessary feature of modern business activity, and their aggregated capital has become the source of nearly all great enterprises."[47] The Court then concluded that the subpoena at issue was too sweeping to be regarded as reasonable. Justices Brewer and Fuller, in dissent, insisted that corporations were protected by both amendments. The different result on the applicability of the Fourth and Fifth Amendments to corporations is not readily explainable. Indeed, the justices offered no rationale for their position. One may speculate that the Court's reading of the Fourth Amendment was prompted in part by a desire to safeguard corporate property rights. But this consideration would have also pertained to the self-incrimination rights of corporations. In any event, the Fuller Court's line between the Fourth and Fifth Amendment rights of corporations, however unsatisfactory, has proved to be an enduring feature of constitutional jurisprudence.

Fuller and his colleagues also put teeth into the Sixth Amendment right to confront witnesses. The case of *Kirby v. United States* (1899) involved a prosecution for receiving stolen property. An act of Congress provided that the conviction of the thieves was conclusive evidence that the property had been stolen. Speaking for a 6 to 2 majority, Justice Harlan concluded that such a presumption impaired the defendant's right to confront the witnesses against him.

In other areas as well the Fuller Court moved to protect criminal defendants by giving an expanded meaning to the Bill of Rights. The justices dealt with the Eighth Amendment ban on cruel and unusual punishments in *Weems v. United States* (1910), a case that originated in the Philippine Islands. Convicted of falsifying public documents, the defendant was sentenced under Philippine law to a heavy fine, fifteen years in prison at hard labor in chains, and perpetual loss of civil liberties. This draconian punishment, derived from the Spanish penal code, continued in effect following acquisition of the Philippines by the United States. The central issue for the Court was whether the prohibition on cruel and unusual punishments applied to the severity of the penalty in relation to

---

47. *Hale v. Henkel,* 201 U.S. 43, 76 (1906).

the offense. Justice Joseph McKenna, who delivered the opinion for a plurality of the Court, adopted as a precept of constitutional law that "punishment for crime should be graduated and proportioned to offense." Rejecting a historical interpretation of the Eighth Amendment, McKenna asserted that the ban on cruel punishments "is not fastened to the obsolete but may acquire meaning as public opinion becomes enlightened by a humane justice."[48] Justices White and Holmes, dissenting, complained that the majority was limiting legislative authority to define and punish crime. The *Weems* decision made clear that the Supreme Court under Fuller was prepared, at least in some situations, to promote the rights of criminal defendants as vigorously as it safeguarded the rights of property owners.

A few other decisions by the Fuller Court pertaining to federal criminal procedure warrant brief comment. The respective functions of judge and jury in criminal cases was a matter of controversy during the nineteenth century. In some jurisdictions the jury had the right to determine the law as well as the facts. But in *Sparf and Hansen v. United States* (1895) the Supreme Court emphatically rejected this approach and affirmed that juries in federal criminal trials must follow the judge's instructions as to the law. The jury was merely to apply the law, as declared by the trial court, to the facts. "Public and private safety alike would be in peril," Justice Harlan reasoned, "if the principle be established that juries in criminal cases may, of right, disregard the law as expounded to them by the court and become a law unto themselves."[49]

Last, Fuller and his associates approved congressional legislation enlarging the Court's appellate jurisdiction over criminal matters. In the Criminal Appeals Act of 1907, Congress provided that the federal government be allowed a writ of error in criminal cases in which the trial court quashed an indictment for an alleged offense against the United States. Contrary to the trend of restricting appeals to the Supreme Court, this measure brought new business before the justices. The Fuller Court had no difficulty in upholding the statute in *Taylor v. United States* (1907) and *United States v. Bitty* (1908). Abruptly dismissing the argument that the statute violated the double jeopardy clause of the Fifth Amendment, the justices explained that the act created a means by which trial judges could be instructed as to the validity and meaning of criminal statutes.

---

48. *Weems v. United States,* 217 U.S. 349, 367, 378 (1910). For a treatment of *Weems* see Michael Meltsner, *Cruel and Unusual: The Supreme Court and Capital Punishment* (New York: Random House, 1973), 173–175; Fellman, "Cruel and Unusual Punishments," 37–38.
49. *Sparf and Hansen v. United States,* 156 U.S. 51, 101 (1895).

7

Issues of Government

During the late nineteenth century the needs of a changing and more complex society posed novel challenges to established modes of governance. As the federal government gradually expanded in size and function, the Supreme Court was called upon to adjudicate the constitutional boundaries of the political branches and police the separation of powers. Moreover, the notion of divided sovereignty inherent in federalism produced bruising clashes between claims of states' rights and federal authority. Foreign affairs occupied an increasingly vital place in American public life following the Spanish-American War of 1898, and the acquisition of overseas territories raised contentious political and legal issues. Under Fuller's leadership the Supreme Court began to play a more active role in determining structural developments and defining governmental power. In addressing these matters the justices engaged in a searching examination of constitutional procedures and institutions. There was often intense conflict between traditional values and the perceived needs of the emerging social order. Pulled by contrary forces, the Fuller Court found it difficult to formulate tidy solutions to perplexing governmental and jurisdictional issues. Although they were committed to federalism and respect for state autonomy, Fuller and his associates enhanced the authority of the federal judiciary to review state legislation.

FOREIGN RELATIONS

The conduct of foreign affairs emerged as a controversy in American public life during the 1890s. As a result, the Supreme Court under Fuller had to settle many disputes pertaining to foreign policy. The general trend of these decisions was to strengthen the hand of the executive branch and Congress over relations with foreign nations.

This current was demonstrated by *Geofroy v. Riggs* (1890), in which a unanimous Court gave a capacious reading to the treaty power. The case involved the right of French citizens to inherit land in the District of Columbia. Justice Stephen J. Field, for the Court, construed a treaty with France as modifying the common-law doctrine that prevented aliens from inheriting land. He broadly declared that the treaty power "extends to all proper subjects of negotiation between our government and the governments of other nations."[1] Field intimated that Congress might by treaty provision accomplish results that it could not achieve directly through legislation. The outcome in *Geofroy* set the stage for expansion of the treaty power following Fuller's tenure.

Fuller and his associates also confronted a group of prize cases arising from the Spanish-American War. In most instances the justices sustained the maritime seizure of Spanish vessels as prizes of war. Fuller was especially inclined to uphold the seizure of prizes and wrote for the Court in four such cases.[2] But in the important case of *The Paquete Habana* (1900) the Supreme Court asserted that the federal government was bound by the rules of international law that exempted coastal fishing ships from seizure. Writing for a majority of six, Justice Horace Gray formulated a much quoted proposition:

> International law is part of our law, and must be ascertained and administered by the courts of justice of appropriate jurisdiction, as often as questions of right depending upon it are duly presented for their determination. For this purpose, where there is no treaty, and no controlling executive or legislative act or judicial decision, resort must be had to the customs and usages of civilized nations.[3]

He qualified the binding effect of customary international law, however, by observing that courts should apply international law in the absence of any federal statute that mandated a different result. Fuller, speaking for the dissent, denied that there was "any such established rule" exempting fishing vessels and urged deference to the president's decisions in carrying on war. Despite Fuller's protest, the *Paquete Habana* decision was a

---

1. *Geofroy v. Riggs*, 133 U.S. 258, 266 (1890).

2. Willard L. King, *Melville Weston Fuller: Chief Justice of the United States, 1888–1910* (New York: Macmillan, 1950, reprint Chicago: University of Chicago Press, 1967), 248.

3. *The Paquete Habana*, 175 U.S. 677, 700 (1900).

milestone in the recognition of customary international law as part of the law of the United States.[4]

The acquisition of Puerto Rico and the Philippines following the war with Spain sparked an intense but short-lived debate concerning the emergence of the United States as an imperial power. Previous territorial acquisitions had been made with the implicit understanding that they would eventually become states. But the new possessions were not contiguous to the United States and were already populated by persons with racial and cultural backgrounds different from those of most Americans. Imperialists espoused the position that the United States was simply fulfilling its destiny as a great nation and that the federal government had ample authority to dominate and govern overseas territories. In contrast, anti-imperialists condemned the notion that the United States could legitimately hold overseas possessions as colonies. They pictured colonial rule as a betrayal of the ideals of the Declaration of Independence and insisted that "the Constitution follows the flag." The status of the new possessions therefore raised fundamental questions about the nature of American constitutionalism.[5]

Congressional legislation establishing governments for Puerto Rico and the Philippines gave rise to a group of some fourteen decisions, known as the Insular Cases, in which the Supreme Court wrestled with the constitutional relationship of these territories to the United States. The Insular Cases presented three core issues: 1) whether the United States could acquire new possessions by treaty, 2) whether Congress could govern the new territories as it saw fit, and 3) whether the Bill of Rights applied to the inhabitants of these territories. Decided between 1901 and 1904, the Insular Cases made clear the sharp divisions that characterized both popular and judicial attitudes. Indeed, the eminent attorney John W. Davis declared that "there may be found in these opinions the most hotly contested and long continued duel in the life of the

---

4. Louis Henkin, "The Constitution and United States Sovereignty: A Century of *Chinese Exclusion* and Its Progeny," 100 *Harvard Law Review* 872–878 (1987). On *The Paquete Habana* litigation see King, *Fuller*, 248; John E. Semonche, *Charting the Future: The Supreme Court Responds to a Changing Society, 1890–1920* (Westport, Conn.: Greenwood Press, 1978), 124–125.

5. James Edward Kerr, *The Insular Cases: The Role of the Judiciary in American Expansionism* (Port Washington, N.Y.: Kennikat Press, 1982); Alfred H. Kelly, Winfred A. Harbison, and Herman Belz, *The American Constitution: Its Origins and Development*, 7th ed. (New York: Norton, 1991), vol. 2, 383–385; Melvin I. Urofsky, *A March of Liberty: A Constitutional History of the United States* (New York: Alfred A. Knopf, 1988), 484–487; David P. Currie, *The Constitution in the Supreme Court: The Second Century, 1888–1986* (Chicago: University of Chicago Press, 1990), 59–65.

Supreme Court."[6] The Insular Cases also marked a disappointment for Fuller because he was unable to persuade a majority of the Court to adopt his views.

In *DeLima v. Bidwell* (1901) the Court affirmed that the United States had the authority to acquire new lands. The justices experienced more difficulty in deciding whether goods brought into the United States from Puerto Rico after ratification of the treaty were subject to import duties. Resolution of this issue turned upon whether Puerto Rico was a foreign country for purposes of tariff laws. By a 5 to 4 vote the Court determined that when the United States established control over Puerto Rico the island ceased to be a foreign country. The sharp division among the justices on this point foreshadowed continuing controversy over the legal status of the overseas territories.

The Fuller Court again addressed this question in *Downes v. Bidwell* (1901), the most important of the Insular Cases. At issue was the constitutionality of the Foraker Act of 1900, which established a civil government for Puerto Rico and levied a duty on imports from the island. The measure was challenged as a violation of the constitutional requirement that duties be "uniform throughout the United States." A majority of five sustained the statute, but they differed widely in the reasoning that led to their conclusion. Describing Puerto Rico as "a territory appurtenant and belonging to the United States" but not part of the United States for revenue purposes, Justice Henry Billings Brown ruled that Congress had broad power to determine the status of annexed possessions. "The Constitution," he emphasized, "was created by the people of the *United States,* as a union of *States,* to be governed solely by representatives of the *States.*" Reflecting the influence of the imperialistic spirit, Brown spoke in terms of "alien races" and "Anglo-Saxon principles." Nonetheless, he stopped short of allowing Congress unfettered authority over the overseas territories. He suggested that "certain natural rights enforced in the Constitution," including religious freedom, "the right to personal liberty and individual property", and freedom of speech, restrained the power of Congress in dealing with territorial inhabitants.[7]

Justice Edward D. White rejected Brown's analysis and, in his influential concurring opinion, provided a separate justification for his vote. After a lengthy review of history, White took the position that constitutional protections applied to a territory only after the territory had been "in-

---

6. As quoted in Henry Steele Commager and Milton Cantor, eds., *Documents of American History,* 10th ed. (Englewood Cliffs, N.J.: Prentice Hall, 1988), 13.

7. *Downes v. Bidwell,* 182 U.S. 244, 287, 251, 282 (1901).

corporated" by Congress into the United States. White was unclear as to how incorporation was to be achieved, but he maintained that it did not occur "until in the wisdom of Congress it is deemed that the acquired territory had reached that state where it is proper that is should enter into and form a part of the American family."[8] Since no congressional action appeared to incorporate Puerto Rico, he concluded that the political status of the inhabitants was a matter for Congress. According to the majority, then, the Constitution did not necessarily extend by its own force to the newly acquired possessions. The residents of these territories were left in a sort of constitutional limbo, largely subject to the control of Congress.

Speaking for the four dissenters, Fuller stressed that under the Constitution, Congress possessed only enumerated powers. In Fuller's view Congress had no authority to govern territories according to different rules from those pertaining in the United States. He also derided Justice White's concept of incorporation "as if possessed of some occult meaning" and argued that in any event, by passing the Foraker Act, Congress had accepted Puerto Rico as part of the United States.[9] Fuller's dissent was consistent with his propensity to construe strictly the powers of Congress and his distrust of unrestricted legislative authority. Moreover, as a Democrat, he was no doubt influenced by that party's anti-imperialist stance.

Notwithstanding the opinion of the chief justice, a majority of his colleagues adopted White's incorporation theory as law in *Dorr v. United States* (1904). Fred Dorr was convicted of libel in the Philippines after a trial without a jury. He attacked his conviction on grounds that the Sixth Amendment guarantee of trial by jury was applicable to the Philippines. Brushing aside this argument, Justice William R. Day, speaking for the majority, declared that territories were to be governed by Congress until they were incorporated into the United States. Reflecting the prevalent imperialist attitude, Justice Day explained that Congress was not constitutionally required to provide trial by jury:

> If the right to trial by jury were a fundamental right which goes wherever the jurisdiction of the United States extends, or if Congress, in framing laws for outlying territory belonging to the United States, was obliged to establish that system by affirmative legisla-

---

8. *Ibid.*, 339. For a discussion of Justice White's role in formulating the incorporation doctrine see Robert B. Highsaw, *Edward Douglass White: Defender of the Conservative Faith* (Baton Rouge: Louisiana State University Press, 1981), 170–174.

9. *Downes v. Bidwell*, 182 U.S. 244, 373 (1901). Fuller's views are examined in King, *Fuller*, 265–266.

tion, it would follow that, no matter what the needs or capacities of the people, trial by jury, and in no other way, must be forthwith established, although the result may be to work injustice and provoke disturbance rather than to aid the orderly administration of justice. If the United States, impelled by its duty or advantage, shall acquire territory peopled by savages, and of which it may dispose or not hold for ultimate admission to Statehood, if this doctrine is sound, it must establish there the trial by jury. To state such a proposition demonstrates the impossibility of carrying it into practice.[10]

Three justices, including Fuller, concurred in result but again declined to accept the incorporation theory. Only Justice John M. Harlan insisted that the right to a jury trial was fundamental in nature and was guaranteed by the Constitution to all inhabitants of the newly acquired possessions.[11]

In the spate of Insular Cases the Supreme Court placed its imprimatur on the imperialist policy of overseas expansion. Although they were plagued by division and cloudy analysis, the justices moved in step with dominant public opinion and confirmed congressional authority over the annexed territories. In 1900 the electorate had overwhelmingly rejected the anti-imperialist appeal of the Democrats. As the fictional humorist Mr. Dooley, created by journalist Finley Peter Dunne, colorfully observed, "No matther whether th' constitution follows th' flag or not, th' supreme court follows th' illection returns."[12]

The Fuller Court likewise upheld the power of Congress to construct the Panama Canal. In *Wilson v. Shaw* (1907) a taxpayer brought suit to enjoin the secretary of the treasury from disbursing money for canal purposes. The case had marked political overtones because it called into question the actions of the president and Congress in acquiring the canal zone. Fuller and his associates had no difficulty in unanimously dismissing the action. Justice David J. Brewer, writing for the Court, noted that under the commerce clause Congress was empowered to build highways and canals within ceded territory. He further pointed out that the Court had "no supervising control over the political branch of the Government in its action within the limits of the Constitution."[13]

---

10. *Dorr v. United States,* 195 U.S. 138, 148 (1904).

11. For an assessment of Justice Harlan's attitude toward overseas possessions see Loren P. Beth, *John Marshall Harlan: The Last Whig Justice* (Lexington: University Press of Kentucky, 1992), 249–256.

12. Edward J. Bander, ed., *Mr. Dooley on the Choice of Law* (Charlottesville, Va: Michie, 1963), 52.

13. *Wilson v. Shaw,* 204 U.S. 24, 32 (1907).

GOVERNMENT OF THE TERRITORIES

Congressional management of domestic territories, unlike that of the new overseas possessions, created few constitutional problems for the Fuller Court. Still, the case of *Late Corporation of the Church of Jesus Christ of Latter-Day Saints v. United States* (1890) elicited an extensive discussion of the authority of Congress over the territories. As part of the drive to suppress polygamy, in 1887 Congress abrogated the charter of the Mormon Church and directed legal proceedings to seize the church's property. Although this measure went well beyond the prohibition of polygamy, the justices sustained the legislation by a vote of 6 to 3. Likening polygamy to barbarism and abruptly dismissing claims of religious freedom, the majority defined the plenary power of Congress to legislate for the territories in sweeping terms.

Writing for the dissenters, Fuller agreed that Congress could extirpate polygamy by criminal penalties but insisted that it had no authority to confiscate the property of persons or corporations who might have been guilty of criminal practices. Emphasizing that Congress could exercise only the powers expressed in the Constitution, Fuller tellingly observed, "I regard it of vital consequence, that absolute power should never be conceded as belonging under our system of government to any one of its departments."[14] The chief justice's opinion, described by his biographer as "one of the greatest glories of Fuller's career," was soon vindicated. By joint resolution in 1893 Congress restored most of the confiscated property to the Mormons.[15] This case is noteworthy also because it was the only major constitutional decision in which the Fuller Court split along partisan lines.

TOWARD THE ADMINISTRATIVE STATE

The Constitution vests all legislative authority in Congress. By the late nineteenth century, however, Congress began increasingly to delegate discretionary power to the executive branch. Clearly neither Congress nor the courts could provide detailed oversight, which necessitated a host of small decisions. The Supreme Court under Fuller recognized that legislators could not anticipate every contingency and uniformly sustained the delegation of legislative power. In so doing, it facilitated the emergence of the administrative state in which substantial lawmaking authority is exercised by the president and administrative agencies.

---

14. *Late Corporation of the Church of Jesus Christ of Latter-Day Saints v. United States,* 136 U.S. 1, 67 (1890). See also Semonche, *Charting the Future,* 29.

15. King, *Fuller,* 147. See *United States v. Late Corporation of the Church of Jesus Christ of Latter-Day Saints,* 150 U.S. 145, 148–149 (1893).

The tendency of Congress to grant the executive branch discretion to make regulations came before the Fuller Court in *Field v. Clark* (1892). The case involved a challenge to the reciprocity provision of the 1890 tariff, which empowered the president to suspend the free importation of certain goods from any country if he deemed the duties imposed by that nation on American products to be unreasonable. The justices sustained the measure by a vote of 7 to 2. Paying lip service to the separation of powers doctrine, the majority declared, "That Congress cannot delegate legislative power to the President is a principle universally recognized as vital to the integrity and maintenance of the system of government ordained by the Constitution."[16] But the Court denied that the president was making law. Rather, the majority asserted that he was "the mere agent of the law-making department" to ascertain the existence of specific facts and act in obedience to congressional directive. This fiction set the stage for broader delegations of the law-making function. In their dissent, Justice Lucius Q. C. Lamar and Fuller argued that Congress had improperly delegated to the president the power to impose duties upon his own judgment. The decision in *Field* became the foundation for subsequent rulings upholding statutes that conferred wide regulatory authority upon executive departments.

A more extensive transference of legislative power to the president was sustained in *Butterfield v. Stranahan* (1904). Under the Tea Inspection Act of 1897, a board appointed by the secretary of the treasury was empowered to establish quality standards for imported teas. An importer attacked the constitutionality of the statute on grounds that, in effect, it vested legislative power in the executive. A unanimous Court concluded that Congress determined to exclude unwholesome tea and merely delegated to the secretary an executive duty to carry out the policy declared in the statute. "Congress legislated on the subject as far as was reasonably practicable," Justice White observed for the Court, "and from the necessities of the case was compelled to leave the executive officials the duty of bringing about the result pointed out by the statute."[17] By the end of Fuller's term, therefore, the justices had accepted the delegation of a large amount of discretionary authority to the executive. This approach weakened the separation of powers doctrine and vastly enlarged the extent of presidential power.

---

16. *Field v. Clark*, 143 U.S. 649, 692 (1892). See Kelly, Harbison, and Belz, *The American Constitution*, 412–414, for the rise of the administrative state.

17. *Butterfield v. Stranahan*, 192 U.S. 470, 496 (1904).

FEDERAL JUDICIAL POWER

As discussed earlier, during Fuller's tenure the Supreme Court became increasingly active in defending economic rights against state infringement. Yet the Eleventh Amendment, which deprived the federal
courts of jurisdiction over suits against states by the citizens of other
states, posed a major obstacle to effective use of federal judicial power to
enforce state contractual obligations. Prior to Fuller's appointment, the
Supreme Court had construed the Eleventh Amendment to bar federal
judicial relief in cases in which states repudiated their bonded indebtedness. This line of decisions frustrated most efforts to compel the southern states to honor their debts.[18] Under Fuller's leadership, however, the
justices began to reinterpret the Eleventh Amendment and to restore the
original narrow understanding of the provision. This expansion of federal judicial authority over the states stood in marked contrast to Fuller's
tendency to limit the reach of congressional power and defer to the states
in areas of social policy.

At the beginning of Fuller's chief justiceship, the Supreme Court took a
restrictive view of federal judicial power in a leading case, *Hans v. Louisiana*
(1890), which involved a federal-court suit by a Louisiana citizen against his
own state for bond interest. By its own terms the Eleventh Amendment did
not prohibit such a lawsuit, but the justices unanimously invoked the concept of sovereign immunity and held that a state could not be sued by individuals in federal court without its consent. Although cast in jurisdictional
terms, the outcome in *Hans* further contracted judicial protection of contract rights. The *Hans* decision can best be understood as part of the Supreme Court's refusal, on claimed jurisdictional grounds, to confront the
widespread repudiation of bonds by southern states.[19]

In other important respects, however, Fuller and his colleagues moved
to enlarge the suability of localities and states in federal court. The justices unanimously ruled in *Lincoln County v. Luning* (1890) that the Eleventh Amendment pertained only to suits against states and did not
prevent political subdivisions from being sued in federal court. The defaulting county was ordered to pay its bonded obligations. Since, as the
Court recognized, municipalities and counties are part of the state that
created them, the rationale of the holding in *Lincoln County* is not readily
apparent. In political terms, on the other hand, the decision is easily ap-
prehended. Judicial coercion of defaulting municipalities, many of

---

18. John V. Orth, *The Judicial Power of the United States: The Eleventh Amendment in American History* (New York: Oxford University Press, 1987), 7–9, 58–89.

19. *Ibid.*, at 74–76; Currie, *The Constitution in the Supreme Court*, 7–9.

which were located in sparsely settled western states, did not portend the same threat to judicial authority as that presented by unified southern resistance to payment of state bonds. The distinction between states and localities for purposes of the Eleventh Amendment, if not strictly logical, has proved a lasting one.[20] Moreover, as a practical matter, the Fuller Court's insistence on fiscal probity by local government strengthened the credit rating of municipal bonds.[21]

The justices also entertained a suit in which a state sued another to collect on defaulted bonds. A group of creditors arranged a test case by making a gift of certain North Carolina bonds to South Dakota. By a margin of 5 to 4 the Fuller Court held in *South Dakota v. North Carolina* (1904) that a state could sue in federal court on its own behalf to enforce its property rights in bonds acquired by gift. Emphasizing that the Supreme Court had long exercised jurisdiction over actions by one state against another concerning property rights, Justice Brewer, for the majority, rejected an Eleventh Amendment defense. In a further display of judicial resolve, he ordered that unless North Carolina paid the judgment, the Court's marshal should sell at public auction the state's interest in stock that secured the bonded obligation. The dissenters charged that the issue in substance was between private individuals and North Carolina and that the majority winked at evasion of the Eleventh Amendment. Armed with the majority opinion, the creditors were able to negotiate a compromise settlement with North Carolina for the bonds owned by private holders.[22]

In the same spirit, the Fuller Court found the Eleventh Amendment no obstacle to a suit by Virginia seeking to allocate one-third of its pre-Civil War debt to West Virginia. After decades of fruitless negotiations Virginia instituted an original action in the Supreme Court to procure an accounting between the states. West Virginia questioned the Supreme Court's jurisdiction to hear the complaint. Speaking for a unanimous Court in *Virginia v. West Virginia* (1907), Fuller pointed out that the Eleventh Amendment did not comprehend controversies between states. He concluded that the Supreme Court had jurisdiction over the suit and ex-

---

20. Orth, *Judicial Power of the United States*, 110–120.

21. One contemporary authority observed "that the firm moral fibre displayed in the opinions upon bond cases has been of incalculable value to the whole country." Frank W. Hackett, "A Recent Decision of the Supreme Court upon Municipal Cases," 5 *Harvard Law Review* 159 (1891).

22. This case is examined in Robert F. Durden, *Reconstruction Bonds & Twentieth Century Politics: South Dakota v. North Carolina* (Durham, N.C.: Duke University Press, 1962). See also Orth, *Judicial Power of the United States*, 83–84.

pressed his confidence that the West Virginia legislature would make adequate provision to satisfy any decree. Fuller did not address the merits of Virginia's claim, and in 1908 the Court referred the case to a special master. The outcome was eminently sensible since the Supreme Court was the only tribunal capable of resolving such controversies between states. This was the first in a series of cases between these states concerning allocation of fiscal responsibilities, and the matter was eventually resolved after Fuller's death when the Supreme Court coerced payment of West Virginia's share of the debt.[23]

Torn between the conflicting demands of state sovereignty and protection of contractual obligations, the Fuller Court handled monetary suits against the states in a piecemeal and inconsistent fashion. But the justices were not writing on a fresh slate; the Supreme Court under Fuller's predecessor, Chief Justice Morrison R. Waite, had given the Eleventh Amendment a broad interpretation. In general the Court during Fuller's tenure endeavored to limit the reach of the Eleventh Amendment by fashioning various exceptions. Although a tidy solution eluded them, the justices curtailed use of the Eleventh Amendment as a shield for defaulting states and localities.

Fuller and his associates more dramatically strengthened the federal judiciary by affirming the issuance of injunctions against state officials. After 1890 there was a steady increase of cases in which suits were instituted in federal courts to prevent state officers from executing state laws that allegedly violated the Constitution.[24] The Eleventh Amendment seemingly raised a barrier to such actions, but the Fuller Court revived an earlier doctrine that held that suits against state officials were not suits against the state. This trend became evident in *Pennoyer v. McConnaughy* (1891), in which the plaintiff sought to enjoin Oregon's land commissioners from conveying certain real property to which the plaintiff asserted title based on prior contractual rights. The defendant commissioners argued that the suit was, in effect, against the state within the meaning of the Eleventh Amendment. Rejecting this contention, the justices unanimously ruled that "an officer of a State may be enjoined from executing a statute of the State which is in conflict with the Constitution of the United States, when such execution would violate and destroy the

---

23. For the prolonged controversy between Virginia and West Virginia see Orth, *Judicial Power of the United States,* 106–109; Thomas Reed Powell, "Coercing a State to Pay a Judgment: Virginia v. West Virginia," 17 *Michigan Law Review* 1 (1918).

24. Charles Warren, *The Supreme Court in United States History,* rev. ed. (Boston: Little, Brown, 1926), vol. 2, 715–716.

rights and privileges of the complainant."[25] The Court also observed that the plaintiff was not seeking any affirmative relief against the state. Finding a violation of the contract clause, the justices sustained an injunction preventing the defendant officials from selling the land.

Railroad companies promptly took advantage of this jurisdictional development by obtaining federal court injunctions in several cases to restrain enforcement of rates fixed by state commissions. This was a less hazardous means of challenging the constitutionality of statutes than violating laws and running the risk of stiff penalties. Thus the Supreme Court's willingness to entertain injunction suits against state officers was closely linked with the emergence of substantive due process review of economic regulations.

This line of decisions culminated in the landmark case of *Ex Parte Young* (1908).[26] It originated as part of the long struggle over state legislation regulating railroads. A 1907 Minnesota law mandated reduction in passenger and commodity rates and imposed enormous fines and severe criminal penalties on railroads and their agents for violations of the act. The evident purpose of the penalties was to intimidate the railroads and their officers from resorting to the courts to test the validity of the law. Arguing that the reduced rates were confiscatory and hence infringed the due process clause of the Fourteenth Amendment, railroad stockholders obtained a temporary injunction from the federal circuit court prohibiting Edward T. Young, the Minnesota attorney general, from enforcing the act. Young violated the injunction by attempting to enforce the new rates in state court. Found guilty of contempt, Young was fined, directed to dismiss the state court proceedings, and jailed until he obeyed the federal court order. Young petitioned the Supreme Court for a writ of habeas corpus. He asserted that the suit was in reality an action against the state in contravention of the Eleventh Amendment.

Speaking for a majority of eight, Justice Rufus W. Peckham declared the penalty provisions unconstitutional on their face because they effectively denied resort to the courts. Peckham then rejected the Eleventh Amendment defense and maintained that a state could not impart to an official any immunity from the supreme authority of the United States. He declared that when a state officer sought to enforce an unconstitutional act, "he is in

---

25. *Pennoyer v. McConnaughy*, 140 U.S. 1, 11 (1891).

26. The decision in *Ex Parte Young* receives careful examination in Orth, *Judicial Power of the United States*, 121–135; Semonche, *Charting the Future*, 221–224; Currie, *The Constitution in the Supreme Court*, 52–54; Richard C. Cortner, *The Iron Horse and the Constitution: The Railroads and the Transformation of the Fourteenth Amendment* (Westport, Conn.: Greenwood Press, 1993), 181–211.

that case stripped of his official or representative character and is subjected in his person to the consequences of his individual conduct." The Court's distinction between suits against states and suits against state officers alleged to be acting unconstitutionally rested on a convenient legal fiction that facilitated circumvention of the Eleventh Amendment. Justice Harlan emphasized this point in his solitary dissent. Discarding his usual nationalist stance, Harlan warned that the majority opinion "would work a radical change in our governmental system" and "place the States of the Union in a condition of inferiority."[27] He complained that the decision had practically obliterated the Eleventh Amendment.

The *Young* case was a milestone in the Fuller Court's transformation of federal judicial power. It provided the jurisdictional counterpart to the Court's oversight of economic legislation.[28] The justices were strongly influenced by their suspicion of state railroad regulation and their desire to safeguard property rights. Justice Peckham explained that a company should not be required to risk heavy fines in order to obtain judicial review of regulatory legislation. Protection of investment capital was a persistent theme for Fuller and his associates. "Over eleven thousand millions of dollars it is estimated, are invested in railroad property, owned by many thousands of people who are scattered over the whole country from ocean to ocean," Peckham pointedly observed, "and they are entitled to equal protection from the laws and from the courts, with the owners of all other kinds of property, no more, no less."[29]

Although the *Young* decision aroused a storm of protest from Progressives and champions of states' rights, Congress largely accepted the Court's activist role. To placate critics, in 1910 Congress established the requirement that injunctions preventing state officials from enforcing allegedly unconstitutional state laws be issued by a three-judge court, but it did not limit the authority of the Supreme Court. Federal judicial power was fundamentally unchanged. Thus *Young* established a basic precept of modern Eleventh Amendment law. Indeed, in time the three-judge panels proved cumbersome, and Congress repealed the requirement in 1976. Despite detractors, *Ex Parte Young* has survived because the power

---

27. *Ex Parte Young*, 209 U.S. 123, 160, 175 (1908).

28. For a rewarding discussion of judicial power and the Eleventh Amendment see William F. Duker, "Mr. Justice Rufus W. Peckham and the Case of *Ex Parte Young*: Lochnerizing *Munn v. Illinois*," 1980 *Brigham Young University Law Review*, 539–558. See also Edward A. Purcell, Jr., *Litigation and Inequality: Federal Diversity Jurisdiction in Industrial America, 1870–1958* (New York: Oxford University Press, 1992), 284–285.

29. *Ex Parte Young*, 209 U.S., 165.

to enjoin state officials from violating the Constitution proved essential to maintaining the federal system and safeguarding individual rights.

In addition to threading its way through the complexities of Eleventh Amendment jurisprudence, the Fuller Court instituted a unique contempt proceeding for willful disregard of its order staying the execution of a prisoner pending appeal. The case arose from a 1906 lynching of a black defendant convicted of rape in Chattanooga. It was alleged that Sheriff John F. Shipp and his deputies aided and abetted the lynch mob. Fuller was outraged by the murder and promptly called the justices to his home for an emergency meeting. The Court requested that the attorney general investigate the incident. The attorney general filed an information charging a contempt of the Supreme Court. Brushing aside arguments that the Court lacked jurisdiction, the justices unanimously ruled that they had the authority to preserve the existing conditions until the appeal was resolved.[30] The Court then appointed a commissioner who heard testimony concerning the contempt charges during 1907 and 1908.

Fuller initially assigned preparation of the Court's opinion to Holmes but later decided to handle the matter himself. Fuller may well have decided that, given the novel nature of this contempt proceeding, the chief should deliver the opinion. Writing for a majority of five in *United States v. Shipp* (1909), he found the sheriff, one of his deputies, and four members of the mob guilty of contempt of the Supreme Court. He declared that once the Court granted stay of execution it became the duty of the sheriff to protect the defendant. Fuller unsparingly condemned the lynching. "It is apparent," he observed, "that a dangerous portion of the community was seized with the awful thirst for blood which only killing can quench, and that considerations of law and order were swept away in the overwhelming flood." He concluded that "this lamentable riot was the direct result of opposition to the administration of the law by this Court."[31] The three dissenters maintained that there was inadequate evidence to support contempt findings against the sheriff and the deputy. Holmes felt that Shipp deserved imprisonment for one year, but his recommendation did not prevail.[32] Shipp and his deputy were sentenced to ninety days in the District of Columbia jail, and the other de-

---

30. *United States v. Shipp,* 203 U.S. 563 (1906).
31. *United States v. Shipp,* 214 U.S. 386, 414, 425 (1909). Helpful treatment of the *Shipp* litigation can be found in King, *Fuller,* 323–327; Semonche, *Charting the Future,* 231–233; Liva Baker, *The Justice from Beacon Hill: The Life and Times of Oliver Wendell Holmes* (New York: HarperCollins, 1991), 431–432.
32. Holmes to Fuller, May 18, 1909, Fuller Papers, LC.

fendants received lesser sentences.[33] These punishments seem trivial to modern eyes. But Fuller was making an extraordinary use of the contempt power of the federal judiciary to reach offenses that were otherwise outside normal legal proceedings. The early part of the twentieth century was an intense period of lynching in the South, and the state courts had made only a feeble response. Although it was prompted in large part by a desire to vindicate the authority of the Court, Fuller's firm stand helped to publicize the unsavory practice of lynching at a time when many government bodies looked the other way.

FEDERALISM

The contested nature of the federal union presented the Fuller Court with many opportunities to delineate the balance between state and federal authority. As discussed earlier, debate over the appropriate role of the states figured prominently in the Court's handling of economic issues, criminal justice, and race relations. In several cases, moreover, Fuller and his associates addressed jurisdictional matters that pertained directly to the place of the states in the constitutional order.

In an unusual case, *In re Neagle* (1890), the Supreme Court broadly construed its power to grant a writ of habeas corpus to a federal marshal arrested under state law. This case arose from a colorful episode in which Justice Field was personally involved. There was long-standing animosity between Field and David S. Terry, growing out of Field's handling of a celebrated divorce action concerning a prior marriage of Terry's wife. Because Terry had threatened to kill Field, the attorney general assigned special deputies to protect the justice when he performed circuit duty in California in 1889. When Terry attacked Field in a restaurant, deputy David Neagle shot and killed Terry. Neagle was arrested for murder by the California authorities. The federal circuit court promptly granted a writ of habeas corpus releasing Neagle from state custody.[34]

Field recused himself from hearing the appeal, but his strong support for Neagle was no secret to his colleagues. Likewise, public sentiment leaned heavily toward Neagle. At issue on the appeal was whether the

---

33. For the imposition of punishments see *United States v. Shipp,* 215 U.S. 580 (1909). Fuller received many requests for his help in obtaining a pardon for Shipp. For example, see John Allison to Fuller, December 8, 1909, George W. Yerger to Fuller, December 13, 1909, Fuller Papers (microfilm), CHS. Shipp, however, declined to authorize any consideration of a pardon application. Docket of Pardon Cases, vol. 26, 148, National Archives.

34. Carl Brent Swisher, *Stephen J. Field: Craftsman of the Law* (Washington: Brookings Institution, 1930, reprint Chicago: University of Chicago Press, 1969), 321–361.

federal court was authorized to interfere with the state's administration
of criminal justice in these circumstances. A federal statute provided that
the courts could issue a writ of habeas corpus when a prisoner was held
for an act done "in pursuance of a law of the United States." Although no
statute expressly empowered the federal government to protect judicial
officers from violence, Justice Samuel F. Miller, writing for a majority of
six, interpreted the term "law" to encompass the actions of a federal marshal within the scope of his duties. He emphasized the need to safeguard
judges from the malice of disgruntled litigants. Since Neagle was acting
under the authority of the United States, the Court declared that he was
innocent of any crime against California and could not be tried in the
state courts. Justice Lucius Q. C. Lamar, joined by Fuller, dissented. Contending that the word "law" as used in the habeas corpus act referred
only to federal statutes, they protested that the Court was invading state
criminal jurisdiction. The dissenters expressed confidence that California courts would have acquitted Neagle. To the majority, however, the
power of the federal government to protect its officials outweighed deference to state autonomy.[35]

Fuller and his colleagues also had occasion to pass upon the compact
clause of the Constitution, which declares that no state shall without the
consent of Congress "enter into any agreement or compact" with another state. The leading case of *Virginia v. Tennessee* (1893) grew out of a
conflict between the two states concerning their boundary. Invoking the
original jurisdiction of the Supreme Court, Virginia asked the justices to
set aside an 1803 survey accepted by both parties for many years. Virginia asserted that the arrangement was void because it had not been approved by Congress. Justice Field, for a unanimous Court, rejected
Virginia's position. He reasoned that the clause did not apply to every
agreement between states. Rather, Congress need approve only those
compacts that tended to increase the power of the states and thus to en-
croach upon federal authority. Field added that approval by Congress
did not require formal action but could be implied from subsequent legislation. Because the determination of a boundary had no effect upon
political influence, he ruled that the boundary settlement at issue did not
require the consent of Congress. Although it did not fit comfortably with
the language of the compact clause, Field's opinion had two virtues. It

35. King, *Fuller,* 139–142; Semonche, *Charting the Future,* 25–27. See also Richard Maxwell
Brown, "Law and Order on the American Frontier: The Western Civil War of Incorpora-
tion," in John McLaren, Hamar Foster, and Chet Orloff, eds., *Law For the Elephant, Law
For the Beaver: Essays in the Legal History of the North American West* (Pasadena, Cal.: Ninth
Judicial Circuit Historical Society and Canadian Plains Research Center, 1992), 80–81.

harmonized with the Fuller Court's persistent attempts to preserve state autonomy within the federal union, and it relieved Congress of the burden of reviewing every agreement between the states.

The Fuller Court heard several other cases under its original jurisdiction that raised far-reaching questions about the constitutional order. In *Kansas v. Colorado* (1907) Kansas brought suit to enjoin Colorado from diverting water from the Arkansas River for the purpose of reclaiming arid land. Kansas maintained that under common law it was entitled to the continuous flow of the water, while Colorado asserted that it had a right to diminish the flow of water for irrigation.[36] The United States intervened in the lawsuit, arguing that the states were subject to superior right of the federal government to control the reclamation of arid land. The government urged the Court to recognize congressional authority to direct water distribution. Writing for the Court, Justice Brewer emphasized the limited nature of federal power under the Constitution. He dismissed the contention of the United States on grounds that it conflicted with the basic design for a government of enumerated power. Brewer pointed to the Tenth Amendment as a check on the unwarranted exercise of federal power and observed that the Tenth Amendment should "be considered fairly and liberally so as to give effect to its scope and meaning."[37] It followed that the federal government could not interfere with the allocation of water within a state. Although recognizing the rights of each state to allocate water internally, Brewer nonetheless refused to apply the water law of either Colorado or Kansas. Instead, he declared that the dispute must be resolved by an application of "interstate common law" to be fashioned by the Court. Noting that the advantages of irrigation in Colorado outweighed the harm to southwestern Kansas, Brewer declined on equitable principles to disturb the existing division of water. The outcome was a qualified victory for Colorado. But Brewer warned that greater diversion of water by Colorado might destroy the equitable apportionment between the states and require judicial correction. *Kansas v. Colorado* established that federal common law governed water disputes between states. The opinion had broad implications because the justices in effect elevated the power of the federal courts to handle interstate controversies above congressional authority.[38]

---

36. For the dispute that culminated in *Kansas v. Colorado* see James Earl Sherow, *Watering the Valley: Development Along the High Plains Arkansas River, 1870–1950* (Lawrence: University Press of Kansas, 1990), 103–119.

37. *Kansas v. Colorado*, 206 U.S. 46, 90–91 (1907).

38. Warren, *The Supreme Court in United States History*, vol. 2, 714; Semonche, *Charting the Future*, 203–205; Purcell, *Litigation and Inequality*, 285–286.

During the same term the Fuller Court considered another case that had an important bearing on the power of the states to control pollution across state lines. Georgia filed an original action in the Supreme Court seeking to enjoin a corporation located in Tennessee from discharging noxious fumes over Georgia territory. Georgia claimed that the air pollution was causing wholesale destruction to forests and crops. There was little dispute about the extent of the damage, so the case turned upon the standing of Georgia to maintain the action. Although the state owned little of the affected land, Justice Holmes, speaking for the Court in *Georgia v. Tennessee Copper Company* (1907), proclaimed that Georgia had "an interest independent of and behind the titles of its citizens, in all the earth and air within its domain."[39] Holmes concluded that the state in its capacity as quasi-sovereign had standing to sue on behalf of its citizens, and he ordered that an injunction should issue. This early environmental case demonstrated again that Fuller and his colleagues were not blind champions of business and that they were prepared to deal with the negative consequences of industrial growth.

FULL FAITH AND CREDIT

Article IV, section 1 of the Constitution declares that "Full Faith and Credit shall be given in each State to the public Acts, Records and judicial proceedings of every other State." This clause was intended to promote uniformity and certainty among the states concerning judgments rendered in the courts in other states. The full faith and credit provision did not feature prominently in constitutional adjudication before Fuller's appointment. In a series of cases he and his associates grappled with the scope of this clause and sought to delineate the extent to which judgments rendered in one state have conclusive effect in others.[40]

Much of this litigation concerned claimed exceptions to the full faith and credit obligation. As a general proposition, Fuller and his colleagues insisted that states give effect to judgments obtained elsewhere. Before Fuller became chief, the Supreme Court had ruled that a state need not enforce judgments based on the penal statutes of other jurisdictions. In

---

39. *Georgia v. Tennessee Copper Co.*, 206 U.S. 230, 237 (1907). The entry of a final decree was delayed for years while the parties sought a practical means of diminishing the sulfur fumes. After Fuller's death the Court entered an injunction restraining plant operations and appointing an inspector to monitor the character of gases emitted. *Georgia v. Tennessee Copper Co.*, 237 U.S. 474 (1915).

40. On the full faith and credit clause see Currie, *The Constitution in the Supreme Court*, 65–78; Willis L. M. Reese, "Full Faith and Credit to Foreign Equity Decrees," 42 *Iowa Law Review* 183 (1957).

Huntington v. Attrill (1892), however, the justices, by a 6 to 1 vote, narrowly construed the penal judgment exception. They decided that a New York statute making officers of corporations who sign false statements liable for corporate debts was not penal in nature, and therefore a judgment under the law was entitled to full faith and credit in Maryland. The Court defined penal in terms of punishment and determined that the penal exception did not embrace private damage actions.

The Court similarly held that a state was bound to give full faith and credit even to judgments of other states that were contrary to its public policy. At issue in the well-known case of *Fauntleroy v. Lum* (1908) was a Missouri judgment awarding monetary damages for breach of a contract concerning cotton futures made in Mississippi. Speaking for a majority of five, Justice Holmes took the position that the judgment must receive full faith and credit in Mississippi even if the underlying transaction was void under Mississippi law. The four dissenters protested that the full faith and credit clause did not override a state's police power to prohibit certain transactions within its borders. In *Fauntleroy* the Fuller Court signaled that the national policy served by the full faith and credit clause would customarily outweigh the interests of particular states.

The power of courts in one state to affect title to land located in other states has long been a source of controversy. Fuller and his associates addressed this thorny problem in *Fall v. Eastin* (1909). As part of a divorce proceeding, a Washington court appointed a commissioner to convey to the wife certain land situated in Nebraska. Justice Joseph McKenna, in an opaque opinion, declared that a state court could compel the parties before it to transfer land in other jurisdictions, but a state could not directly convey title by a commissioner's deed. The distinction drawn in *Fall* is open to question, but the decision remains the Supreme Court's most definitive pronouncement on the subject.

Under Fuller's leadership the justices tended to give a broad reading to the full faith and credit clause. Interpreting the provision in a nationalist spirit, the Court strengthened the policy of uniformity in legal proceedings among the states. This outcome comported comfortably with the Fuller Court's efforts to protect the emerging national market.

8

PRIVATE LITIGATION

Although constitutional and public law litigation occupied an increasingly large share of the Supreme Court's time during Fuller's tenure, the justices continued to hear a heavy volume of private disputes concerning property, contracts, and torts. The bulk of this litigation arose under diversity of citizenship jurisdiction. Another category of private controversies arose from congressional legislation dealing with patents, copyright, bankruptcy, and railroad safety. The Supreme Court's resolution of these cases had a direct bearing on the development of the national economy. An analysis of the Fuller Court's private litigation is therefore essential in providing a full picture of its work in aiding economic growth and strengthening federal judicial power.

DIVERSITY JURISDICTION

Under article III of the Constitution federal judicial power extends to suits between citizens of different states or foreign nations.[1] Reflecting concern about local bias against out-of-state claimants, this jurisdiction was designed to provide a neutral forum for the adjudication of inter state lawsuits. Thus diversity jurisdiction gave nonresidents a federal alternative to the state courts. But states' rights advocates worried that a broad federal diversity jurisdiction would eclipse state tribunals. Consequently, the Judiciary Act of 1789 sought to constrain the exercise of diversity jurisdiction. Section 34 of the act required federal courts to follow state laws in cases in which they applied. The Supreme Court did not for-

---

1. In treating diversity jurisdiction I have relied heavily on Tony A. Freyer, *Forums of Order: The Federal Courts and Business in American History* (Greenwich, Conn.: JAI Press, 1979), and Edward A. Purcell, Jr., *Litigation and Inequality: Federal Diversity Jurisdiction in Industrial America, 1870–1958* (New York: Oxford University Press, 1992).

mulate a definitive interpretation of section 34 until the landmark decision in *Swift v. Tyson* (1842). There the justices ruled that the term "laws" referred only to state statutes and that, in dealing with contracts and commercial instruments, the federal courts were free to decide cases in accord with general principles of commercial law. This opened the door for federal judges to render judgments independent of state law as to the substantive rules governing commercial transactions. In effect, the federal courts formulated a federal common law for diversity cases. Responding to rapid changes in technology and the development of a national market for goods, the Supreme Court soon extended the *Swift* principle into other areas of law. By the late nineteenth century multistate business corporations regularly invoked diversity jurisdiction to escape local antipathy and the uncertainty of state laws. Corporate defendants also took advantage of the Removal Act of 1875 to remove cases that were brought against them in state tribunals to federal court. Hence the exercise of diversity jurisdiction was closely linked with the growth of interstate business enterprise.

Business interests gained both substantive and tactical advantages from resort to federal diversity jurisdiction. The extent to which federal judges consciously fashioned legal doctrine favorable to corporations has been overstated, but federal judges were generally sympathetic to the emerging national economy and less likely than state tribunals to aid local interests. Aside from fear of local prejudice, corporate defendants had other valid reasons to distrust state courts. Corporations conducting business across state lines faced a bewildering morass of antiquated, diverse, and unsettled legal rules at the state level. The resulting confusion placed a considerable burden on the growing interstate commercial economy. Multistate businesses naturally preferred the unifying application of federal common law based on the *Swift* principle to the uncertainties of state laws. In an age with little national economic regulation, diversity jurisdiction served the important purpose of providing an impartial and consistent application of law involving interstate transactions.[2] Additionally, corporate attorneys, more familiar with federal procedures and appellate practice than local counsel, could often use access to the federal courts as a means of engineering favorable settlements of private disputes. By the late nineteenth century railroads and insurance companies were particular beneficiaries of diversity jurisdiction.

---

2. Herbert Hovenkamp, *Enterprise and American Law, 1836–1937* (Cambridge, Mass.: Harvard University Press, 1991), 83–91.

The ever-widening exercise of diversity jurisdiction prompted an assault on federal judicial power. Critics charged that such authority served corporate interests, gave unfair advantages to out-of-state companies, and weakened state courts as separate law-making authorities. Bills to curtail diversity jurisdiction were debated in Congress but failed to win passage. As with the income tax and bankruptcy legislation, the controversy over diversity jurisdiction laid bare pronounced sectional differences. Southerners and westerners sought to narrow federal judicial power, while eastern investors defended the federal courts as guarantors of credit and capital investment.[3]

Despite the occasional misgivings of individual justices, the Fuller Court consistently expanded both the right of corporations to use diversity jurisdiction and the reach of federal common law. The ability of corporations to initiate suits in or remove cases to the federal courts rested upon a determination of corporate citizenship for jurisdictional purposes. Prior to Fuller's appointment, the Supreme Court, in a series of cases, formulated the doctrine that a corporation was to be treated as a citizen of the chartering state. Several states attempted to curtail corporate resort to the federal courts by providing that out-of-state corporations were deemed to become domestic corporations. Such "adoption" statutes had the effect of destroying diversity of citizenship between the corporation and residents of the adopting state. In keeping with its policy of allowing corporations easy access to the federal courts, the Fuller Court in *St. Louis and San Francisco Railway Company v. James* (1896) declined to permit the states to treat such adopted corporations as citizens and thus defeat federal jurisdiction. "The presumption that a corporation is composed of citizens of the state which created it," Justice George Shiras explained, "accompanies such corporation when it does business in another state, and it may sue or be sued in the Federal courts in such other states as a citizen of the state of its original creation."[4] The upshot of the *James* rule was to preserve diversity between corporations and citizens of all states other than the state of incorporation. In *Louisville, New Albany & Chicago Railway Company v. Louisville Trust Company*

---

3. Felix Frankfurter and James M. Landis, *The Business of the Supreme Court: A Study in the Federal Judicial System* (New York: Macmillan, 1928), 89–93. For southern hostility to federal diversity jurisdiction see Harry N. Scheiber, "Federalism, the Southern Regional Economy, and Public Policy Since 1865," in David J. Bodenhamer and James W. Ely, Jr., eds., *Ambivalent Legacy: A Legal History of the South* (Jackson: University Press of Mississippi, 1984), 74–78.

4. *St. Louis and San Francisco Railway Company v. James,* 161 U.S. 545, 562 (1896); Purcell, *Litigation and Inequality,* 18–19.

(1899) the justices went a step further, holding that even if a corporation was rechartered in another state, it remained for purposes of diversity a citizen of the original state of incorporation.

During Fuller's tenure the *Swift* principle was applied to numerous categories of law, including negotiable instruments, torts, corporations, real property, and insurance. In resolving diversity issues the chief and his associates were guided for the most part by an instrumentalist conception of law. A study of representative cases illustrates how the justices molded a body of private law to facilitate commercial transactions and foster economic growth. It also demonstrates that Fuller and his associates did not automatically decide every case in favor of corporations. With the conspicuous exception of cases involving the fellow servant rule, they were engaged in a search for the most appropriate and commercially reasonable rules of law. This is not to deny that many substantive issues were resolved in a manner helpful to business. Since much of the nation's economic activity was conducted by corporations, the Court's attempts to formulate a uniform commercial jurisprudence inevitably assisted multistate business enterprise. In a real sense, then, the Supreme Court under Fuller functioned as the leading commercial tribunal in the United States.

The Court, for instance, adopted a modern approach to the scope of the powers of a corporation under its charter. In *Jacksonville, Mayport, Pablo Railway and Navigation Company v. Hooper* (1896), the defendant railroad leased a hotel situated on a beach at the terminus of its line for the use of passengers. At issue was a suit by the landowner for back rent and losses suffered when the hotel was destroyed by fire. The railroad relied on a defense of *ultra vires*, contending that the lease was void because it was not within the contractual powers of a railroad company. Brushing aside this argument, the Supreme Court unanimously held that a railroad had the power to conduct transactions incidental to its main business and could operate a hotel. By softening a strict application of the *ultra vires* rule, the Court recognized broad corporate authority to engage in business and encouraged corporations to make vertical acquisitions. But the decision was also an example of reliance on general federal law to defeat the interests of a particular corporate defendant when they were inconsistent with broader commercial interests.

The Fuller Court, too, addressed the law governing private contracts.[5]

---

5. For a helpful study of the transformation of contract law at the end of the nineteenth century see Walter F. Pratt, "American Contract Law at the Turn of the Century," 39 *South Carolina Law Review* 415 (1988).

Embracing modern commercial values, the justices approved new contractual practices. A key decision was *Roehm v. Horst* (1900), in which the justices accepted the doctrine of anticipatory breach. Writing for a unanimous bench, Fuller held that when a contract is repudiated before performance is due, the injured party may sue at once for damages. This sensible ruling brought contract law into conformity with the underlying commercial realities. The Court was also willing to grant specific performance of corporate contracts on grounds that the legal remedy of monetary damages was not sufficient. Fuller, speaking for the Court in *Union Pacific Railway Company v. Chicago, Rock Island and Pacific Railway Company* (1896), demonstrated a keen understanding of business transactions. "It must not be forgotten," he observed, "that in the increasing complexities of modern business relations equitable remedies have necessarily and steadily been expanded, and no inflexible rule has been permitted to circumscribe them."[6]

Although the Supreme Court generally followed state laws dealing with the ownership and transfer of land, the justices did not always adhere to local law interpreting deeds and grants of land. In *Moelle v. Sherwood* (1893), for example, the Court was called upon to ascertain the title to certain real property in Nebraska. The technical question before the Court was whether the grantee of a quitclaim deed could qualify as a bona fide purchaser for purposes of protection under the recording system. Ignoring Nebraska decisions that denied bona fide purchaser status to parties who received land by quitclaim deed, the Supreme Court forcefully asserted that there was no sound reason to prevent a grantee from claiming protection under the recording acts because of the form of the conveyance. In a frequently cited opinion, Justice Stephen J. Field explained that quitclaim deeds were widely used and were appropriate in many situations. The *Moelle* case exemplifies an instrumental use of the federal common law to make land easier to transfer and to encourage recording of deeds.

Perhaps the most contentious subject of diversity litigation concerned the tort liability of corporations. The federal courts heard many actions in which individual plaintiffs sued railroads or manufacturing concerns for personal injuries caused by negligence. Since railroading was an especially hazardous occupation, the docket of the Fuller Court was full of suits against railroads by injured employees. A critical point in such litigation was application of the fellow servant rule. According to this com-

---

6. *Union Pacific Railway Company v. Chicago, Rock Island and Pacific Railway Company*, 163 U.S. 564, 600–601 (1896).

mon-law doctrine, an employer was not responsible for an injury to one employee caused by a fellow employee engaged in common service.[7] Liability therefore often turned upon the test of what constituted common service. In an effort to ameliorate the harsh results of the fellow servant rule, courts formulated the vice-principal exception. This exception held that a superior official represented the company as a vice-principal and was not a fellow servant with subordinate employees. It followed that the employer was responsible for the negligence of a vice-principal.

The leading case of *Baltimore and Ohio Railroad Company v. Baugh* (1893) involved a fireman injured by the negligence of an engineer who drove a locomotive over a section of track without following established safety procedures. Justice David J. Brewer, writing for the Court, asserted that the liability of railroads to their employees was a matter of general law and that the decisions of state courts were not authoritative.[8] Noting that railroads were "the main channels through which this interstate commerce passes," he stressed the need for uniform rules governing the obligations of carriers.[9] Brewer proceeded to define common service in sweeping terms and to severely limit the vice-principal exception. He then determined that the engineer and fireman were fellow servants and that the fireman could not recover from the railroad for injuries due to the engineer's negligence. The adoption of a federal rule of decision in *Baugh* rested on the implicit premise that tort rules had a direct impact on interstate commerce. Justice Field, in an impassioned dissent, maintained that state law should control. Seemingly attacking the very basis of the *Swift* principle, he stated that the general law "is often little less than what the judge advancing the doctrine thinks at the time should be the general law on a particular subject." This argument was out of character for Field, who generally supported reliance on federal common law in diversity cases. But it can be understood as an expression of Field's long-standing dislike of the fellow servant rule. He pointedly observed that the Court should adopt a rule of law "in accor-

---

7. On the fellow servant rule see Morton Keller, *Affairs of State: Public Life in Nineteenth Century America* (Cambridge, Mass.: Harvard University Press, 1977), 401–404; Kermit L. Hall, *The Magic Mirror: Law in American History* (New York: Oxford University Press, 1989), 202–203.

8. The *Baugh* case is explored in Purcell, *Litigation and Inequality*, 79–82; John E. Semonche, *Charting the Future: The Supreme Court Responds to a Changing Society, 1890–1920* (Westport, Conn.: Greenwood Press, 1978), 42–43.

9. *Baltimore and Ohio Railroad Company v. Baugh,* 149 U.S. 368, 378 (1893).

dance with justice and humanity to the servants of a corporation."[10] Fuller dissented separately on grounds that the employees were not fellow servants and that the majority ruling unreasonably enlarged an employer's freedom from liability for employee injuries.

The justices repeatedly enforced the broad fellow servant rule established in *Baugh* throughout Fuller's tenure as chief. For instance, in *New England Railroad Company v. Conroy* (1899) the Court, by a vote of 8 to 1, held that the conductor of a freight train and a brakeman were fellow servants despite the conductor's supervision of other employees on the train. This line of decisions culminated in *Northern Pacific Railway Company v. Dixon* (1904), in which a sharply divided Court decided that a railroad station agent was the fellow servant of a fireman. Hence the railroad was not responsible for the death of the fireman, caused by a collision resulting from the negligence of the station agent. In a sharply worded dissent, Justice White, joined by Fuller and two other justices, protested that the fellow servant rule was inapplicable because the law placed a positive duty on employers to furnish a safe workplace.

The Court adhered to an expansive fellow servant rule despite the fact that by the early twentieth century some states had abolished or modified this defense. Hence, as the Court itself observed, the fellow servant rule was administered differently in federal diversity cases from the way it was administered in some state courts. One must be careful, however, not to exaggerate the extent of this disparity. As late as 1906 only seven states had entirely abrogated the fellow servant rule, and many jurisdictions continued to apply the common-law doctrine.[11] The *Baugh* decision, therefore, was not markedly out of step with the prevailing law governing industrial accidents.

Rigorous application of the fellow servant rule contributed to the public's perception of a federal forum that favored corporate interests over injured workers. The Supreme Court's dogged dedication to the fellow servant rule helped to bring the notion of a federal common law of torts into disrepute. Fuller was uncomfortable with the Court's strict application of the fellow servant rule. He never wrote an opinion that invoked the rule, and he endeavored to restrict its operation as much as possible. Fuller appeared to realize instinctively that the fellow servant rule originated in an earlier day and was not a suitable vehicle through which to

---

10. *Ibid.*, at 401, 411. For a discussion of Field's views see Freyer, *Forums of Order*, 124–125; Semonche, *Charting the Future*, 42–43.

11. Lester P. Schoene and Frank Watson, "Workmen's Compensation on Interstate Railways," 47 *Harvard Law Review* 389, 391–393 (1934).

decide liability for workplace injuries in a modern industrial society.[12] His dislike of the rule was vindicated when Congress abolished it for railroad employees in 1906 as part of the Employers' Liability Act.[13] Likewise, states began to enact workmen's compensation laws early in the twentieth century, thus inaugurating a new scheme for compensating injured employees and gradually displacing the federal common law of industrial accidents.[14]

A preoccupation by scholars with fellow servant cases, however, has produced an unduly bleak assessment of the Fuller Court's handling of industrial accidents. The justices often proved sympathetic to tort claimants. For example, the Court imposed a nondelegable obligation on employers to provide safe tools and a safe workplace. In a line of decisions the justices found railroads liable for injuries arising from faulty roadbeds or defective machinery. "The general rule," Fuller insisted in 1896, "undoubtedly is that a railroad company is bound to provide suitable and safe materials and structures in the construction of its roads and appurtenances."[15] In a related development, in *Chicago, Kansas and Western Railroad Company v. Pontius* (1895), Fuller wrote an opinion sustaining application of a Kansas statute that made railroads liable for injuries to employees caused by negligence of other employees.

Moreover, under Fuller the Court adhered to a number of procedural rules favorable to plaintiffs. In *Inland and Seaboard Coasting Company v. Tolson* (1891) the justices placed the burden of proof of contributory negligence on the defendant. The Court also adopted the last clear chance doctrine, which held that the contributory negligence of an injured party will not defeat an action if the defendant by reasonable care might have avoided the consequences of the injured party's negligence.[16] The justices assisted plaintiffs in another way. They ruled in *Union Pacific Railway Company v. Botsford* (1891) that in federal suits an injured plaintiff was not required to submit to a medical examination before trial. At the least,

---

12. Willard L. King, *Melville Weston Fuller: Chief Justice of the United States, 1888–1910* (New York: Macmillan, 1950, reprint Chicago: University of Chicago Press, 1967), 183–184; Robert P. Reeder, "Chief Justice Fuller," 59 *University of Pennsylvania Law Review* 1, 11 (1910).

13. The Fuller Court struck down the Employers' Liability Act on grounds that the measure exceeded congressional power over commerce. See chapter 5.

14. See Lawrence M. Friedman and Jack Ladinsky, "Social Change and the Law of Industrial Accidents," 67 *Columbia Law Review* 59–72 (1967).

15. *Union Pacific Railway Company v. O'Brien,* 161 U.S. 451, 457 (1896). For a list of opinions by Fuller that sustained verdicts in favor of injured employees see Robert P. Reeder, "Chief Justice Fuller," 11 (1910).

16. *Grand Trunk Railway Company v. Ives,* 144 U.S. 408 (1892).

these decisions call into question the image of federal diversity jurisdiction as a forum uniformly supportive of corporate defendants.

Late in Fuller's tenure the Supreme Court decided a case that foreshadowed the eventual overthrow of the *Swift* doctrine. At issue in *Kuhn v. Fairmont Coal Company* (1910) was the liability of a mining company for failure to furnish adequate support to surface land in West Virginia while it exercised its contractual rights to excavate coal.[17] After commencement of the federal action, the West Virginia Court of Appeals construed a similar deed in favor of the mining company. The company argued that the federal courts were bound to accept the West Virginia decision as determinative of the rights of the parties. By a 4 to 3 margin the justices disagreed, ruling that the case presented questions of general law in which the federal courts could exercise an independent judgment. The case aroused controversy because it vividly demonstrated the displacement of state law even with respect to real property, a matter that was historically seen as local in nature and subject to state regulation. Justice Oliver Wendell Holmes, for the dissenters, inveighed against what he considered an inappropriate extension of diversity jurisdiction and an invasion of state authority. Taking aim at "the uncertainty and vacillation of the theory" behind the *Swift* principle,[18] he maintained that state law was the source of legal authority in federal diversity cases. The Holmes dissent initiated a new round of criticism of federal common law and led in time to abandonment of the *Swift* doctrine in *Erie Railroad Company v. Tompkins* (1938).

There was a close affinity between the Fuller Court's expansive assertion of diversity jurisdiction and its constitutional jurisprudence. Reliance on federal common law in diversity cases paralleled the Court's aggressive review of state regulatory legislation under the due process clause and the dormant commerce power and its willingness to enjoin the enforcement of unconstitutional state laws. Fuller and his associates generally sought to bring economic activity within the protective orbit of the federal judiciary. Whatever the shortcomings of the *Swift* principle,[19] the justices discerningly recognized the pressing need for a national law to govern the conduct of business across state lines.

---

17. The *Kuhn* litigation is discussed in Freyer, *Forums of Order*, 144–145; Semonche, *Charting the Future*, 241–242.

18. *Kuhn v. Fairmont Coal Company*, 215 U.S. 349, 370 (1910).

19. For the larger controversy surrounding the *Swift* and *Erie* decisions see Tony A. Freyer, *Harmony & Dissonance: The Swift and Erie Cases in American Federalism* (New York: New York University Press, 1981).

FEDERAL RAILROAD SAFETY LEGISLATION

As the number of railroad accidents mounted in the late nineteenth century, Congress moved to assure the safety of employees and travelers by passing the Safety Appliance Act in 1893.[20] This measure required railroads to equip their engines with power brakes and their cars with automatic couplers. It also provided that an employee injured by any train operating in violation of the statute was deemed not to have assumed the risk of unsafe conditions.

The Fuller Court was called upon to interpret the Safety Appliance Act in *Johnson v. Southern Pacific Company* (1904). The plaintiff, a brakeman, was hurt while coupling an engine and a dining car. Although both vehicles were equipped with automatic couplers, they were of different types and were not compatible upon impact. Fuller, for a unanimous bench, gave a generous reading to the statute and ordered a new trial for the plaintiff. As he aptly observed,

> the object was to protect the lives and limbs of railroad employees by rendering it unnecessary for a man operating the couplers to go between the ends of the cars, and that object would be defeated, not necessarily by the use of automatic couplers of different kinds, but if those different kinds would not automatically couple with each other. The point was that the railroad companies should be compelled, respectively, to adopt devices, whatever they were, which would act so far uniformly as to eliminate the danger consequent on men going between cars.

More important, Fuller emphasized that the act was remedial in nature and should be broadly construed "to promote the public welfare by securing the safety of employees and travelers."[21] The *Johnson* decision invigorated enforcement of the Safety Appliance Act and again demonstrated that Fuller and his colleagues did not always take the side of corporate defendants in tort litigation. It also signaled the Supreme Court's readiness to accept legislative reform of the common law of industrial accidents.

Indeed, three years later the justices interpreted the Safety Appliance Act to furnish enhanced protection to injured employees. Despite the act's elimination of the defense of assumption of the risk, railroads continued to invoke contributory negligence as a bar to actions. In *Schlemmer*

---

20. See Ari and Olive Hoogenboom, *A History of the ICC: From Panacea to Palliative* (New York: Norton, 1976), 34.

21. *Johnson v. Southern Pacific Company*, 196 U.S. 1, 16, 17 (1904). On *Johnson* see Purcell, *Litigation and Inequality*, 164.

v. Buffalo, Rochester and Pittsburgh Railway Company (1907) a widow brought a suit for the wrongful death of her husband caused by the failure of the defendant railroad to equip its cars with automatic couplers in accordance with the act. The Pennsylvania courts dismissed the action on the basis of contributory negligence by the deceased brakeman. Writing for a majority of five, Holmes, joined by Fuller, tellingly pointed out that statutory modification of common law negligence principles "is due to an opinion that men who work with their hands have not always the freedom and equality of position assumed by the doctrine of *laissez faire* to exist." He declared that assumption of the risk "in this broad sense obviously shades into negligence as commonly understood." Holmes in effect equated the two doctrines for purposes of applying the statute. The remedial purpose of the statute, Holmes concluded, would be undercut if an employee's rights could be "sacrificed by simply charging him with assumption of the risk under another name."[22] Justice Brewer, in dissent, stressed the distinction between assumption of the risk and contributory negligence and argued that the act did not set aside the defense of contributory negligence.

In *St. Louis, Iron Mountain and Southern Railway Company v. Taylor* (1908) the Fuller Court confirmed this broad construction of the Safety Appliance Act. The justices unanimously ruled that the purpose of the act was to supplant the common law and impose an absolute duty on railroads. Use of railroad cars without required safety devices constituted a violation of the act and gave rise to tort liability. Acknowledging that the statute burdened railroads, the Court added, "It is quite conceivable that Congress, contemplating the inevitable hardship of such injuries, and hoping to diminish the economic loss to the community resulting from them, should deem it wise to impose their burdens upon those who could measurably control their causes, instead of upon those who are in the main helpless in that regard."[23] This record makes plain that the Court under Fuller vigorously implemented the Safety Appliance Act and supported congressional efforts to improve railroad safety.

CORPORATE GOVERNANCE

As business enterprise grew rapidly in size during the late nineteenth century, corporate management was as a practical matter increasingly divorced from the stockholders. As a consequence, stockholders resorted to lawsuits to obtain redress for fraud or mismanagement by

---

22. *Schlemmer v. Buffalo, Rochester and Pittsburg Railway Company*, 205 U.S. 1, 12, 13 (1907).
23. *St. Louis, Iron Mountain and Southern Railway Company v. Taylor*, 210 U.S. 281, 295–296 (1908).

officers and directors. The courts were called upon to formulate appropriate standards of responsibility to govern corporate managers. Fuller made a major contribution to this process with his landmark opinion in *Briggs v. Spaulding* (1891). The suit was instituted by the receiver of an insolvent national bank against the bank directors to recover losses caused by mismanagement of the officers. The receiver did not contend that the directors were guilty of any dishonesty but rather that they had failed to supervise the officers and thus breached their fiduciary duties.

Rejecting this argument, Fuller, for a majority of five, devised the business judgment rule. He denied that directors functioned as guarantors of the fidelity of corporate officers. Instead, he maintained that directors were bound to that degree of care "which ordinarily prudent and diligent men would exercise under similar circumstances." In a classic and much quoted articulation of the duties of directors, Fuller stated,

> Directors must exercise ordinary care and prudence in the administration of the affairs of a bank, and this includes something more than officiating as figure heads. They are entitled under the law to commit banking business, as defined, to their duly authorized officers, but this does not absolve them from the duty of reasonable supervision, nor ought they to be permitted to be shielded from liability because of want of knowledge of wrongdoing, if that ignorance is the result of gross inattention.

On the facts presented he concluded that the directors were not guilty of passive negligence in allowing the bank president to continue in office. The four dissenters, in an opinion by Justice Harlan, asserted that the directors had been supinely negligent in supervising the bank officers and had not used such care "as men of ordinary diligence exercise in respect to their own business."[24] Fuller may well have been unduly generous in assessing the prudence of the bank directors, but he established an enduring standard of care for directors of corporations. Under the business judgment rule courts have refrained from reviewing good faith business decisions and have rarely found directors liable for negligence. As a practical matter the rule increased power in the hands of corporate directors and underscored the separation of stockholders and corporate management.[25]

---

24. *Briggs v. Spaulding,* 141 U.S. 132, 152, 165, 166 (1891).
25. Hovenkamp, *Enterprise and American Law,* 62–63.

EQUITY RECEIVERSHIPS

The Fuller Court gave further evidence of its instrumentalist approach to law by approving a pioneering use of equity receiverships. The receivership issue stemmed from the chaotic financial conditions in the railroad industry during the late nineteenth century. Since there was no bankruptcy law in force in the 1880s, financially troubled railroads turned to the federal courts and requested the appointment of a receiver. Despite lack of statutory authority, federal judges relied on their general equity powers to establish receiverships. Historically, courts of equity had named an outside person to collect the assets of an insolvent business for the limited purpose of distributing the property among the creditors. In 1884 the receivership of the Wabash, St. Louis and Pacific Railway Company broke new ground in several respects. This marked the first occasion that a receiver had been named on motion of a railroad rather than by its creditors. In addition, the court named the managers of the Wabash as receivers. Last, the receivers were expected to operate the railroad, conserve its assets, defer payments of debt, and reorganize the line on a financially viable basis.[26]

This unprecedented resort to equity receivership rested on important policy considerations. Unlike many other types of property, a railroad was an economic unit and could be disposed of only as a going concern. Public interest, moreover, dictated that transportation services be continued if at all possible. Consequently, the contractual rights of creditors and bondholders had to be subordinated to preservation of the line. The result of this reasoning was a greatly enlarged conception of receivership in which the federal courts were drawn into the business of supervising railroads.[27]

Despite strong criticism of equity railroad receiverships, a unanimous Supreme Court, in an opinion by Fuller, had no difficulty sustaining the practice. Although they recognized the extraordinary nature of these receiverships, the justices upheld the Wabash appointment in *Quincy, Missouri and Pacific Railroad Company v. Humphreys* (1892). Fuller explained that the relief sought "was obviously framed upon the theory that an insolvent railroad corporation has a standing in a court of equity to surrender its property into the custody of the court, to be preserved and

---

26. Albro Martin, "Railroads and the Equity Receivership: An Essay on Institutional Change," 34 *Journal of Economic History* 685 (1974). See also Charles Warren, *The Supreme Court in United States History*, rev. ed. (Boston: Little, Brown, 1926), vol. 2, 639.

27. Keller, *Affairs of State*, 425–427. For a skeptical contemporary reaction see Seymour D. Thompson, "The Court Management of Railroads," 27 *American Law Review* 31 (1893).

disposed of according to the rights of its various creditors, and, in the meantime, operated in the public interest."[28] The Wabash precedent soon became the model for many railroad receiverships during the 1890s. Viewed in its most positive light, railroad receivership administration showed the ingenuity of the federal courts in devising a means to balance competing economic interests while keeping an insolvent carrier in operation.

The widespread use of railroad receivers was soon engulfed in a heated political controversy. Federal judges sometimes instructed receivers, as officers of the court, to disregard state laws regulating or taxing railroads. Attempts by state officials to enforce state laws against lines under receivership were treated as contempt of court. Such actions aroused bitter attacks in the South, where political leaders charged that railroad receivers favored northern creditors rather than local interests.[29] Feelings were exacerbated by the fact that many insolvent railroads remained under receivership for years. In 1894 the South Carolina legislature adopted a memorial to Congress bitterly protesting that the federal courts were usurping authority to control railroads and thus were invading state autonomy. The lawmakers took particular aim at Fuller for an 1893 ruling in which he stressed that railroad property in the hands of a receiver was not subject to a state tax levy in violation of court order.[30]

But in economic terms the equity receivership was a highly successful legal mechanism. It helped many railroads weather the depression of the 1890s. Congress incorporated the equity receivership into the bankruptcy laws in 1933 and thus provided a statutory basis for the reorganization of insolvent lines. With equity receiverships the Fuller Court embraced a bold innovation that, on the whole, served the nation well. Indeed, current reorganization law under the Bankruptcy Act is a direct descendant of this novel device.

BANKRUPTCY

The Constitution vests power in Congress "to establish . . . uniform laws on the subject of bankruptcies throughout the United States." After years of acrimonious debate, much of it sectional in nature, Congress fi-

---

28. *Quincy, Missouri and Pacific Railroad Company v. Humphreys*, 145 U.S. 82, 95 (1892).

29. Scheiber, "Federalism, the Southern Regional Economy, and Public Policy Since 1865," 78–80.

30. Memorial of the General Assembly of the State of South Carolina . . . in the Matter of Receivers of Railroad Corporations and Equity Jurisdiction of the Courts of the United States, 28 *American Law Review* 161 (1894). See *In re Tyler*, 149 U.S. 164 (1893).

nally enacted an enduring bankruptcy law in 1898, taking account of the competing interests of debtors and creditors and seeking to achieve an equitable distribution of the bankrupt's property.[31] A national bankruptcy system was closely linked to federal control of interstate commerce and to the maturing national market, both matters of vital concern to the Fuller Court.

Fuller and his associates repeatedly upheld far-reaching congressional authority over bankruptcy and, in so doing, helped establish the foundations of modern bankruptcy practice. In the important case of *Hanover National Bank v. Moyses* (1902) Fuller, for a unanimous Court, sustained the constitutionality of the 1898 act against a variety of challenges. He established three basic propositions. First, he adopted a broad view of the class of persons subject to the bankruptcy power. Rejecting the English practice of applying bankruptcy acts only to traders, Fuller determined that the authority of Congress was not limited by English law in force when the Constitution was adopted. Rather, he stated, Congress had plenary power over the whole subject of bankruptcies and could provide that individuals other than traders might be adjudged bankrupts. Second, Fuller affirmed the authority of Congress to authorize the retroactive impairment of contracts. "The subject of 'bankruptcies'", Fuller observed, "includes the power to discharge the debtor from his contracts and legal liabilities, as well as to distribute his property. The grant to Congress involves the power to impair the obligation of contracts, and this the States were forbidden to do."[32] Third, he addressed the uniformity requirement of the bankruptcy clause. Fuller held that uniformity was geographic, not personal, and therefore Congress could give effect to exemptions prescribed by state laws even though this produced different results for debtors in different states.

Closely related to the reach of congressional power under the bankruptcy clause was the jurisdiction of the federal courts in bankruptcy matters. At issue in *In re Watts and Sachs* (1903) was a conflict between the state-appointed receiver of an insolvent corporation and a federal district court enforcing the bankruptcy statute. Fuller, again writing for the Court, maintained that "the operation of the bankruptcy laws of the United States cannot be defeated by insolvent commercial corporations

---

31. Charles Warren, *Bankruptcy in United States History* (Cambridge, Mass: Harvard University Press, 1935). See also Peter J. Coleman, *Debtors and Creditors in America: Insolvency, Imprisonment for Debt, and Bankruptcy, 1607–1900* (Madison: State Historical Society of Wisconsin, 1974), 269–293, and F. Regis Noel, *A History of the Bankruptcy Law* (Washington: Charles H. Potter, 1919), 157–180.

32. *Hanover National Bank v. Moyses,* 186 U.S. 181, 188 (1902).

applying to be wound up under state statutes. The bankruptcy law is paramount, and the jurisdiction of the Federal courts in bankruptcy, when properly invoked in the administration of the affairs of insolvent persons and corporations, is essentially exclusive."[33] This ruling established the superior jurisdiction of the federal courts sitting in bankruptcy to administer the affairs of insolvent individuals or corporations.

The question of the extent to which the Bankruptcy Act relieved a bankrupt from debts also occupied the time of the justices. Fuller and his colleagues fashioned the policy of excepting spousal and child support payment from discharge in bankruptcy. In *Audubon v. Shufeldt* (1901) the justices anticipated subsequent legislation by unanimously declaring that "alimony does not arise from any business transaction, but from the relation of marriage. It is not founded on contract, express or implied, but on the natural and legal duty of the husband to support the wife."[34] From this premise the Court found that a claim for alimony was a duty rather than a debt within the meaning of the act and was therefore not barred by a discharge. The Bankruptcy Act was amended in 1903 to expressly exempt alimony and child support from discharge. Finding that the amendment was merely declaratory of the true meaning of the statute, the Fuller Court reiterated its position in *Wetmore v. Markoe* (1904): "The bankruptcy law should receive such an interpretation as will effectuate its beneficent purposes and not make it an instrument to deprive dependent wife and children of the support and maintenance due them from the husband and father, which it has ever been the purpose of the law to enforce."[35]

The creation of a permanent bankruptcy system reflected the push by corporate enterprise in the late nineteenth century for a systematic and national method of discharging insolvent debtors while safeguarding the interests of creditors. Not surprisingly, Fuller and his associates gave forceful approval to the new bankruptcy scheme. Their decisions provided the building block for subsequent developments in bankruptcy law.

PATENTS

The Constitution vested Congress with authority to award an "exclusive Right" to inventors "for limited Times." In the Patent Act of 1790 Congress made patents available for new and useful inventions. Con-

---

33. *In re Watts and Sachs,* 190 U.S. 1, 27 (1903).
34. *Audubon v. Shufeldt,* 181 U.S. 575, 577 (1901).
35. *Wetmore v. Markoe,* 196 U.S. 68, 77 (1904).

gress revamped the patent statute in 1836 and created a separate Patent Office to handle patent applications. The patent system rested on the rationale that grants of limited monopoly protection promoted the public interest by encouraging mechanical innovation. Such thinking, however, ran counter to a deep-seated aversion to monopoly and belief in competition as the best stimulus for technological advance.[36] The late nineteenth century witnessed an extraordinary outpouring of inventive activity. The number of patents granted by the Patent Office mounted dramatically. As a consequence, Fuller and his colleagues heard a steady stream of cases in which inventors alleged infringement of their patents. The patent jurisprudence of the Fuller Court reflected the unresolved tension between exclusive privilege for inventors and the public interest in access to new devices.

A recurring issue concerned the standard of patentability. The Fuller Court tended to construe patent requirements strictly, in keeping with its suspicion of state-conferred monopoly and preference for free-market competition. The Patent Act of 1790 specified novelty and utility as the primary criteria for patentability. Fuller, however, speaking for the Court in *Smith v. Whitman Saddle Company* (1893), stressed "genius or invention" as an additional prerequisite for a patent, a concept that persisted until enactment of the present patent statute in 1952. This insistence upon inventive faculty set a high standard of patentability and led the Court to invalidate many patents during Fuller's tenure. Moreover, the chief and his colleagues placed particular emphasis on the level of innovation necessary to secure a patent. Thus in *McClain v. Ortmayer* (1891) they invalidated a patent for a horse collar pad and pointed out that the patent system "is strictly limited to the invention of what is new and useful."[37] At the same term the justices in *Patent Clothing Company v. Glover* (1891) also voided a patent to strengthen pants on grounds that there was no patentable novelty. Similarly, the Court struck down a patent for an apparatus to transfer grain in *Richards v. Chase Elevator Company* (1895). In reaching this result the justices reaffirmed the rule that a mere aggregation of familiar elements producing no new result does not constitute a patentable combination.

Still other objections were found to patent claims. In *The Incandescent Lamp Patent* (1895), which arose out of an infringement suit between competing inventors of electric lighting, the Court took the position that

---

36. Bruce W. Bugbee, *Genesis of American Patent and Copyright Law* (Washington: Public Affairs Press, 1967), 125–158; Kermit L. Hall, *The Magic Mirror: Law in American History* (New York: Oxford University Press, 1989), 92.
37. *McClain v. Ortmayer,* 141 U.S. 419, 428 (1891).

a vague and uncertain description of the patented device could not serve as the basis for a valid patent. The justices expressed concern that an ambiguous patent monopoly would prevent other inventors from conducting further experiments to improve products. Fuller and his associates also pointed out that the patent system protected actual inventions, not mere ideas. "A conception of the mind," the Court declared in *Clark Thread Company v. Willimantic Linen Company* (1891), "is not an invention until represented in some physical form."[38]

On the other hand, the Fuller Court was not uniformly hostile to patent claims. The justices sustained a number of patents when the requisite innovation and inventive genius were demonstrated. In several cases the Court relied on commercial success to buttress its conclusion that particular patents were valid. For example, the justices in *Magowan v. New York Belting and Packing Company* (1891) upheld a patent for india-rubber packing and observed that extensive public use was "pregnant evidence of its novelty, value and usefulness."[39] Despite doubtful evidence of novelty, the Fuller Court in *The Barbed Wire Patent* (1892) likewise recognized the validity of a wire fence patent. The justices cited the widespread use of the barbed wire fence in cattle districts as demonstrating patentability.

Moreover, in *United States v. Bell Telephone Company* (1897) Fuller and his associates resolved a complex and prolonged conflict over telephone patents in favor of the Bell Telephone Company. In so doing the justices rebuffed an attempt by the federal government to set aside the telephone patents on grounds that they were wrongfully issued. Writing for the Court, Justice Brewer found no evidence of any fraud or error sufficient to justify cancellation. He broadly stressed the property rights of the inventor and suggested that one purpose of the patent system was to encourage disclosure of inventions. Brewer observed, "The inventor is one who has discovered something of value. It is his absolute property. He may withhold the knowledge of it from the public, and he may insist upon all the advantages and benefits which the statute promises to him who discloses to the public his invention."[40] This comment underscored the notion that the patent protection rested on an implicit contractual basis whereby the inventor exchanged public disclosure of his work for a limited monopoly.

The Fuller Court also professed a willingness to safeguard patent holders against infringement by the federal government. In *Belknap v. Schild* (1896) the justices declared that "the United States have no more

---

38. *Clark Thread Company v. Willimantic Linen Company,* 140 U.S. 481, 489 (1891).
39. *Magowan v. New York Belting and Packing Company,* 141 U.S. 332, 343 (1891).
40. *United States v. Bell Telephone Company,* 167 U.S. 224, 250 (1897).

right than any private person to use a patented invention without license of the patentee or making compensation to him." They robbed this protection of meaning, however, by holding that under the doctrine of sovereign immunity the government was not subject to a patent infringement suit. Moreover, officers and agents acting for the government were not individually liable because they had not made any profits from the wrongful use of plaintiff's invention. Little wonder that Harlan and Field, in dissent, complained that "the government may well be regarded as organized robbery so far as the rights of patentees are concerned."[41] Despite their protest, the notion of governmental immunity remains embedded in contemporary patent law.

It is not surprising that the justices were called upon to determine whether the exercise of patent rights conflicted with the Sherman Anti-Trust Act. A frequent complaint was that corporate patent holders attempted to fix the price at which patented products could be resold, a move that lessened competition. In this regard Fuller and his colleagues affirmed the right of a patent holder to set the price of patented articles and to assign the right to sell such goods upon condition that the licensee charge a fixed price. Declaring that the "very object of these [patent] laws is monopoly," Justice Rufus W. Peckham ruled in *Bement v. National Harrow Company* (1902) that price-fixing conditions imposed by the patent holder would be enforced.[42] He concluded that patent license arrangements to maintain retail prices were not illegal under the Sherman Act.

As patents became an increasingly important aspect of national economic life, Fuller and his associates were caught up in the tension between the need to stimulate creativity and the desire to protect the public from unwarranted special privilege. Although the justices broke little new ground with respect to patent jurisprudence, they wrestled with difficult issues that remain in contention to the present.[43]

COPYRIGHT

The Constitution also confers on Congress authority to grant authors the sole right to their writings. Congress enacted the first copyright law in 1790 and made major amendments in 1831, 1870, and 1909. In several cases the Fuller Court was called upon to define the nature

---

41. *Belknap v. Schild*, 161 U.S. 10, 28 (1896).

42. *Bement v. National Harrow Company*, 186 U.S. 70, 91 (1902). See Horace R. Lamb, "The Relation of the Patent Law to the Federal Anti-Trust Laws," 12 *Cornell Law Quarterly* 261, 265–269 (1927).

43. Morton Keller, *Regulating a New Economy: Public Policy and Economic Change in America, 1900–1933* (Cambridge, Mass.: Harvard University Press, 1990), 107–109.

and scope of copyright protection. The Court's handling of copyright privilege, like its handling of patent jurisprudence, was marked by the competing goals of monopoly protection to encourage intellectual production and the public's interest in free access to information.[44]

Two early decisions concerning the rights of judicial reporters in their volumes of cases illustrate this point. In *Banks v. Manchester* (1888) the Fuller Court invalidated an Ohio law permitting the state supreme court's official reporter to claim copyright in the court's opinions on grounds that such matter properly belonged in the public domain. But in *Callaghan v. Myers* (1888) the Court approved protection for original material contributed to case reports by the reporter himself, such as headnotes, statements of facts, and arguments of counsel.

In considering the amount and quality of originality required for copyright, the justices walked a similar fine line. The Fuller Court maintained that under the Constitution, copyright protection was confined to writings produced by intellectual labor. Justice Field, speaking for the Court in *Higgins v. Keuffel* (1891), held that advertising labels that merely described a product were not a subject for copyright. "To be entitled to a copyright," he explained, "the article must have by itself some value as a composition, at least to the extent of serving some purpose other than as a mere advertisement or designation of the subject to which it is attached."[45]

But the justices were prepared to sustain copyright protection for pictorial illustrations that served advertising purposes. The case of *Bleistein v. Donaldson Lithographing Company* (1903) raised the question whether colored lithographs designed to promote a circus were proper subjects of copyright. By a 7 to 2 vote the Court sensibly ruled that advertising posters could be copyrighted. Justice Holmes, who wrote the opinion, noted that the pictures had commercial value and that they had aesthetic appeal to the general public. Pointing to the artistic controversy initially surrounding the paintings of Goya and Manet, he cautioned against a narrow understanding of the worth of illustrations. "It would be a dangerous undertaking," Holmes added, "for persons trained only to law to constitute themselves final judges of the worth of pictorial illustrations."[46]

---

44. Bugbee, *Genesis of American Patent and Copyright Law*, 125–158; Keller, *Regulating a New Economy*, 109–110; Richard Rogers Bowker, *Copyright: Its History and Its Law* (Boston: Houghton Mifflin, 1912); Lyman Ray Patterson, *Copyright in Historical Perspective* (Nashville: Vanderbilt University Press, 1968), 180–221.

45. *Higgins v. Keuffel,* 140 U.S. 428, 431 (1891).

46. *Bleistein v. Donaldson Lithographing Company,* 188 U.S. 239, 251 (1903).

The Fuller Court's determination to balance the rights of authors and those of the public was also evident in *Holmes v. Hurst* (1899). This case presented the question whether serial publication of a book in a monthly magazine before securing a copyright vitiated the author's rights. The Court affirmed the long-standing rule that copyright protection was wholly statutory and rested upon compliance with certain statutory formalities, not upon common-law principles. Therefore, the author's rights in the subsequent book were lost by virtue of its prior publication in the form of magazine articles.

The only major stumble in the Fuller Court's copyright jurisprudence occurred when it confronted the vexing problems posed by the emergence of new technologies. In *White-Smith Music Publishing Company v. Apollo Company* (1908) the Court determined that perforated rolls of music used in player pianos were not copyrightable works. This dubious decision unnecessarily restricted the scope of copyright. Mindful that copyright protection was statutory in nature, however, the Fuller Court was reluctant to ascribe to Congress an intention to permit copyright of mechanical musical instruments despite adverse economic consequences to manufacturers. In a concurring opinion Justice Holmes bowed to precedent but lamented that denying protection to developing media "give[s] to copyright less scope than its rational significance and the ground on which it is granted seems to me to demand."[47] The approach adopted by the Fuller Court in *White-Smith* would not be corrected by Congress until passage of the Copyright Act of 1976.

---

47. *White-Smith Music Publishing Company v. Apollo Company*, 209 U.S. 1, 19.

9

Betting on The Future

Fuller began to experience ill health during the 1909–10 term of the
Supreme Court and became visibly more feeble. He died at his summer
home in Sorrento, Maine, on July 4, 1910, at the age of seventy-seven
and was buried in Chicago. He had served as chief justice for twenty-two
years, a period longer than that of any other chief in American history
except John Marshall and Roger B. Taney.

While he was a student at Bowdoin College Fuller wrote an essay addressing the question "Are great intellectual powers preferable to energy
and decision of character?" He revealingly answered in the negative.
"The world furnishes many examples," he observed, "of the superiority
of the truly earnest and laborious mind over the merely intellectual."[1]
Much of Fuller's subsequent career vindicated this thesis. Perseverance,
hard work, a convivial personality, distinguished achievements at the bar,
and a measure of luck propelled him into the center chair of the Supreme Court. There he became an institutional and administrative
leader of the justices rather than a dominant intellectual force. Although
he wrote some significant opinions dealing with constitutional and private law issues, he preferred to guide the Court behind the scenes. Fuller
was instrumental in orchestrating a conservative majority and directing
the Court toward a more active role in American society.

The most important dimension of jurisprudence during the Fuller era
was dedication to entrepreneurial liberty and the rights of property owners. Closely related to this judicial policy was a determination to protect
the free flow of trade among the states and to fashion a general common
law to govern interstate commercial transactions. To these ends Fuller
and his colleagues developed the doctrine of substantive due process, be-

---

1. Willard L. King, *Melville Weston Fuller: Chief Justice of the United States, 1888–1910* (New
York: Macmillan, 1950, reprint Chicago: University of Chicago Press, 1967), 22–23.

gan to apply the takings clause, and strengthened the place of the federal judiciary in the constitutional system. The Fuller Court's efforts to safeguard economic rights should be understood as a fulfillment of the property-conscious values that shaped the constitution-making process in 1787.[2] Supporting the Court's decisions was the classical economic theory dominant in the late nineteenth century that saw government intervention in the free market as usually harmful to the public welfare. Utilitarian considerations also influenced the justices. The need to encourage investment capital as the engine of economic growth was repeatedly emphasized in rulings during the Fuller period.

Yet the pattern of decision making by the Fuller Court was complex and took account of other constitutional principles. Foremost among these was a commitment to federalism. At the turn of the century large segments of society still looked to the states rather than the federal government to solve social problems. Consistent with this preference for limited and balanced government, the Supreme Court, and Fuller in particular, sought to preserve a large measure of autonomy for the states in handling social issues and criminal justice. Nor did the justices act as the single-minded champions of corporate interests so often depicted by historians. On the contrary, a wide variety of regulatory measures passed constitutional muster during Fuller's tenure. There was, in other words, a degree of tension between judicial solicitude toward property rights and the growing national market on one hand and the pull of traditional states' rights sentiment on the other. Resolution of this conflict was not free from difficulty.

It also deserves emphasis that Fuller and his associates usually operated within the general climate of public sentiment. As one scholar has aptly concluded, "*Lochner* era jurists realized the importance of public opinion in the evolution of constitutional law. In propounding laissez-faire constitutionalism, they believed public opinion was on their side."[3] The justices shared the economic and social views of the age and spoke for the dominant political alliance. In many respects the Fuller Court's approach to jurisprudential issues mirrored the attitudes of American society as a whole. Like most Americans of the period, for instance, the justices displayed little sympathy for the claims of social outsiders, such as unions and racial minorities. The Court tended to ratify majoritarian preferences and rarely challenged legislation clearly reflecting the wishes

---

2. James W. Ely, Jr., *The Guardian of Every Other Right: A Constitutional History of Property Rights* (New York: Oxford University Press, 1992), 42–58.

3. Stephen A. Siegel, "*Lochner* Era Jurisprudence and the American Constitutional Tradition," 70 *North Carolina Law Review* 108 (1991).

of the majority. To be sure, Fuller and his colleagues made aggressive use of judicial review, but it was typically directed against statutes that were enacted at the behest of special-interest groups or that appeared to lack majority support. Even with respect to such controversial decisions as *Pollock* and *E. C. Knight*, the Fuller Court acted in harmony with what it perceived to be the prevailing current of public opinion. Notwithstanding an activist bent, the Court under Fuller was mindful of its limits.

It remains to examine the legacy of the Fuller Court. Any assessment of segments of the history of the Supreme Court is a hazardous enterprise. Evaluations of judicial performance are subjective; they depend in the last analysis largely upon value preferences. At the outset one must recognize that Supreme Court decisions initiate a dialogue between the justices and the public. To be effective, decisions must accord with the march of history. The justices of the Fuller Court, in Alexander M. Bickel's phrase, "placed their own bet on the future."[4] The legacy of Fuller and his colleagues rests upon how one reads the verdict of history.

There is no denying that over time many of Fuller's judicial achievements have been eclipsed. The nation no longer embraces a constitutional order founded on the principles of limited government, states' rights, and respect for private property. Fuller's attempts to cabin congressional tax and regulatory authority ultimately proved futile. After a lacerating struggle over the New Deal program, the Supreme Court largely abandoned its long-standing concern with economic rights in 1937. Likewise, the post-World War II civil rights movement has discredited the Fuller Court's acquiescence in the policy of racial segregation in the South. To modern eyes, much of Fuller's handiwork seems to belong to a distant era.

From another perspective, however, the jurisprudence of the Fuller years may be seen as pointing toward modern American society. The justices glimpsed a future based on capitalist enterprise and attempted, in the main, to encourage the emerging industrial order. Indeed, the Fuller Court directly contributed to growth of large corporations, massive industrialization, a national market for goods, and increased national wealth. The new industrial order, legitimated by the justices, has become a permanent feature of American life. Reflecting its faith in private economic ordering, the Court under Fuller viewed nascent government regulations with great skepticism. Although a web of regulations gradually displaced the free market after 1937, interest in property rights and

---

4. Alexander M. Bickel, *The Supreme Court and the Idea of Progress* (New York: Harper & Row, 1970), 99.

entrepreneurial liberty did not expire with the coming of New Deal. The American polity remained suspicious about governmental control of the economy.[5] Recent decades have produced efforts to deregulate some industries, to revive constitutional protection for the rights of property owners, and even to restore the Tenth Amendment as a constraint on Congressional power. The takings clause has figured prominently in recent constitutional adjudication. Thus many of the issues addressed by Fuller and his colleagues have reemerged as part of the constitutional dialogue. Seen in this light, the Fuller Court was a better prophet than historians have generally recognized.

The work of the Fuller Court was important for another reason. It made an enduring contribution to the constitutional system by establishing the Supreme Court as a key participant in American governance. Fuller and his associates enhanced the power of the federal courts to enforce the Constitution. Fuller's tenure marked a turning point in the evolution of judicial authority; under his leadership, the Supreme Court rejected a passive position and became increasingly activist in reviewing economic legislation. On a broad range of issues the Court showed vitality as a substantive policymaker. Expansive use of federal judicial power in the late twentieth century has built upon precedent from the Fuller era. The doctrine of substantive due process, for instance, while no longer used to protect economic liberty, has been revamped to guarantee a host of noneconomic rights.

Fuller's tenure as chief, then, left a lasting imprint on American law and society. This is not to claim that Fuller and his colleagues were uniquely gifted or always reached meritorious conclusions. But the justices were conscientious individuals who faced a myriad of new and nettlesome challenges in an age of rapid change. In view of recent scholarly criticism of the purposes and effects of governmental regulation of the economy, the conventional view of the Fuller Court needs to be reconsidered.

---

5. Morton Keller, *Regulating a New Economy: Public Policy and Economic Change in America, 1900–1933* (Cambridge, Mass.: Harvard University Press, 1990), 228–230.

APPENDIX

MEMBERS OF THE SUPREME COURT
DURING FULLER'S CHIEF JUSTICESHIP,
1888–1910

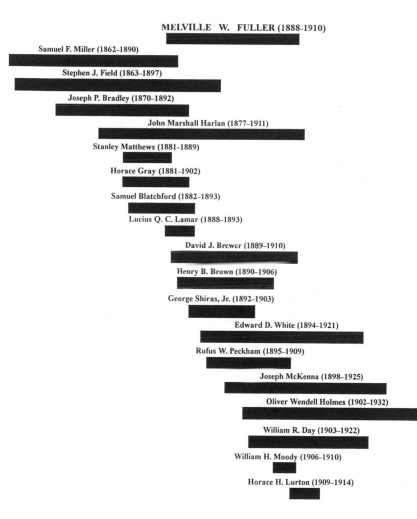

MELVILLE W. FULLER (1888–1910)

Samuel F. Miller (1862–1890)

Stephen J. Field (1863–1897)

Joseph P. Bradley (1870–1892)

John Marshall Harlan (1877–1911)

Stanley Matthews (1881–1889)

Horace Gray (1881–1902)

Samuel Blatchford (1882–1893)

Lucius Q. C. Lamar (1888–1893)

David J. Brewer (1889–1910)

Henry B. Brown (1890–1906)

George Shiras, Jr. (1892–1903)

Edward D. White (1894–1921)

Rufus W. Peckham (1895–1909)

Joseph McKenna (1898–1925)

Oliver Wendell Holmes (1902–1932)

William R. Day (1903–1922)

William H. Moody (1906–1910)

Horace H. Lurton (1909–1914)

DATES OF SERVICE
ON THE FULLER COURT
(ARRANGED IN ORDER OF APPOINTMENT)

Samuel F. Miller	Confirmed July 16, 1862
	Died October 13, 1890
Stephen J. Field	Confirmed March 10, 1863
	Retired December 1, 1897
Joseph P. Bradley	Confirmed March 21, 1870
	Died January 22, 1892
John Marshall Harlan	Confirmed November 29, 1877
	Died October 14, 1911
Stanley Matthews	Confirmed May 12, 1881
	Died March 22, 1889
Horace Gray	Confirmed December 20, 1881
	Died September 15, 1902
Samuel Blatchford	Confirmed March 27, 1882
	Died July 7, 1893
Lucius Q. C. Lamar	Confirmed January 16, 1888
	Died January 23, 1893
Melville W. Fuller	Confirmed July 20, 1888
	Died July 4, 1910
David J. Brewer	Confirmed December 18, 1889
	Died March 28, 1910
Henry B. Brown	Confirmed December 29, 1890
	Retired May 28, 1906
George Shiras, Jr.	Confirmed July 26, 1892
	Retired February 23, 1903
Edward D. White	Confirmed February 19, 1894
	Died May 19, 1921
Rufus W. Peckham	Confirmed December 9, 1895
	Died October 24, 1909
Joseph McKenna	Confirmed January 21, 1898
	Retired January 5, 1925
Oliver Wendell Holmes	Confirmed December 2, 1902
	Retired January 12, 1932
William R. Day	Confirmed February 23, 1903
	Retired November 13, 1922
William H. Moody	Confirmed December 12, 1906
	Retired November 20, 1910
Horace H. Lurton	Confirmed December 20, 1909
	Died July 12, 1914

BIBLIOGRAPHY

PRIMARY SOURCES

Writings of Melville W. Fuller (in chronological order)

"Annual Address," 1877 *Proceedings of the Illinois State Bar Association* 59.

"Sidney Breese. Address delivered on the 9th day of January, 1879, before the State Bar Association on his Life, Character and Services," 11 *Chicago Legal News* 145 (January 25, 1879).

"Constitutional Construction at the Ballot-Box," 1886 *Proceedings of the Illinois State Bar Association* 76.

"The Supreme Court," speech at annual dinner of New England Society of Pennsylvania, December 22, 1888, in Thomas B. Reed, ed., *Modern Eloquence*, vol. 2 (Philadelphia: J. D. Morris, 1900), 513.

"Address in Commemoration of the Inauguration of George Washington . . . Delivered Before the Two Houses of Congress December 11, 1889" (Washington, D.C.: Government Printing Office, 1890, reprinted in 132 U.S. 706 [1889]).

"Anniversary Address," June 28, 1894, in *Addresses and Poem on the Occasion of the One Hundredth Anniversary of . . . Bowdoin College* (Brunswick, Maine, 1894).

"Remarks of Chief Justice Fuller," the Marshall Centennial, February 4, 1901, in 180 U.S. 645 (1901).

Editor, *The Professions* (Boston: Hall and Locke, 1911).

Manuscripts

Correspondence and Reports Relating to the Nomination of Melville W. Fuller, Records of the United States Senate, 50th Congress, National Archives.

Grover Cleveland Papers, Manuscript Division, Library of Congress (LC).

John Chandler Bancroft Davis Papers, Manuscript Division, Library of Congress (LC).

Melville Weston Fuller Papers, Manuscript Division, Library of Congress (LC).
Melville Weston Fuller Papers, Chicago Historical Society (CHS).
Personal Files of Melville W. Fuller, Records Relating to Members of the
    Supreme Court, Record Group 60, General Records of the Department
    of Justice, National Archives.

Government Records and Documents

Journal of the Constitutional Convention of the State of Illinois Convened at
    Springfield, January 7, 1862.
Journal of the House of Representatives of the Twenty-Third General
    Assembly of the State of Illinois . . . January 5, 1863 (Springfield, Ill.:
    Baker and Phillips, 1865).
Journal of the Executive Proceedings of the Senate of the United States of
    America from December 5, 1887, to March 3, 1889. Vol. 26 (Washington,
    D.C.: Government Printing Office, 1901).

Contemporary Published Sources

Bench and Bar of Chicago (Chicago: American Biographical Publishing
    Company, 1883).
Brewer, David J., "Protection to Private Property From Public Attack," 55 *New
    Englander and Yale Review* 97 (1891).
Brown, Henry B., "The Distribution of Property," *Report of the Sixteenth Annual
    Meeting of the American Bar Association* 213 (1893).
"Chief Justice Fuller," 1 *Green Bag* 2 (1889).
Clark, Malcolm, Jr., ed., *Pharisee among the Philistines: The Diary of Judge
    Matthew P. Deady* (2 vols., Portland: Oregon Historical Society, 1975).
Cooley, Thomas M., *A Treatise on the Constitutional Limitations Which Rest upon the
    Legislative Power of the States* (Boston: Little, Brown, 1868, reprint New
    York: Da Capo Press, 1972).
"Correspondence of President Cleveland to Melville W. Fuller," 3 *American
    Scholar* 245 (1934).
"Document: The Appointment of Mr. Justice Harlan," 29 *Indiana Law Journal*
    46 (1953).
Field, Stephen J., "The Centenary of the Supreme Court," February 4, 1890,
    in 134 U.S. 729 (1890).
[Gorham, George C.], *Biographical Notice of Stephen J. Field* [Washington, D.C.,
    1892].
Hicks, Frederick C., ed., *Arguments and Addresses of Joseph Hodges Choate* (St.
    Paul: West, 1926).
Holmes, Oliver W., "The Path of the Law," 10 *Harvard Law Review* 457 (1897).
Howe, Mark DeWolfe, ed., *Holmes-Pollock Letters: The Correspondence of Mr.
    Justice Holmes and Sir Frederick Pollock, 1874–1932*, 2 vols., 2nd ed.
    (Cambridge, Mass.: Harvard University Press, 1961).

"Judge Putnam's Recollections of Chief Justice Fuller," 22 *Green Bag* 526 (1910).

Kent, Charles A., *Memoir of Henry Billings Brown* (New York: Duffield, 1915).

Memorial of the General Assembly of the State of South Carolina . . . in the Matter of Receivers of Railroad Corporations and Equity Jurisdiction of the Courts of the United States, 28 *American Law Review* 161 (1894).

Proceedings of the Bar and Officers of the Supreme Court of the United States in Memory of Melville Weston Fuller, December 10, 1910 (Washington, D.C., 1911).

"Mr. Justice Peckham," 30 *American Law Review* 100 (1896).

Roosevelt, Theodore, "Judges and Progress," 100 *Outlook* 40 (January 6, 1912).

Roosevelt, Theodore, "The New Nationalism", in Roosevelt, *Social Justice and Popular Rule* (New York: Charles Scribner's Sons, 1926).

Taft, William H., "The Right of Private Property," 3 *Michigan Law Journal* 215 (1894).

Tiedeman, Christopher G., "The Income Tax Decisions As An Object Lesson in Constitutional Construction," 6 *Annals of the American Academy of Political and Social Science* 268 (1895).

Tiedeman, Christopher G., *A Treatise on the Limitations of Police Power in the United States* (St. Louis: F. H. Thomas, 1886).

Williston, Samuel, *Life and Law: An Autobiography* (Boston: Little, Brown, 1940).

Wilson, George Grafton, comp., *The Hague Arbitration Cases* (Boston: Ginn and Company, 1915; reprint Littleton, Colo: Fred B. Rothman Co., 1990).

SECONDARY SOURCES

Books

Abraham, Henry J., *Justices and Presidents: A Political History of Appointments to the Supreme Court,* 3rd ed. (New York: Oxford University Press, 1992).

Andreas, A. T., *History of Chicago,* 3 vols. (Chicago: A. T. Andreas, 1884–86, reprint New York: Arno Press, 1975).

Anthony, Elliott, *The Constitutional History of Illinois* (Chicago: Chicago Legal News Print, 1891).

Badger, Reid, *The Great American Fair: The World's Columbian Exposition & American Culture* (Chicago: Nelson Hall, 1979).

Baer, Judith A., *The Chains of Protection: The Judicial Response to Women's Labor Legislation* (Westport, Conn.: Greenwood Press, 1978).

Baker, Liva, *The Justice From Beacon Hill: The Life and Times of Oliver Wendell Holmes* (New York: HarperCollins, 1991).

Bakken, Gordon Morris, *Rocky Mountain Constitution Making, 1850–1912* (Westport, Conn.: Greenwood Press, 1987).

Bannister, Robert C., *Social Darwinism: Science and Myth in Anglo-American Social Thought* (Philadelphia: Temple University Press, 1979).

Barnes, Catherine A., *Journey from Jim Crow: The Desegregation of Southern Transit* (New York: Columbia University Press, 1983).

Barrows, Charles L., *William M. Evarts: Lawyer, Diplomat, Statesman* (Chapel Hill: University of North Carolina Press, 1941).

Beth, Loren P., *John Marshall Harlan: The Last Whig Justice* (Lexington: University Press of Kentucky, 1992).

———, *The Development of the American Constitution, 1877–1917* (New York: Harper & Row, 1971).

Bickel, Alexander M. *The Supreme Court and the Idea of Progress* (New York: Harper & Row, 1970).

Blaustein, Albert P., and Roy M. Mersky, *The First One Hundred Justices: Statistical Studies on the Supreme Court of the United States* (Hamden, Conn.: Archon Books, 1978).

Bodenhamer, David J., *Fair Trial: Rights of the Accused in American History* (New York: Oxford University Press, 1992).

Bowker, Richard Rogers, *Copyright: Its History and Its Law* (Boston: Houghton Mifflin, 1912).

Braeman, John, *Before the Civil Rights Revolution: The Old Court and Individual Rights* (Westport, Conn.: Greenwood Press, 1988).

Brodhead, Michael J., *David J. Brewer: The Life of a Supreme Court Justice*, 1837–1910 (Carbondale, Ill.: Southern Illinois University Press, 1994).

Bugbee, Bruce W., *Genesis of American Patent and Copyright Law* (Washington, D.C.: Public Affairs Press, 1967).

Burg, David F., *Chicago's White City of 1893* (Lexington: University Press of Kentucky, 1976).

Butler, Charles Henry, *A Century at the Bar of the Supreme Court of the United States* (New York: G.P. Putnam's Sons, 1942).

Cole, Arthur Charles, *The Centennial History of Illinois, Volume Three: The Era of the Civil War, 1848–1870* (Springfield: Illinois Centennial Commission, 1919).

Coleman, Peter J., *Debtors and Creditors in America: Insolvency, Imprisonment for Debt, and Bankruptcy, 1607–1900* (Madison: State Historical Society of Wisconsin, 1974).

Conant, Michael, *The Constitution and the Economy: Objective Theory and Critical Commentary* (Norman: University of Oklahoma Press, 1991).

Cortner, Richard C., *The Supreme Court and the Second Bill of Rights: The Fourteenth Amendment and the Nationalization of Civil Liberties* (Madison: University of Wisconsin Press, 1981).

———, *The Iron Horse and the Constitution: The Railroads and the Transformation of the Fourteenth Amendment* (Westport, Conn.: Greenwood Press, 1993).

Corwin, Edwin S., *Court Over Constitution* (Princeton, N.J.: Princeton University Press, 1938).

Cullom, Shelby M., *Fifty Years of Public Service*, 2nd ed. (Chicago: A. C. McClurg, 1911).

Currey, J. Seymour, *Chicago: Its History and Its Builders,* 5 vols. (Chicago: S. J. Clarke, 1912).

Currie, David P., *The Constitution in the Supreme Court: The Second Century, 1888–1986* (Chicago: University of Chicago Press, 1990).

Curry, J. L. M., *A Brief Sketch of George Peabody and a History of the Peabody Education Fund* (Cambridge, Mass.: University Press, 1898).

Dawley, Alan, *Struggles for Justice: Social Responsibility and the Liberal State* (Cambridge, Mass.: Harvard University Press, 1991).

Dickerson, Oliver M., *The Illinois Constitutional Convention of 1862* (Urbana, Ill.: University Press, 1905).

Dunn, Arthur Wallace, *From Harrison to Harding: A Personal Narrative, Covering a Third of a Century, 1888–1921* (New York: G. P. Putnam's Sons, 1922).

Durden, Robert F., *Reconstruction Bonds & Twentieth Century Politics: South Dakota v. North Carolina* (Durham, N.C.: Duke University Press, 1962).

Ely, James W., Jr., *The Guardian of Every Other Right: A Constitutional History of Property Rights* (New York: Oxford University Press, 1992).

Epstein, Richard A., *Takings: Private Property and the Power of Eminent Domain* (Cambridge, Mass.: Harvard University Press, 1985).

Ewing, Cortez, *The Judges of the Supreme Court, 1789–1937* (Minneapolis: University of Minnesota Press, 1938).

Fairman, Charles, *Mr. Justice Miller and the Supreme Court, 1862–1890* (Cambridge, Mass.: Harvard University Press, 1939).

Faulkner, Harold U., *Politics, Reform, and Expansion: 1890–1900* (New York: Harper and Row, 1959).

Frankfurter, Felix, and James M. Landis, *The Business of the Supreme Court: A Study in the Federal Judicial System* (New York: Macmillan, 1928).

Freyer, Tony A., *Harmony & Dissonance: The Swift and Erie Cases in American Federalism* (New York: New York University Press, 1981).

_____, *Forums of Order: The Federal Courts and Business in American History* (Greenwich, Conn.: JAI Press, 1979).

Friedman, Lawrence M., *A History of American Law,* 2nd ed. (New York: Simon and Schuster, 1985).

Furer, Howard B., ed., *The Fuller Court 1888–1910* (Millwood, N.J.: Associated Faculty Press, 1986).

Galloway, Russell W., *Justice for All? The Rich and Poor in Supreme Court History 1790–1990* (Durham, N.C.: Carolina Academic Press, 1991).

Gates, John B., *The Supreme Court and Partisan Realignment* (Boulder, Colo.: Westview Press, 1991).

Gillman, Howard, *The Constitution Besieged: The Rise and Demise of Lochner Era Police Powers Jurisprudence* (Durham, N.C.: Duke University Press, 1993).

Ginger, Ray, *Altgeld's America: The Lincoln Ideal Versus Changing Realities* (New York: Funk & Wagnalls, 1958).

Goldman, Sheldon, *Constitutional Law and Supreme Court Decision-Making* (New York: Harper and Row, 1982).

Graber, Mark A., *Transforming Free Speech: The Ambiguous Legacy of Civil Libertarianism* (Berkeley: University of California Press, 1991).

Hall, Kermit L., *The Magic Mirror: Law in American History* (New York: Oxford University Press, 1989).

———, Ely, James W., Jr., Joel B. Grossman, and William M. Wiecek, eds., *The Oxford Companion to the Supreme Court of the United States* (New York: Oxford University Press, 1992).

Handy, Robert T., *Undermined Establishment: Church-State Relations in America, 1880–1920* (Princeton, N.J.: Princeton University Press, 1991).

Harbaugh, William Henry, *The Life and Times of Theodore Roosevelt* (New York: Collier, 1963).

Hatch, Louis Clinton, *Maine: A History: Biographical* (New York: American Historical Society, 1919).

Hatch, Louis C., *The History of Bowdoin College* (Portland: Loring, Short & Harmon, 1927)

Heller, Francis H., *The Sixth Amendment to the Constitution: A Study in Constitutional Development* (Lawrence: University of Kansas Press, 1951).

Highsaw, Robert B., *Edward Douglass White: Defender of the Conservative Faith* (Baton Rouge: Louisiana State University Press, 1981).

Hoff, Joan, *Law, Gender, and Injustice: A Legal History of U.S. Women* (New York: New York University Press, 1991).

Hofstadter, Richard, *Social Darwinism in American Thought*, rev. ed. (New York: George Braziller, 1959).

Hoogenboom, Ari and Olive, *A History of the ICC: From Panacea to Palliative* (New York: Norton, 1976).

Horwitz, Morton J., *The Transformation of American Law, 1870–1960: The Crisis of Legal Orthodoxy* (New York: Oxford University Press, 1992).

Hovenkamp, Herbert, *Enterprise and American Law, 1836–1937* (Cambridge, Mass.: Harvard University Press, 1991).

Hurst, J. Willard, *Law and the Conditions of Freedom in the Nineteenth-Century United States* (Madison: University of Wisconsin Press, 1956).

Jackson, Percival E., *Dissent in the Supreme Court: A Chronology* (Norman: University of Oklahoma Press, 1969).

Johnson, Rossiter, ed., *A History of the World's Columbian Exposition*, 4 vols. (New York: D. Appleton, 1897–98).

Keller, Morton, *Affairs of State: Public Life in Nineteenth Century America* (Cambridge, Mass.: Harvard University Press, 1977).

———, *Regulating a New Economy: Public Policy and Economic Change in America, 1900–1933* (Cambridge, Mass.: Harvard University Press, 1990).

Kelly, Alfred H., Winfred A. Harbison, and Herman Belz, *The American Constitution: Its Origins and Development*, 7th ed. (New York: Norton, 1991).

Kens, Paul, *Judicial Power and Reform Politics: The Anatomy of Lochner v. New York* (Lawrence: University Press of Kansas, 1990).

Kerr, James Edward, *The Insular Cases: The Role of the Judiciary in American Expansionism* (Port Washington, N.Y.: Kennikat Press, 1982).

King, Willard L., *Melville Weston Fuller: Chief Justice of the United States, 1888–1910* (New York: Macmillan, 1950, reprint Chicago: University of Chicago Press, 1967).

Kull, Andrew, *The Color-Blind Constitution* (Cambridge, Mass.: Harvard University Press, 1992).

Lofgren, Charles A., *The Plessy Case: A Legal-Historical Interpretation* (New York: Oxford University Press, 1987).

Lusk, D. W., *Eighty Years of Illinois: Politics and Politicians, 1809-1889*, 3rd ed. (Springfield, Ill.: H. W. Rokker, 1889).

Martin, Albro, *Railroads Triumphant: The Growth, Rejection, and Rebirth of a Vital American Force* (New York: Oxford University Press, 1992).

_____, *Enterprise Denied: Origins of the Decline of American Railroads, 1897–1917* (New York: Columbia University Press, 1971).

McCloskey, Robert Green, *American Conservatism in the Age of Enterprise, 1865–1910* (Cambridge, Mass.: Harvard University Press, 1951).

McCormick, Richard L., *From Realignment to Reform: Political Change in New York State, 1893–1910* (Ithaca, N.Y.: Cornell University Press, 1981).

McDevitt, Matthew, *Joseph McKenna: Associate Justice of the United States* (Washington: Catholic University of America Press, 1946, reprint New York: Da Capo Press, 1974).

Meltsner, Michael, *Cruel and Unusual: The Supreme Court and Capital Punishment* (New York: Random House, 1973).

Myers, Gustavus, *History of the Supreme Court of the United States* (Chicago: Charles H. Kerr, 1912).

Nedelsky, Jennifer, *Private Property and the Limits of American Constitutionalism: The Madisonian Framework and Its Legacy* (Chicago: University of Chicago Press, 1990).

Nevins, Allan, *Grover Cleveland: A Study in Courage* (New York: Dodd, Mead, 1933).

Noel, F. Regis, *A History of the Bankruptcy Law* (Washington: Charles H. Potter, 1919).

North, James W., *The History of Augusta* (Augusta, Maine: Clapp and North, 1870).

Orth, John V., *The Judicial Power of the United States: The Eleventh Amendment in American History* (New York: Oxford University Press, 1987).

Palmer, John M., ed., *The Bench and Bar of Illinois*, 2 vols. (Chicago: Lewis, 1899).

Patterson, Lyman Ray, *Copyright in Historical Perspective* (Nashville: Vanderbilt University Press, 1968).

Paul, Arnold M., *Conservative Crisis and the Rule of Law: Attitudes of Bar and Bench, 1887–1895* (Ithaca, N.Y.: Cornell University Press, 1960).

Pfeffer, Leo, *This Honorable Court: A History of the United States Supreme Court* (Boston: Beacon Press, 1965).

Posner, Richard A., *Cardozo: A Study in Reputation* (Chicago: University of Chicago Press, 1990).

_____, *Law and Literature: A Misunderstood Relation* (Cambridge, Mass.: Harvard University Press, 1988).

Pringle, Henry F., *The Life and Times of William Howard Taft,* 2 vols. (New York: Farrar & Rinehart, 1939).

Purcell, Jr., Edward A., *Litigation and Inequality: Federal Diversity Jurisdiction in Industrial America, 1870–1958* (New York: Oxford University Press, 1992).

Roche, John P., *Sentenced to Life* (New York: Macmillan, 1974).

Ross, William G., *A Muted Fury: Populists, Progressives, and Labor Unions Confront the Courts, 1890–1937* (Princeton, N.J.: Princeton University Press, 1994).

Schlesinger, Keith R., *The Power That Governs: The Evolution of Judicial Activism in a Midwestern State, 1840–1890* (New York: Garland, 1990).

Schultz, David A., *Property, Power, and American Democracy* (New Brunswick: Transaction, 1992).

Selvin, Molly, *This Tender and Delicate Business: The Public Trust Doctrine in American Law and Economic Policy, 1789–1920* (New York: Garland, 1987).

Semonche, John E., *Charting the Future: The Supreme Court Responds to a Changing Society, 1890–1920* (Westport, Conn.: Greenwood Press, 1978).

Shattuck, Petra T., and Jill Norgren, *Partial Justice: Federal Indian Law in a Liberal Constitutional System* (New York: Berg, 1991).

Sherow, James Earl, *Watering the Valley: Development along the High Plains Arkansas River, 1870–1950* (Lawrence: University Press of Kansas, 1990).

Shiras, George III, *Justice George Shiras, Jr., of Pittsburgh* (Pittsburgh: University of Pittsburgh Press, 1953).

Siegan, Bernard H., *Economic Liberties and the Constitution* (Chicago: University of Chicago Press, 1980).

Stanley, Robert, *Dimensions of Law in the Service of Order: Origins of the Federal Income Tax, 1861–1913* (New York: Oxford University Press, 1993).

Steamer, Robert J., *Chief Justice: Leadership and the Supreme Court* (Columbia, S.C.: University of South Carolina Press, 1986).

_____, *The Supreme Court in Crisis: A History of Conflict* (Amherst: University of Massachusetts Press, 1971).

Stover, John F., *The Life and Decline of the American Railroad* (New York: Oxford University Press, 1970).

Surrency, Erwin C., *History of the Federal Courts* (New York: Oceana Publications, 1987).

Swindler, William F., *Court and Constitution in the Twentieth Century: The Old Legality, 1889–1932* (Indianapolis: Bobbs-Merrill, 1969).

Swisher, Carl Brent, *Stephen J. Field: Craftsman of the Law* (Washington: Brookings Institution, 1930, reprint Chicago: University of Chicago Press, 1969).

Tomlins, Christopher L., *The State and the Unions: Labor Relations, Law, and the Organized Labor Movements in America, 1880–1960* (Cambridge: Cambridge University Press, 1985).

Tsai, Shih-shan Henry, *The Chinese Experience in America* (Bloomington: Indiana University Press, 1986).

Twiss, Benjamin R., *Lawyers and the Constitution: How Laissez-Faire Came to the Supreme Court* (Princeton, N.J.: Princeton University Press, 1942).

Umbreit, Kenneth Bernard, *Our Eleven Chief Justices* (New York: Harper & Brothers, 1938).

Urofsky, Melvin I., *A March of Liberty: A Constitutional History of the United States* (New York: Alfred A. Knopf, 1988).

Waltman, Jerold L., *Political Origins of the U.S. Income Tax* (Jackson: University Press of Mississippi, 1985).

Warren, Charles, *The Supreme Court in United States History*, 2 vols., rev. ed. (Boston: Little, Brown, 1926).

_____, *Bankruptcy in United States History* (Cambridge, Mass.: Harvard University Press, 1935).

White, G. Edward, *The American Judicial Tradition: Profiles of Leading American Judges* (New York: Oxford University Press, 1976).

_____, *Justice Oliver Wendell Holmes: Law and the Inner Self* (New York: Oxford University Press, 1993).

Wiecek, William M., *Liberty Under Law: The Supreme Court in American Life* (Baltimore: Johns Hopkins University Press, 1988).

Willis, William, *A History of the Law, the Courts, and the Lawyers of Maine* (Portland: Bailey & Noyes, 1863).

Wright, Benjamin Fletcher, *The Contract Clause of the Constitution* (Cambridge, Mass.: Harvard University Press, 1938).

Articles and Book Chapters

Aitchison, Clyde B., "The Evolution of the Interstate Commerce Act: 1887–1937," 5 *George Washington Law Review* 289 (1937).

Anderson, Alexis J., " The Formative Period of First Amendment Theory, 1870-1915," 24 *American Journal of Legal History* 56 (1980).

Benedict, Michael Les, "Laissez-Faire and Liberty: A Re-Evaluation of the Meaning and Origins of Laissez-Faire Constitutionalism," 3 *Law and History Review* 293 (1985).

_____, "Victorian Moralism and Civil Liberty in the Nineteenth-Century United States," in Donald G. Nieman, ed., *The Constitution, Law, and American Life: Critical Aspects of the Nineteenth-Century Experience* (Athens: University of Georgia Press, 1992).

Bergan, Francis, "Mr. Justice Brewer: Perspective of A Century," 25 *Albany Law Review* 191 (1961).

Cushman, Barry, "A Stream of Legal Consciousness: The Current of Commerce Doctrine From *Swift* to *Jones & Laughlin*, 61 *Fordham Law Review* 105 (1992).

_____, "Doctrinal Synergies and Liberal Dilemmas: The Case of the Yellow-Dog Contract, *1992 Supreme Court Review* 235.

Diamond, Stephen, "The Death and Transfiguration of Benefit Taxation: Special Assessments in Nineteenth-Century America," 12 *Journal of Legal Studies* 201 (1983).

Duker, William F., "The Fuller Court and State Criminal Process: Threshold of Modern Limitations on Government," 1980 *Brigham Young University Law Review* 275.

―――, "Mr. Justice Rufus W. Peckham and the Case of *Ex Parte Young:* Lochnerizing *Munn v. Illinois*," 1980 *Brigham Young University Law Review* 539.

Ellis, Elmer, "Public Opinion and the Income Tax, 1860–1900," 27 *Mississippi Valley Historical Review* 225 (1940).

Ely, James W., Jr., " 'That due satisfaction may be made' " The Fifth Amendment and the Origins of the Compensation Principle," 36 *American Journal of Legal History* 1 (1992).

―――, "The Railroad Question Revisited: *Chicago, Milwaukee & St. Paul Railway v. Minnesota* and Constitutional Limits on State Regulations," 12 *Great Plains Quarterly* 121 (1992).

―――, "Melville Weston Fuller," in Melvin I. Urofsky, ed., *Biographical Directory of U.S. Supreme Court Justices* (New York: Garland, 1994).

Epstein, Richard A., "The Proper Scope of the Commerce Power," 73 *Virginia Law Review* 1387 (1987).

―――, "Toward a Revitalization of the Contract Clause," 51 *University of Chicago Law Review* 703 (1984).

Ernst, Daniel R., "The Labor Exemption, 1908–1914," 74 *Iowa Law Review* 1151 (1989).

Fairman, Charles, "What Makes a Great Justice? Mr. Justice Bradley and the Supreme Court, 1870–1892," 30 *Boston University Law Review* 49 (1950).

Farrelly, David, "Justice Harlan's Dissent in the Pollock Case," 24 *Southern California Law Review* 175 (1951).

Fellman, David, "Cruel and Unusual Punishments," 19 *Journal of Politics* 34 (1957).

Fish, Peter G., "A New Court Opens: The United States Court of Appeals for the Fourth Circuit," 2 *Georgia Journal of Southern Legal History* 171 (1993).

Frank, John P., "The Appointment of Supreme Court Justices: Prestige, Principles and Politics," 1941 *Wisconsin Law Review* 172.

―――, "Supreme Court Appointments: II," 1941 *Wisconsin Law Review* 343.

Frankfurter, Felix, "Chief Justices I Have Known," 39 *Virginia Law Review* 884 (1953).

Friedman, Lawrence M., and Jack Ladinsky, "Social Change and the Law of Industrial Accidents," 67 *Columbia Law Review* 50 (1967).

Gamer, Robert E., "Justice Brewer and Substantive Due Process: A Conservative Court Revisited," 18 *Vanderbilt Law Review* 615 (1965).

Glennon, Robert J., Jr., "Justice Henry Billings Brown: Values in Tension," 44 *University of Colorado Law Review* 553 (1973).

Gordon, David, "Swift & Co. v. United States: The Beef Trust and the Stream of Commerce Doctrine," 28 *American Journal of Legal History* 244 (1984).

Graham, Howard Jay, "Justice Field and the Fourteenth Amendment," 52 *Yale Law Journal* 851 (1943).

Hackett, Frank W., "A Recent Decision of the Supreme Court Upon Municipal Bonds," 5 *Harvard Law Review* 157 (1891).

Hartley, Katha G., "Spring Valley Water Works v. San Francisco: Defining Economic Rights in San Francisco," 3 *Western Legal History* 287 (1990).

Henkin, Louis, "The Constitution and United States Sovereignty: A Century of *Chinese Exclusion* and its Progeny," 100 *Harvard Law Review* 853 (1987).

Hovenkamp, Herbert, "Regulatory Conflict in the Gilded Age: Federalism and the Railroad Problem," 97 *Yale Law Journal* 1017 (1988).

Hylton, J. Gordon, "The Judge Who Abstained in *Plessy v. Ferguson:* Justice David Brewer and the Problem of Race," 61 *Mississippi Law Journal* 315 (1991).

_____, "David Brewer and the Rights of Property: A Conservative Justice Reconsidered," unpublished paper.

Kay, Richard S., "The Equal Protection Clause in the Supreme Court, 1873–1903," 29 *Buffalo Law Review* 667 (1980).

Kens, Paul, "The Source of a Myth: Police Powers of the States and Laissez Faire Constitutionalism, 1900–1937," 35 *American Journal of Legal History* 70 (1991).

Kousser, J. Morgan, "Separate but *not* Equal: The Supreme Court's First Decision on Racial Discrimination in Schools," 46 *Journal of Southern History* 17 (1980).

Lamb, Horace R., "The Relation of the Patent Law to the Federal Anti-Trust Laws," 12 *Cornell Law Quarterly* 261 (1927).

Martin, Albro, "Railroads and the Equity Receivership: An Essay on Institutional Change," 34 *Journal of Economic History* 685 (1974).

May, James, "Antitrust in the Formative Era: Political and Economic Theory in Constitutional and Antitrust Analysis, 1880–1918," 50 *Ohio State Law Journal* 257 (1989).

Mayer, David N., "The Jurisprudence of Christopher G. Tiedeman: A Study in the Failure of Laissez-Faire Constitutionalism," 93 *Missouri Law Review* 93 (1990).

McCurdy, Charles W., "Justice Field and the Jurisprudence of Government-Business Relations: Some Parameters of Laissez-Faire Constitutionalism, 1863–1897," 61 *Journal of American History* 970 (1975).

_____, "The Roots of 'Liberty of Contract' Reconsidered: Major Premises in the Law of Employment, 1867–1937," *Yearbook 1984 Supreme Court Historical Society* 20.

_____, "The *Knight* Sugar Decision of 1895 and the Modernization of American Corporation Law, 1869–1903," 53 *Business History Review* 304 (1979).

Miller, Geoffrey P., "Public Choice at the Dawn of the Special Interest State: The Story of Butter and Margarine," 77 *California Law Review* 83 (1989).

Morris, Jeffrey B., "The Era of Melville Weston Fuller," *Yearbook 1981 Supreme Court Historical Society* 37.

Neely, Alfred S., " 'A humbug based on economic ignorance and incompetence'— Antitrust in the Eyes of Justice Holmes," 1993 *Utah Law Review* 1.

Newmyer, R. Kent, "Harvard Law School, New England Legal Culture, and the Antebellum Origins of American Jurisprudence," 74 *Journal of American History* 814 (1987).

Newton, Nell Jessup, "Federal Power Over Indians: Its Sources, Scope, and Limitations," 132 *University of Pennsylvania Law Review* 195 (1984).

Note, "Judgments of the Supreme Court Rendered by A Majority of One," 24 *Georgetown Law Review* 984 (1936).

Porter, Mary Cornelia, "That Commerce Shall Be Free: A New Look at the Old Laissez-Faire Court," *1976 Supreme Court Review* 135.

_____, "Lochner and Company: Revisionism Revisited," in Ellen Frankel Paul and Howard Dickman, eds., *Liberty, Property and Government: Constitutional Interpretation Before the New Deal* (Albany: State University of New York Press, 1989).

Powell, Thomas Reed, "Coercing A State To Pay A Judgment: Virginia v. West Virginia," 17 *Michigan Law Review* 1 (1918).

Pratt, Walter F., "Rhetorical Styles on the Fuller Court," 24 *American Journal of Legal History* 189 (1980).

_____, "American Contract Law at the Turn of the Century," 39 *South Carolina Law Review* 415 (1988).

Reeder, Robert P., "Chief Justice Fuller," 59 *University of Pennsylvania Law Review* 1 (1910).

Reese, Willis L. M., "Full Faith and Credit to Foreign Equity Decrees," 42 *Iowa Law Review* 183 (1957).

Riggs, Robert E., "Substantive Due Process in 1791," 1990 *Wisconsin Law Review* 941.

Roche, John P., "Civil Liberty in the Age of Enterprise," 31 *University of Chicago Law Review* 103 (1963).

_____, "Entrepreneurial Liberty and the Commerce Power: Expansion, Contraction and Casuistry in the Age of Enterprise," 30 *University of Chicago Law Review* 680 (1963).

Salyer, Lucy, "Captives of Law: Judicial Enforcement of the Chinese Exclusion Laws, 1891–1905," 76 *Journal of American History* 91 (1989).

Scheiber, Harry N., "Federalism, the Southern Regional Economy, and Public Policy Since 1865," in David J. Bodenhamer and James W. Ely, Jr., eds., *Ambivalent Legacy: A Legal History of the South* (Jackson: University Press of Mississippi, 1984).

_____, "Instrumentalism and Property Rights: A Reconsideration of American 'Styles of Judicial Reasoning' in the 19th Century," 1975 *Wisconsin Law Review* 1.

Schiffman, Irving, "Melville Fuller," in Leon Friedman and Fred L. Israel, eds., *The Justices of the United States Supreme Court, 1789–1978*, 5 vols. (New York: Chelsea House, 1980), II, 1471.

Schoene, Lester P., and Frank Watson, "Workmen's Compensation on Interstate Railways," 47 *Harvard Law Review* 389 (1934).

Siegel, Stephen A., "Understanding the Lochner Era: Lessons From the Controversy Over Railroad and Utility Rate Regulation," 70 *Virginia Law Review* 187 (1984).

———, "*Lochner* Era Jurisprudence and the American Constitutional Tradition," 70 *North Carolina Law Review* 1 (1991).

Soltow, Lee C., "Evidence on Income Inequality in the United States, 1866–1965," 29 *Journal of Economic History* 279 (1969).

Spector, Robert M., "Legal Historian on the United States Supreme Court: Justice Horace Gray, Jr., And the Historical Method," 12 *American Journal of Legal History* 181 (1968).

Thompson, Barton H., Jr., "The History of the Judicial Impairment 'Doctrine' and Its Lessons for the Contract Clause," 44 *Stanford Law Review* 1373 (1992).

———, "Judicial Takings," 76 *Virginia Law Review* 1449 (1990).

Thompson, Seymour D., "The Court Management of Railroads," 27 *American Law Review* 31 (1893).

Urofsky, Melvin I., "Myth and Reality: The Supreme Court and Protective Legislation in the Progressive Era," *Yearbook 1983 Supreme Court Historical Society* 53.

Walker, Thomas G., Lee Epstein, and William J. Dixon, "On the Mysterious Demise of Consensual Norms in the United States Supreme Court," 50 *Journal of Politics* 361 (1988).

Wall, Joseph Frazier, "Social Darwinism and Constitutional Law with Special Reference to *Lochner v. New York*," 33 *Annals of Science* 465 (1976).

Wallenstein, Peter, " 'These New and Strange Beings': Women in the Legal Profession in Virginia, 1890–1990," 101 *Virginia Magazine of History and Biography* 193 (1993).

Westin, Alan Furman, "The Supreme Court, the Populist Movement and the Campaign of 1896," 15 *Journal of Politics* 3 (1953).

Westin, Alan F., "Stephen J. Field and the Headnote to O'Neil v. Vermont: A Snapshot of the Fuller Court at Work," 67 *Yale Law Journal* 363 (1958).

White, G. Edward, "John Marshall Harlan I: The Precursor," 19 *American Journal of Legal History* 1 (1975).

Wiecek, William M., "State Protection of Personal Liberty: Remembering the Future," in Paul Finkelman and Stephen E. Gottlieb, eds., *Toward A Usable Past: Liberty Under State Constitutions* (Athens: University of Georgia Press, 1991).

Widerman, Rivka, "Tobacco Is A Dirty Weed. Have We Ever Liked It? A Look at Nineteenth Century Anti-Cigarette Legislation," 38 *Loyola Law Review* 387 (1992).

Wright, Charles Alan, "Authenticity of 'A Dirtier Day's Work' Quote in Question," 13 *Supreme Court Historical Society Quarterly* 6 (1990).

ZoBell, Karl M., "Division of Opinion in the Supreme Court: A History of Judicial Disintegration," 44 *Cornell Law Quarterly* 186 (1959).

TABLE OF CASES

The Table of Cases includes only those decisions discussed in the text. The full citation for cases mentioned in the footnotes is given in the appropriate note.

Index